the
stocked
kitchen

sarah kallio & stacey krastins

ATRIA BOOKS

new york   london   toronto   sydney

the

stocked

kitchen

one grocery list . . . endless recipes

ATRIA B O O K S

A Division of Simon & Schuster, Inc.
1230 Avenue of the Americas
New York, NY 10020

First Atria Books hardcover edition July 2011

ATRIA B O O K S and colophon are trademarks of Simon & Schuster, Inc.

For information about special discounts for bulk purchases, please contact Simon & Schuster Special Sales at 1-866-506-1949 or business@simonandschuster.com.

The Simon & Schuster Speakers Bureau can bring authors to your live event. For more information or to book an event, contact the Simon & Schuster Speakers Bureau at 1-866-248-3049 or visit our website at www.simonspeakers.com.

Designed by Suet Yee Chong

Manufactured in the United States of America

10   9   8   7   6   5   4   3   2   1

ISBN 978-1-4516-3535-5
ISBN 978-1-4516-3537-9 (ebook)

To Craig, Andrew, Charlie, Larry, Lexie, and Ella—
thank you for all your unwavering love and support.

—S.K.s

the system

using the system

recipes

contents

the
stocked
kitchen

the
system

start with the list

We've all had that moment during the day when we ask, with a knot in our stomach, "What am I going to make for dinner?" We stand in our kitchens having a conversation with ourselves (hopefully, silently): *I don't have anything to make. . . . What I planned for doesn't sound good. . . . I don't have any time to cook, let alone get to the store.*

We are all searching for a way to make the process easier. Many of us get discouraged into prepackaged complacency, which doesn't satisfy any real cravings. (We've never heard anyone say, "You know what sounds good? Powdered milk with dehydrated broccoli!") Bookstores contain a myriad of cookbooks touting catchphrases like "quick and simple" or "cheap and easy." The recipes may be quick, but they often require us to purchase random ingredients that we need a pinch of and then will never use again. We have, in the past, cluttered our pantries, refrigerators, and cupboards with hundreds of dollars' worth of cookbooks and specialty items like red pepper paste. We were still left missing an easy-to-use, versatile, and effective system for getting dinner on the table. This is why we created The Stocked Kitchen.

The Stocked Kitchen is the first complete meal creation system with only one standard list of groceries. If your kitchen is "stocked" with these ingredients, you will always have what you need to create any of our recipes. These recipes have been used for all our own dining needs, including meals for drop-in guests, special occasions, and every-night dinners for our families. This system encompasses all parts of the meal creation process from shopping to storing to cooking to serving. The results are delicious, "guestworthy" meals made from real, basic ingredients. We have proved The Stocked Kitchen system works. It has reduced our grocery bills, our stress levels, our trips to the market, and our food waste. We create more delicious meals while removing the handcuffs of preplanning. It is so simple—"Start with the list"— but once you've incorporated it into your life, you will see how powerful The Stocked Kitchen philosophy can be. One grocery list, endless recipes!

how it all started

Looking back, we can't believe what two women and a Mac can do.

A third-birthday party actually brought us together. Stacey's son Andrew invited Sarah's daughter Lexie to his big day. We met, connected, and began to meet for playdates. While sitting and chatting, we soon realized that we have more in common with each other than just our children's ages. We both have engineering degrees and marketing experience, and had always desired to start our own businesses. (You could say we had entrepreneurial spirits in us that were struggling to come out.) In addition, we love to cook and entertain. We both often found ourselves offering or being asked to host and organize bridal showers, baby showers, holiday parties, and reunions for family and friends. We were the only people we knew who had guests over regularly (up to fifty people in the backyard on a random Friday night). Friends and family would make comments like "How do you do it?" We decided to collaborate on an entertaining book to make it easier for everyone.

We wanted this book to be something that we ourselves could and would use in our own kitchens. We began by questioning why entertaining is so much work and so expensive. Over countless playdates, we started to realize that what made hosting people costly and time consuming was the fact that most recipes call for random ingredients that require extra cost and trips to the market. To alleviate some of the burden on us, we would often ask our husbands to pick up missing ingredients on their way home from work. They were even more confused than we were as to where to find items like tahini paste. So, for our entertaining book, we decided to list all of the specialty items, explain where they could be found, and describe what they looked like. We also decided to limit each dinner party to only three specialty items . . . hmmm . . . actually, no, how about only one item?

Wait! Why do we need any specialty items at all?

In fact, we already owned too many ingredients that didn't get used enough and didn't work together. We decided that what we needed was to invent a way to standardize the items in our kitchens without limiting our ability to create a wide variety of dishes. Plus, we realized that this wasn't just important for entertaining: this system could be incredibly beneficial for cooking in general.

We investigated our own pantries and asked ourselves what items could be used in multiple ways, what more common items could be used to substitute for specialty items, and more obviously, what items we didn't ever use. We researched what would be found in traditional ethnic pantries and how to derive those flavors from ingredients that we already used. We then began to create recipes using only these ingredients to prove the system worked. After a year of ingredient negotiation and recipe development, we created The Stocked Kitchen Grocery List. This list is now the only list we use to make all our meals.

We had a list and a lot of recipes, and were in awe of what we had created. We couldn't wait to share it with all of our friends and family because we believed that they could benefit so much from the list and recipes. We did know, however, that we needed to protect our idea properly, so we copyrighted the list and trademarked our brand name, The Stocked Kitchen. We then began to share The Stocked Kitchen philosophy and get people's opinions. We developed a prototype book called *Taste* and in just seven months sold nine hundred copies, mostly in our small community through home shows, our website, and local retail stores. The world should never underestimate a woman's—let alone two mothers'—ability to find creative and realistic solutions to a problem.

The Stocked Kitchen system is so integrated into our lives and has made cooking so much easier that it's hard to remember how we did it before. Since we've limited the ingredients we use, we feel that we have so many more options. There are no more Sunday evening recipe planning sessions. There is no more grocery list making. There is no more standing in front of an open pantry, full of random ingredients, saying, *I have nothing to make.* There is no more prepackaged lasagna taking up room in our freezers for "just in case." In fact, the most "planning" we do for meals is thawing some meat and then choosing a recipe to cook it with, late in the afternoon. This system allows us to make delicious dinners with little or no preplanning, lower our grocery bills, and waste a lot less food.

Dinner doesn't have to be an overwhelming task that you perform just to feed your family. In fact, we consider our most important "guests" to be our husbands and children. We want to make them a meal that is healthy, cost effective, and delicious. We are also determined to be able to serve them options with less processed and prepackaged foods. Because the grocery list is made up of mostly "real" foods, we have the option of making recipes with fewer additives. For the same reasons, it is easy to adapt this system to any dietary preference or need because all the ingredients can be purchased low-fat, sugar free, organic, and so on. Our concept of convenience is adopting a system that works, not just filling our homes with "convenience foods."

This business began with a six-month-old, a twenty-month-old, and two three-year-olds in tow. We've developed it through the loss of jobs, the stress of creating a solid partnership, and potty training. We realize that we could have only traveled this journey together. We are two women who took their creative edge and honed problem-solving skills, followed their dream, and created a business and a future, The Stocked Kitchen.

using
the
system

get stocked

We've provided you with our story. Now . . . let's get you stocked! In this section we will share with you our suggestions for making your kitchen more organized, efficient, and stocked with the ingredients on our list.

check out the grocery list

We're being only slightly melodramatic, but this list will utterly and completely change your life. We have included, at the back of this book, a set of tear-out pages with ingredients divided into categories arranged by how they appear in most grocery stores. The items within each of these categories are listed in alphabetical order. Although every grocery store is slightly different, the list is set up to flow with most markets' layouts. As you use up ingredients during the week, make sure to check the items on your grocery list. When you prepare for a shopping trip, just quickly look to see what else you are missing, and check the box on the list.

the waste factor

There will probably be moments during this process when you feel you are being wasteful. Stop, take a deep breath, and ask yourself if the item that you are considering getting rid of has given you the return on investment that you hoped for. You can't do anything about wasting money in the past. What you can do is begin to build a kitchen full of ingredients that work together and provide great results now.

Also, see the glossary that starts on page 27. This guide provides useful specifics on how to buy, use, and store the items on the list. You might look at the grocery list (page 25) initially and think, "Oh my gosh, do I really have to go and buy all this stuff?" We believe that most of you already have or have recently had about 80 percent of these items in your kitchen. Start going through the list and start pulling out the items that you already have. Feel better?

purge

Take the grocery list and a pen and work on one section at a time. Start going through your pantry, refrigerator, and freezer. Our very basic and absolute rule of thumb is: if you haven't opened or used something in over a year and it's not on the list, get rid of it. Either toss it or give the nonperishable items to charity. Next, make a decision. Are you taking a leap of faith and becoming stocked or are you going to just test the waters? In other words, are you willing to get rid of those packets of taco seasoning and broccoli rice, or are you going to use them up first? If you want to use them up first, that's fine. Come back and see us when your cupboards are bare. If you enjoy the idea of living on the edge and are willing to give yourself to us body and soul . . . welcome! And again, toss or donate!

clean, organize, and prep

No matter how tidy or untidy you are—and we know because we run the gamut in this category—take the time, while items are removed from your cupboards, refrigerators, and freezers, to tidy up. Remove the crud like coffee grounds or garlic skins from your shelves and wash those produce drawers in your refrigerator.

> ## "Honey, can you pick this up on the way home?"
>
> In the past, we think our poor husbands thought that we would send them into the grocery "jungle" on a quest for the most obscure items imaginable just to test their innate hunting skills. Sarah remembers running into a male colleague at the market who looked utterly forlorn. As he stared at the pastas, she asked, "Need some help?" With a bit of desperation he said, "Where are the ramen noodles?" Sarah told him that they were by the soups. With total dismay and sarcasm, he said, "Of course . . . because why would they be by the *noodles*?!?" For all husbands everywhere, The Stocked Kitchen is our gift to you. The list doesn't change. Once you've got it . . . you've got it!

Here are some of our suggestions for kitchen organizing:

- ☑ Store flour and sugars in canisters on your countertop. This makes them much more accessible, which is particularly helpful when you need only a small amount.

- ☑ If possible, store your jelly roll pans, cookie sheets, and cooling racks vertically. This aids so much in getting to them quickly.

- ☑ Keep like canned goods together in your pantry. Stack all of your tomatoes (diced, paste, and sauce) in one area, and your canned beans in another. It will be much easier to find what you are looking for and to determine when you need more.

- ☑ We try to keep like tools together, separating our baking and cooking utensils. We store measuring cups and spoons, spatulas, and whisks in one drawer and slotted spoons, turners, and tongs in another.

the initial shopping trip

Now that you've cleared the clutter, the fun begins. We make check marks on the grocery list next to all of the items that we are missing. This is all the preshopping planning we ever do.

We would suggest in this first shopping trip that you buy the canned goods in quantities of four to six. This should cover any of the recipes in the book. (Go to page 21 to see an additional list of items that we tend to buy in larger quantities.)

If you aren't ready to stock your kitchen all at once, begin by buying the ingredients recipe by recipe. All of a sudden, you will start to accumulate all the items you need to be completely stocked. This process might feel a little less daunting at first, and although it might take a bit longer, you will still get the great benefits of the system.

We wish we had had this book when we were setting up our first homes, because our kitchens would have been stocked the right way the first time. We now do it better—not because we are outstanding chefs, not because we have all the time in the world, but because we have an aid. We are, simply, always prepared.

trust the list

Part of this process is really just a leap of faith. You have to trust that when you have these items in your house, you can always make something. That is our promise to you. By shopping this way, you will always be prepared, you will save money, and you will throw out a lot less spoiled food. The one thing you have to do is believe. Try not to revert back to old habits like frozen pizzas. Believe in the newfound possibilities of your kitchen.

About three years ago we took the plunge. We did exactly what we suggested you do: purged, organized, and shopped stocked. Since then, we've tested the list in the real world and worked hard to perfect it. This single grocery list has taken us through birthday parties, holidays, cocktail parties, and every-night dinners with great success and a barrage of compliments.

The reason the list works is because we created it with very clear objectives. This single grocery list:

- ☑ can be used for every grocery shopping trip.

- ☑ is made up mostly of "real food" and limits the use of prepackaged, highly processed items.

- ☑ can be purchased for varying dietary needs or preferences: low-sodium, low-fat, organic, and so on.

- ☑ is made up of many ingredients that can be stored for at least a few weeks without spoiling.

- ☑ is made up of ingredients that, when combined creatively, can produce exceptional and diverse dishes.

crusty little soldiers

A huge benefit for us has been being able to get rid of all those half-used bottles of salad dressings, cocktail sauce, tartar sauce, etc. We joke that they used to stand at attention along the bottom of our refrigerator door like crusty little soldiers. We now make our own salad dressings as needed and no longer throw away so many half-used containers. Good for the environment and good for our pocketbooks!

never make a wasted trip

Another great result of The Stocked Kitchen is that now we shop smart. Although grocery shopping doesn't necessarily sound like a spree at Saks, we promise that by using this system, it just got a whole lot easier. We have small children and live in Michigan next to a big, beautiful lake that dumps snow on us unrelentingly in the winter. We don't have the time, desire, or energy to bundle up our little ones and make trips to the market for essentials like milk, let alone something called "champagne extract." We want to use our time as efficiently as possible when we are able to get to the market. Here are some of our suggestions for staying stocked:

☑ Always check for sales, but especially on the more expensive items. Whether we are out or not, we always check to see if frozen shrimp, canned lump crabmeat, and the other items on the list are on sale. We bring them home and, when appropriate, put them right in the freezer.

☑ If possible, buy canned goods by the case. They stay good, almost, forever. If you have the room to store them, it's much more economical to buy them in bulk. We love our warehouse retail chains for this!

☑ We recommend buying ingredients in the sizes suggested on the list. We have paid close attention, making sure sizes are usable and the least wasteful. We've erred on the side of opening more cans rather than having half of the cans' contents go to waste.

☑ You don't always have to keep every item on the list in stock. For instance, vanilla ice cream is used only for dessert recipes. If you are not a dessert person, you don't always need to have this on hand. Obviously, Gorgonzola, blue, and feta cheeses have unique flavors that may not be your cup of tea. If this is the case, don't buy them. Although other cheeses will certainly change the taste of your recipes (isn't that the point?), equal amounts of Parmesan or mozzarella can be generally substituted.

☑ Fresh basil, green onions, and the cabbage and carrot mix are probably the most perishable items when it comes to staying fresh. Basil is an excellent herb to keep growing in your kitchen, allowing you the best opportunity to always have it available. Oftentimes your grocer will have fresh basil plants for sale. For all of these items, however, if you find that you are not using them enough, buy them only every other or every third grocery store trip.

☑ Spices are best if used within a year. When we purchase them, we use a permanent marker and write the date on them. Because we've limited the number of spices you need, it is a lot easier to use them up within the year! Also, we purchase chili powder, dried minced onion, cinnamon, Italian seasoning, herbes de Provence, and cumin in large containers to save money. We use them in so many of our recipes that we find ourselves able to use them up.

You will begin to see opportunities to stay stocked everywhere. When we are on vacation, we look in specialty shops for gourmet Dijon mustards, maple syrups, or raspberry jams or jellies, instead of the purposeless items we purchased in the past. Buying stocked is a luxury because you get the value out of the products you are investing in.

use what you have

It was very important to us while we were writing this book to focus on the ingredients, because that is how we cook. We have chicken; what can we make with chicken? We feel that this is the best way to begin to learn to cook with what you have. We now base our meals according to what is available, and not on an arbitrary recipe. If ground beef sounds good for dinner, we choose a recipe from our ground beef section. If we have a bag of potatoes that are starting to sprout, we choose a potato dish. If no meat is thawed for dinner, we look in the bean section for our Kidney Bean–Tortilla Lasagna. It is almost impossible to do this with other cookbooks because most of the time you won't have all of the rest of the ingredients necessary to make a specific recipe.

By shopping with The Stocked Kitchen grocery list, you will shop only for what you need, and in reality, there are going to be days when you are less stocked than others. Don't assume that just because you haven't shopped for a while, you have nothing to make. We tend to shop only every seven to ten days and can always still pull a dinner together. We usually start by looking through the freezer for a meat to thaw. We will also try to find a use for an ingredient that might be on its way to spoiling. For both these reasons, we have set up an ingredient index in the back of this book. The index lists every recipe page on which each ingredient on our grocery list is found (except for salt and pepper). This book allows you to look up a recipe by ingredient because you are generally stocked with the other ingredients needed.

You may find yourself becoming comfortable enough with the ingredients that you start to cook without a recipe. We have found that by using only the ingredients on the list, we know what they taste like and how they pair with other flavors. You may even be able to begin substituting stocked ingredients for other ingredients in your favorite recipes. This is a wonderful result of The Stocked Kitchen system that will help you to continue to add new recipes to your repertoire.

stock support

We have received phone calls from friends saying, "Do you offer tech support?" They have also said they wish we could be there with them while they cook. Although that isn't always possible, we have included, throughout the book, tips and suggestions that we use and trust. We want you to find this system to be realistic and helpful.

Whenever you see Sarah, she will be providing a cooking suggestion. Sarah loves to cook and solve problems. Her motto: "I vill find a way!" She has discovered some handy tips along this journey and is excited to share them with you!

Whenever you see Stacey, she will be providing a serving suggestion. Stacey loves to entertain and set a beautiful table. Her strengths are in organization and presentation. She has great ideas that will make your guests feel welcomed and impressed!

You may also begin to notice a ▬ next to the title of some of our recipes. These are The Stocked Kitchen signature dishes. Although we love all of our recipes, these are some of our favorites.

Below is a list of items that we buy in large quantities. We recommend purchasing canned goods by the case and some spices in the largest sizes available at your warehouse retail chains. Your taste preferences should determine how much you buy, but these ingredients are a great place to start.

Beans	*Garlic powder*
Broth	*Herbes de Provence* (when available)
Cheddar cheese	*Italian seasoning*
Chicken breasts	*Mozzarella cheese*
Chili powder	*Nuts*
Cinnamon	*Oils*
Corn	*Pasta*
Cumin	*Rice*
Diced tomatoes	*Sugar*
Dried minced onion	*Tomato sauce*

This chart aids with equivalents.

CUP	FLUID OUNCES	TABLESPOONS	TEASPOONS
1 cup	8 ounces	16 tablespoons	48 teaspoons
¾ cup	6 ounces	12 tablespoons	36 teaspoons
⅔ cup	5⅓ ounces	10⅔ tablespoons	32 teaspoons
½ cup	4 ounces	8 tablespoons	24 teaspoons
⅓ cup	2⅔ ounces	5⅓ tablespoons	16 teaspoons
¼ cup	2 ounces	4 tablespoons	12 teaspoons
⅛ cup	1 ounce	2 tablespoons	6 teaspoons
¹⁄₁₆ cup	½ ounce	1 tablespoon	3 teaspoons

a stocked week in review

Here is an example of an average week for us, using The Stocked Kitchen system. We all have busy schedules; however, the time that we have to make dinner varies from night to night. The Stocked Kitchen system is flexible enough to be realistic for our lives.

sunday
soups and bread bowls or flank steak roll-ups with mashed potatoes

Our hearty soups are perfect for a day when we have time to let them simmer for a while, and they are especially great for game days! Some Sundays, however, we have the family over for a more formal meal. Our flank steak roll-ups are our answer to the roast!

monday
chicken-rice or pasta bake

On Monday we have the time to let something bake in the oven but not the energy after a busy weekend to be in the kitchen for a long time preparing it. Our baked chicken or pasta dishes are ideal for this.

tuesday
salad and topper

Between their volleyball and golf leagues, our husbands generally want something fast and light. One of our salad recipes topped with a grilled chicken breast or flank steak is perfect for these nights.

wednesday
pasta or rice

We make one of the pasta or rice recipes a complete meal by adding the suggested meat toppings. If we have time, we add a vegetable side dish or salad. If we have thought ahead, we add some fresh bread.

thursday night
fast food or leftovers

With our children's dance classes and soccer practice, Thursday nights seem to be our busiest. When we say "fast food," we don't mean drive-through. Here are some ideas for great food fast.

Pancakes and sausage
Grilled ham and
   cheese sandwiches
Chef salads with ranch
   dressing

Pita pizza
Sloppy Joes
Taco meat and taco salads

friday night
cocktails and appetizers with friends

Many of our appetizers are hearty enough to act as mini meals. Add some cocktails, and you have a perfect night in with friends!

saturday night

This is our free-for-all night. It might be leftovers; we might get a babysitter and go out to dinner (PB&J for the kids); or we might make a homemade pizza. Saturday nights are our wild card.

You are now stocked and ready. It is time to put the system to the test. Our hope for you is that you will experience the same benefits with this system that we have. We wish you more manageable grocery bills, effortless meal planning, and delicious recipes. The only question now is . . . what do you make first?

the grocery list

The only items you need to make any of the recipes in this book!

The Stocked Kitchen Grocery List

pantry

- [ ] applesauce
- [ ] apricot preserves
- [ ] artichoke hearts, marinated
- [ ] barbecue sauce
- [ ] beans, black (15 oz.)*
- [ ] beans, Great Northern/ cannellini (15 oz.)*
- [ ] beans, kidney (15 oz.)*
- [ ] bread crumbs, plain
- [ ] broth, beef (15 oz.)*
- [ ] broth, chicken (15 oz.)*
- [ ] coffee, regular and decaf
- [ ] corn (15 oz.)
- [ ] honey
- [ ] horseradish, prepared
- [ ] ketchup
- [ ] mandarin orange segments (10 oz.)*
- [ ] maple syrup
- [ ] mayonnaise
- [ ] mushrooms (4 oz.)*
- [ ] mustard, Dijon
- [ ] mustard, yellow
- [ ] olives, black (4 oz.)*
- [ ] olives, green or Kalamata
- [ ] pancake mix (not "complete")
- [ ] peanut butter, creamy
- [ ] pears (15 oz.)*
- [ ] pineapple, slices or chunks (20 oz.)*
- [ ] ranch or buttermilk dressing
- [ ] raspberry jam or jelly
- [ ] relish, sweet or dill
- [ ] Tabasco/hot sauce
- [ ] tomatoes, diced (15 oz.)*
- [ ] tomato paste (6 oz.)*
- [ ] tomato sauce (15 oz.)*
- [ ] vinegar, balsamic
- [ ] vinegar, red wine
- [ ] vinegar, white wine
- [ ] Worcestershire sauce

international

- [ ] egg noodles
- [ ] pasta, penne/rotini/ farfalle
- [ ] pasta, string
- [ ] rice, jasmine or brown
- [ ] roasted red peppers (jar)
- [ ] salsa
- [ ] soy sauce

snacks, crackers, and bread

- [ ] bread loaf, white or wheat
- [ ] butter crackers
- [ ] pita bread
- [ ] tortilla chips

spices

- [ ] aniseed or fennel seed
- [ ] black pepper
- [ ] chili powder
- [ ] cinnamon, ground
- [ ] cumin, ground
- [ ] curry powder
- [ ] dill weed
- [ ] garlic powder
- [ ] grill seasoning
- [ ] herbes de Provence
- [ ] Italian seasoning
- [ ] nutmeg, ground
- [ ] onion, dried minced
- [ ] poultry seasoning
- [ ] pumpkin pie spice
- [ ] red pepper flakes
- [ ] salt, table/sea salt

baking

- [ ] baking powder
- [ ] baking soda
- [ ] brownie mix (8 by 8-inch pan size)*
- [ ] cake mix, yellow
- [ ] chocolate chips, semisweet
- [ ] chocolate chips, white
- [ ] cocoa powder

- [ ] extract, almond
- [ ] extract, peppermint
- [ ] extract, vanilla
- [ ] flour, all-purpose
- [ ] food coloring
- [ ] nonstick spray
- [ ] nuts, almonds
- [ ] nuts, peanuts
- [ ] nuts, pecans
- [ ] oil, extra virgin olive
- [ ] oil, vegetable
- [ ] sugar, confectioners'
- [ ] sugar, granulated
- [ ] sugar, light brown

refrigerated

- [ ] butter, unsalted
- [ ] cheese, blue or Gorgonzola
- [ ] cheese, Cheddar
- [ ] cheese, feta
- [ ] cheese, mozzarella
- [ ] cheese, Parmesan
- [ ] cream cheese
- [ ] cream, heavy
- [ ] eggs (large)
- [ ] milk
- [ ] sour cream or plain yogurt
- [ ] tortillas, flour (8-inch fajita size)

freezer

- [ ] bread dough (loaf or ball)
- [ ] broccoli, chopped
- [ ] green beans, cut
- [ ] peas
- [ ] puff pastry sheets
- [ ] shrimp (raw)
- [ ] spinach (bag), chopped
- [ ] vanilla ice cream

meat, chicken, and seafood

- [ ] bacon
- [ ] bulk (ground) breakfast sausage

- [ ] chicken breast (boneless, skinless)
- [ ] chicken thighs (boneless, skinless)
- [ ] crabmeat, imitation or canned lump
- [ ] flank steak or skirt steak
- [ ] ground beef, turkey, or chicken
- [ ] ham, sliced or whole

produce

- [ ] apples
- [ ] basil, fresh
- [ ] bell pepper, red or green
- [ ] cabbage and carrot mix
- [ ] carrots
- [ ] celery
- [ ] cranberries, dried
- [ ] cucumber, English
- [ ] garlic cloves
- [ ] ginger, minced (tube or jar)
- [ ] green onions
- [ ] lemon juice
- [ ] lemons
- [ ] lettuce, head or mixed greens
- [ ] lime juice
- [ ] pine nuts
- [ ] potatoes, russet, sweet, Yukon Gold
- [ ] raisins
- [ ] shallots or onions
- [ ] tomatoes

other supplies

- [ ] aluminum foil
- [ ] parchment paper
- [ ] plastic wrap
- [ ] skewers, wooden
- [ ] storage bags, resealable gallon
- [ ] toothpicks

* approximate sizes

www.thestockedkitchen.com

glossary

8-inch Square Baking Dish—glass or metal dish with an 8-inch square base and approximately 3-inch sides. We prefer glass for its presentation.

9-inch Pie Plate—glass or metal round baking dish. Has shallow slanted sides that are 1 to 1½ inches deep. The most common sizes are 8-, 9-, and 10-inch diameters.

9-inch Round Cake Pan—metal (often aluminum) pan with a 9-inch diameter, and approximately 1½-inch-tall sides. It is best to have at least two.

9 by 13-inch Baking Dish—glass or metal dish with a 9 by 13-inch base and approximately 3-inch-deep sides. We prefer glass for its presentation.

Aluminum Foil—thin, pliable, metal sheets made from aluminum. Great for wrapping food and reducing the cleanup on baking pans.

Aniseed/Fennel Seed—seeds from respective plants that smell and taste similar to licorice. Fennel seed is more aromatic and a bit sweeter. In addition to its use in savory dishes, aniseed is found more often in Italian desserts and liquors.

Apples (fresh)—fruit available in many colors and varieties. We like Fuji, Honeycrisp, and Gala apples for their flavor and versatility. Keep apples in the refrigerator. Apples do not freeze well.

Applesauce—a puree made from cooked and mashed apples. Generally found by the canned fruit. Substitute applesauce for half the oil in any sweet baked-good recipe to reduce calories and fat. We prefer to buy unsweetened applesauce in 4-ounce cups to maintain freshness longer. Four ounces is ½ cup.

Apricot Preserves—apricots cooked in sugar to preserve them. Found by the jams and jellies. Both jam and preserves contain actual fruit; however, jam is made from fruit pulp or crushed fruit, while preserves are comprised of fruit chunks.

Artichoke Hearts, Marinated (jar)—hearts of the artichoke marinated in oil, vinegar, salt, and spices. Generally found by the canned vegetables. Some brands have more oil in their marinated versions, which equals more calories and fat without a lot of added flavor.

Bacon—side, belly, or back cut of pork that has been cured, smoked, or both. Bacon is available in regular or thick-cut versions. We prefer the regular cuts for bacon wraps.

Baking Powder—leavening agent of sodium bicarbonate, cream of tartar, and starch. In general you use baking powder when there is no acidity like buttermilk, chocolate, or honey in the recipe. It works like yeast, but much faster. It is available in nonaluminum versions and found in the baking section of most grocers. Best if kept in the refrigerator (make sure it is airtight).

Baking Soda—leavening agent of sodium bicarbonate. Found in the baking section of most grocers. Store in a resealable storage bag or airtight plastic container in your fridge.

Barbecue Sauce—sauce generally made of tomato puree, onions, sugar, and vinegar. Found near other condiments, like ketchup, in most groceries.

Basil (fresh)—green leafy herb. To keep basil fresh longer, keep it in the refrigerator, wrapped in a damp paper towel, in a resealable storage bag. Growing your own basil is another great option.

Beans, Black (can)—small beans with a glossy black skin canned in water and salt, which becomes a thick syrupy liquid. After draining and rinsing, black beans can be used in salads, nachos, and wraps without cooking.

Beans, Great Northern or Cannellini (can)—white beans that can be used interchangeably. Great Northern beans have a bit of a powdery texture. Cannellini beans are actually thin-skinned white kidney beans. Use either to substitute for garbanzo beans (chickpeas).

Beans, Kidney (can)—a larger kidney-shaped bean with generally a reddish hue, canned in a thick, syrupy liquid. They come in light and dark varieties. Dark varieties have a slightly thicker and tougher skin.

Bell Pepper, Red or Green (fresh)—sweet-fleshed bell-shaped pepper. The different colors of bell peppers show the different stages of maturity. Green peppers are picked first and red peppers are allowed to mature longest. Yellow and orange are in between. Red peppers will be the sweetest, while green are the least sweet and most bitter-tasting. What you keep on hand is your personal preference. Store unwashed in a plastic bag in your refrigerator.

Bread Crumbs, Plain—crumbs of dried bread. Panko are a style of coarse Japanese bread crumbs that can be substituted. Store in an airtight container in the pantry or refrigerator.

To substitute for Italian bread crumbs, add ¼ teaspoon garlic powder and 1 tablespoon Italian seasoning per 1 cup bread crumbs.

To make quick homemade bread crumbs, remove the crusts from bread and place the slices in a 300°F oven on a jelly roll pan. Bake until slightly browned, 10 to 15 minutes. Let the bread cool, then pulse in a food processor.

Bread Dough (frozen)—loaf or ball of raw frozen bread dough. Found bagged in the freezer section of most grocers.

Bread Loaf, White or Wheat—white or wheat sliced sandwich bread. Can be frozen to extend shelf life.

Broccoli (frozen)—green vegetable from the cabbage family. Found in the frozen foods section. Chopped is preferred for these recipes. See the package for cooking directions.

Broth, Beef (can)—liquid made from simmering beef and vegetables. Substitute for water in beef- or tomato-based soups, chilis, and stews to make them taste as if they've been simmering all day. If purchasing larger amounts of broth than recommended, a good rule of thumb is that a 15-ounce can equals approximately 2 cups.

Broth, Chicken (can)—liquid made from simmering chicken and vegetables. Substitute for water in chicken-, seafood-, or green vegetable–based soups, chilis, and stews to make them taste as if they've been simmering all day. Use to cook pasta or rice for extra richness and flavor. For purchasing larger amounts of broth than recommended, a good rule of thumb is that a 15-ounce can equals approximately 2 cups.

Brownie Mix—a prepackaged mix generally made from sugar, flour, vanilla extract, and cocoa powder. Found in the baking section of most grocers. Choose any variety you would like; however, each of our recipes calls for the 8-inch square pan size.

Bulk (Ground) Breakfast Sausage—breakfast sausage without a casing. Found in the meat section of most grocers in plastic-wrapped tubes.

Experiment with other bulk sausages if you like, including Italian sausage. Keep in the freezer to extend shelf life.

Butter Crackers—crispy packaged crackers. Found in the salty snacks section of most groceries.

Butter, Unsalted—made from churning fresh cream or milk. If you do use salted butter, omit ¼ teaspoon salt from the recipe for every 8 tablespoons (1 stick) butter. Keep refrigerated. Sticks at room temperature, however, are easier to spread.

Cabbage and Carrot Mix (Coleslaw Mix)—shredded cabbage and carrots found near the bagged salads section of most grocers. It can be used for coleslaw and also in many Asian dishes, soups, and stews. Store in the refrigerator.

Cake Mix, Yellow—a prepackaged mix generally made from sugar, flour, leavening, salt, and powdered milk. Found in the baking section of most grocers.

Carrots (fresh)—taproot vegetables. We substitute mashed carrots for mashed sweet potatoes in casseroles. Store in a plastic bag in the refrigerator.

Celery (fresh)—slightly bitter stalked vegetable. Store in a plastic bag in the fridge.

Cheese, Blue or Gorgonzola—Blue is a group of strong and tangy cheeses known for their characteristic blue veining. We prefer to buy it crumbled. Gorgonzola is a milder Italian blue cheese. If you do not like blue cheese, substitute equal amounts of mozzarella or Parmesan in our recipes.

Cheese, Cheddar—mild, medium, or sharp hard table cheeses. We like to buy this cheese in blocks because a block provides many more uses; however, buying it preshredded does save a step in many recipes. Can be frozen to increase shelf life.

Cheese, Feta—a brine-cured, tangy Greek cheese generally made from sheep's milk. We prefer to buy it crumbled. If you don't enjoy feta cheese, substitute an equal amount of Parmesan or mozzarella cheese in our recipes.

Cheese, Mozzarella—generally low-moisture white cheese. We choose to have shredded mozzarella on hand because of its ease and versatility. Can be frozen to increase shelf life.

Cheese, Parmesan—hard white grating cheeses. These cheeses can be purchased grated or shredded in a shaker or in chunks. When bought in chunks, Parmesan should always be purchased with a rind. It is a cheese made from raw cow's milk and has a salty, nutty flavor. Parmigiano-Reggiano is a DOP (or Protected Designation of Origin) version of Parmesan cheese.

If buying these cheeses in chunks, wrap in a sheet of parchment paper and then seal in a resealable storage bag in the refrigerator. If you buy in large quantities, they can be frozen to add shelf life.

Chicken Breast (boneless, skinless)—breast of chicken with the bones and skin removed. Chicken can be frozen to add shelf life. Available at many groceries and warehouse stores in large bags, individually frozen. This is generally less expensive and allows you to defrost and cook only what you need.

Chicken Thighs (boneless, skinless)—thighs of chicken with bone and skin removed. Because they have a higher fat content, they are a great option for baked chicken dishes to avoid having dry meat. Chicken can be frozen to add shelf life.

Chili Powder—a ground blend of dehydrated hot chile peppers and other flavors, which can include garlic, cumin, and salt. Found in the spice section of most groceries, the chili powder most commonly available doesn't have a tremendous amount of heat. To retain good flavor and potency, it is best to use dried spices within one year.

Chocolate Chips, Semisweet—small drops of chocolate containing cocoa liquor, sugar, cocoa butter, and vanilla. Found in the baking section of most groceries.

Chocolate Chips, White—small drops of confection containing sugar, cocoa butter, and milk solids. Found in the baking section of most groceries.

Cinnamon, Ground—ground bark of a small evergreen tree. Found in the spice section of most groceries. To retain good flavor and potency, it is best to use dried spices within one year.

Cocoa Powder—made from chocolate liquor pressed to remove most of its cocoa butter. Cocoa powder is found in the baking section of most grocers and is available in regular or dark varieties. Dutch-processed cocoa powder is treated with an alkali to neutralize its acids and has a milder taste than the natural processed cocoa. Keep in a cool, dry pantry out of sunlight.

Coffee (regular and decaf)—berries of the coffee plant. Store coffee in an airtight glass or plastic container in a cool, dark place.

Corn (can)—kernels of corn processed in water and salt. You can substitute equal amounts of pureed corn kernels anytime you see "cream-style corn."

Crabmeat, Imitation/Lump (plastic package or can)—imitation crab is generally made of Alaskan pollack and is found in the refrigerated seafood section of most groceries. Lump crabmeat is real crab from the body of the animal and is found canned near canned tuna.

Cranberries, Dried (Craisins)—dried tart berries. Dried cranberries are generally found in fresh produce sections near raisins and are available sweetened or unsweetened. Dried cranberries should be kept in a resealable container in your pantry.

Cream Cheese—rich, soft cheese made from soured cream and milk. Found in the dairy section of most groceries. We prefer to purchase in a brick form. Light cream cheese (sometimes labeled Neufchâtel) is an acceptable substitute, but we do not recommend "fat free."

Cream, Heavy/Whipping—a high-fat product made from milk. Heavy cream has a higher fat content than whipping cream. Cream can be frozen to add shelf life; however, it will not make whipped cream after freezing.

Cucumber, English (hothouse or seedless)—thin-skinned cucumbers grown in a greenhouse. English cucumbers are the long ones found wrapped in plastic in the fresh produce section of many groceries. We like them because they have very small, soft seeds and a very thin skin, which makes peeling unnecessary. Refrigerate in plastic wrap or a plastic bag.

Cumin, Ground—ground seeds of a flowering plant. Found in the spice section of most groceries, cumin has a distinct, smoky taste. Cumin is found in many Southwest, Mexican, Middle Eastern, and North African dishes. To retain good flavor and potency, it is best to use dried spices within one year.

Curry Powder—spice blend generally made up of ground coriander, turmeric, cumin, fenugreek, red pepper, and other spices. Found in the spice section of most groceries, curry has a very distinct flavor and a bright yellow color. It is often found in Indian and other South Asian cuisines. To retain good flavor and potency, it is best to use dried spices within one year.

Deep-Dish Pizza Pan—round metal pan with 2- to 3-inch-high sides for cooking pizzas.

Dill Weed—dried, chopped dill fronds. To retain good flavor and potency, it is best to use dried spices within one year.

Egg Noodles—wide flat noodles usually made from flour and egg yolks, although "yolkless" varieties are available. Egg noodles (also labeled "Wide Egg Noodles") are found by pastas in most grocers.

Eggs—chicken eggs. If eggs are bad, they will float in a pot of cold water. Keep eggs refrigerated.

Electric Hand Mixer—small handheld appliance with two removable beaters.

Extract, Almond—the extraction of essential almond oil from the nut with alcohol. Found in the baking section of most groceries. We prefer pure versions of all extracts. Almond extract can be substituted for vanilla extract in most recipes. Extracts should be stored in a cool, dark pantry.

Extract, Peppermint—the extraction of essential peppermint oil from the mint with alcohol. Found in the baking section of most groceries. We prefer pure versions of all extracts. Can be substituted anytime you see crème de menthe or peppermint schnapps in recipes. Substitute peppermint extract for peppermint oil at 4 to 1 respectively. Extracts should be stored in a cool, dark pantry.

Extract, Vanilla—the extraction of essential vanilla oil from the bean with alcohol. Found in the baking section of most groceries. We prefer "pure" versions of all extracts. Extracts should be stored in a cool, dark pantry.

Flank Steak/Skirt Steak—slightly different cuts of beef. Flank and skirt steaks are reasonably priced, lean, flavorful cuts of meat. They are generally packaged folded or rolled because they are thin, long slices of meat. Freeze to extend shelf life.

Flour, All-Purpose—a blended wheat flour with an average gluten level. It is available in whole wheat, which can be substituted in any recipe, although it will definitely change the taste and texture of your recipe. Try mixing half and half all-purpose white and whole wheat flour together to avoid texture issues. We prefer unbleached. Store in an airtight container in your refrigerator.

Here are some quick guides when substituting for other flours.

1 cup cake flour = 1 cup minus 2 tablespoons all-purpose

1 cup self-rising flour = 1 cup all-purpose plus 1½ teaspoons baking soda plus ½ teaspoon salt

1 cup pastry flour = 1 cup minus 1 tablespoon all-purpose

Food Coloring—vegetable or chemical dyes for food and drink; most readily available in packages of red, yellow, green, and blue. Found in the baking section of most groceries.

Fry Pan (frying pan or skillet)—a handled pan used for frying and sautéing. Can be made with nonstick surfaces, from aluminum, stainless steel, or cast iron. We prefer to have lid options for all our pots and pans.

Garlic—a bulb made up of cloves, related to the onion family. Garlic is found in the fresh produce section in large bulbs. A clove is one section of the bulb. Store in a cool, dry pantry. To extend shelf life, freeze the entire bulb. Garlic cloves that are still good should feel firm and have a fresh garlic smell.

Substitute 1 clove garlic for every ¼ teaspoon garlic powder.

Garlic Powder—dehydrated garlic cloves ground into a powder. To retain good flavor and potency, it is best to use dried spices within one year.

Substitute ¼ teaspoon garlic powder for every garlic clove.

Ginger (tube or jar)—a vibrant-flavored root. Pureed or minced ginger is widely available in a tube or jar. We prefer the tube because of its ease of use and limited added ingredients. Keep tubes and jars in the refrigerator. They can be kept in the freezer to extend shelf life.

Green Beans (frozen)—podded vegetables found in the frozen food section of most groceries. Cut is preferred for these recipes. See the package for cooking directions.

Green Onions (Spring Onions or Scallions)—an onion with a long, green stalk and a miniature white bulb. Both the green and the white parts of the green onion are edible, although the green stalks are much milder. A good pair of kitchen shears is a quick and easy way to slice them. Green onions should be kept in the refrigerator, sealed in a plastic bag, although it is best to first remove any wilted leaves, and to wrap the green onions in a dry paper towel.

Grill Seasoning—a dried spice blend generally made with garlic, onion, salt, and pepper. Found in the spice section of most groceries or at meat markets. To retain good flavor and potency, it is best to use dried spices within one year.

Ground Beef/Ground Turkey/Ground Chicken—beef, turkey, or chicken meat is ground and packaged. Ground beef can be made from different cuts and qualities of meat. They are listed below from the highest to the lowest fat content.

Ground hamburger	*Ground sirloin*
Ground beef	*Lean ground beef*
Ground chuck	*Extra-lean ground beef*
Ground round	

Ground turkey or ground chicken can be substituted for any of the recipes using ground beef. Keep meat in the freezer to extend shelf life.

Ham (sliced or whole)—a leg cut of pork, most often smoked. Turkey ham is an acceptable substitute. Keep in the freezer to extend shelf life.

Herbes de Provence—a dried spice blend generally made with rosemary, marjoram, basil, bay leaf, thyme, and lavender. Found in the spice section of most groceries, herbes de Provence is a unique spice blend with a Mediterranean flavor. To retain good flavor and potency it is best to use dried spices within one year.

Honey—sweet, thick, sugary liquid made by honeybees. Honey is found near the jams and jellies in most groceries. It is a natural sweetener and an outstanding antioxidant. It can be substituted anytime you see corn syrup, with a 1 to 1 ratio, although it may add just a bit more sweetness. Make sure to keep away from children under a year old. Store in the pantry.

Horseradish, Prepared (Fresh Ground Horseradish)—grated horse-radish root mixed with vinegar. Keep refrigerated. Prepared horserad-ish is generally found in the refrigerated section near cream cheeses or near other condiments such as barbecue and steak sauces.

Italian Seasoning—a dried spice blend generally made with basil, marjoram, oregano, and sage. Found in the spice section of most gro-ceries. To retain good flavor and potency, it is best to use dried spices within one year.

Jelly Roll Pan—a cookie sheet with short (1-inch) sides.

Ketchup (Catsup)—a sweet and tangy condiment made from tomatoes, sugar, vinegar, and spices. Ketchup is such a basic ingredient and so useful in and of itself that we sometimes forget about its versatility. See the index for lots of recipes using ketchup. Also, try it on your copper pots and pans as a cleaner. The acidity of the tomatoes lifts off the tar-nish. Store in the refrigerator after opening. Should last up to a year in the refrigerator.

Lemon Juice—bottled juice of the lemon. Three tablespoons of lemon juice equals about one medium lemon, juiced. Store in the refrigerator to extend shelf life.

Lemons—tart yellow citrus fruit. Keep in the refrigerator fruit drawer.

Lettuce, Head or Mixed Greens—tender leafy green vegetables. Let-tuce comes in many varieties. We love the prewashed organic mixes that are available at most markets and that have a great combination of healthy greens. We prefer darker greens to iceberg for nutritional rea-sons; however, it's best to use a head of iceberg or Bibb lettuce when making lettuce wraps. Keep refrigerated, wrapped in a paper towel and placed in a resealable plastic bag.

Lime Juice— bottled juice of the tart green citrus fruit. You can also use the juice of fresh limes. Keep refrigerated.

Mandarin Orange Segments (can)—small citrus sections canned in either light syrup or pear juice. We prefer the kind that are canned in pear juice to avoid lots of added sugar. To substitute for orange juice in recipes, use an equal volume of mandarin oranges blended with their juice.

Maple Syrup—pure maple syrup is produced from the sap of maple trees. The darker the syrup, the more intense the flavor. Grade A Light Amber, Grade A Medium Amber, Grade A Dark Amber, and Grade B define the syrups' color intensity from lightest to darkest. We prefer pure maple syrup for all different kinds of recipes. Refrigerate maple syrup after opening.

Mayonnaise—a condiment made from oil, egg yolks, lemon juice or vinegar, and seasonings. Reduced-fat or light mayonnaise is an acceptable substitution. Refrigerate after opening.

Milk—generally, cow's milk. Although we usually use skim or low-fat cow's milk, plain soy and rice milk are acceptable alternatives for any of our recipes. Keep refrigerated.

Mini Muffin Pan—a metal pan with 24 small cups that are 1⅜ inches in diameter with 1-inch-tall sides. We prefer the nonstick variety.

Muffin Pan—a metal pan with 12 cups that are 2½ inches in diameter. It is better to have two pans in your inventory. We prefer the nonstick variety.

Mushrooms (can)—mushrooms processed with water and salt. Varieties include whole, sliced, and "pieces and stems." All are suitable for our recipes. We prefer to buy the sliced mushrooms to save us a step. Fresh mushrooms can be used in any of our recipes, although you should use about four times the canned mushroom amount.

Mustard, Dijon—mustard made from brown or black mustard seeds, white wine, vinegar, and spices. Dijon mustard was created by Jean Naigen in Dijon, France, in 1856, when he used the juice of unripe grapes instead of vinegar to make a smoother-tasting mustard. Refrigerate after opening.

Mustard, Yellow (Prepared Mustard)—made from white or yellow mustard seeds, water, vinegar, and spices. Yellow mustard can be substituted for ground mustard. Use 1 tablespoon of yellow mustard for every teaspoon of ground mustard. Refrigerate after opening.

Nonstick Spray—aerosol spray used for creating a nonstick layer on pots and pans to prevent food from adhering to them. It is found in the baking section of most groceries, near the oils. Nonstick spray can be used on most kitchen tool surfaces, including pots, pans, spatulas, and mixing bowls.

Nutmeg (ground)—the seed of a plant found in the South Pacific. It is available already ground in the spice section of your grocery. To retain good flavor and potency, it is best to use dried spices within one year.

Nuts, Almonds—seed of the fruit of the almond tree. Almonds are available raw or roasted and can be found whole, slivered, or sliced. Buying slivered or sliced is very convenient. Because of their high fat content, almonds will become rancid. It is best to store almonds in the refrigerator or freezer in an airtight container.

Nuts, Peanuts—a shelled legume. Peanuts are available in dry-roasted, cocktail, and Spanish varieties. Peanuts are great in desserts, in Asian dishes, in trail mixes, or by themselves. Don't forget G.O.R.P.—"Good Old Raisins and Peanuts"—as a great snack!

Nuts, Pecans—the hard-shelled nut of the pecan tree. Shelled pecans are available halved, chopped, and as chips. Generally, chopped and chips are less expensive. Store in the refrigerator or freezer to extend shelf life.

Oil, Extra Virgin Olive—oil extracted by pressing tree-ripened olives. "Virgin" refers to hand pressing the olives without any chemical treatment. "Extra virgin" refers to olives that are cold-pressed, which makes oil low in acidity and full of fruity flavor. It is great for sautéing but has a lower smoke point, so it is not the best choice for high-heat cooking. Keep in a cool dry place.

Oil, Vegetable—oil extracted from soybeans, cottonseeds, peanuts, safflower seeds, rapeseeds (for canola oil), and sunflower seeds. Refined oils like corn, safflower, canola, and peanut oil have higher smoking points and are better for frying and stir-frying. We like safflower, sunflower, and canola oils for overall cooking and baking. Keep in a cool dry place.

Olives, Black (can)—ripe fruit from the olive tree. American black olives are not allowed to ferment before being packed, which provides a milder flavor. We like to buy these already sliced. Olives add a lot of flavor and act as a great garnish on many dishes. Found in the canned vegetable or condiment aisle of most groceries.

Olives, Green or Kalamata (jar)—Although green olives and Kalamata olives are completely different, we provide the option of using either in our recipes. Depending on your personal preference, the recipes will most likely taste different, but both varieties provide a vibrant, briny taste that is unique. Found in the canned vegetable or condiment aisle of most groceries.

> *Green olives:* fermented green fruit from the olive tree, packed in brine.

> *Kalamata (Greek) olives:* dark, eggplant-colored olives with a salty, fruity flavor and meaty texture. Generally packed in vinegar.

Onion, Dried Minced (Onion Flakes)—dehydrated minced onion. Dried onion is a convenient way to get onions into moist foods. To retain good flavor and potency, it is best to use dried spices within one year.

> 1 small onion = 1 teaspoon onion powder = 1 tablespoon dried minced onion

Pancake Mix—a packaged mix generally made from flour, sugar, powdered milk, and leavening. We choose not to buy the "complete" mixes, which allows us to substitute pancake mix in recipes that call for baking mix. Pancake mix is much easier to find with organic whole wheat flour and without shortening than baking mix is. Keep in a cool, dark pantry.

Parchment Paper—a baking paper infused with silicone to create a nonstick surface. We also love to use it to "quick-thaw" frozen bread dough and to bake chicken. Found either in paper products in most groceries or by the cooking and baking supplies.

Pasta, Penne, Rotini, or Farfalle—dried, shaped pasta, in its most simple form made from a flour and water mixture. We basically want you to have short pasta in your pantry. These shorter, wider shapes can stand up to heavier sauces and provide interest to the dish. The shape choice is up to you, but we suggest:

Penne: Little tubes
Rotini: Corkscrews
Farfalle: Bow ties

Pasta, String—dried, thin, long pasta, in its most simple form made from a flour and water mixture. Again, the specific style is up to you. We don't recommend using angel hair, because it is so fine it can't stand up to some sauces. These are our suggestions from thinnest to thickest:

Thin spaghetti (spaghettini)
Spaghetti
Linguine fine
Linguine
Fettuccine

Peanut Butter, Creamy—paste made from ground peanuts, often combined with oil and sugar. We prefer creamy peanut butter because of its versatility. Peanut butter can generally be stored in the pantry unless it is all-natural or organic. If that is the case, open it, stir in all the oil that has risen to the top, and then refrigerate.

Pears (can)—subtly sweet and fragrant fruit. Available in halves or sliced. We prefer to buy pears in 100 percent juice, although they are also available in heavy or light syrup.

Peas (frozen)—a podded seed, removed from the pod and frozen. Found in the frozen food section, peas are wonderful in recipes or as a quick salad topping. Just thaw and drain, and they are ready to go!

Pepper, Ground Black—ground fermented and dried berries (peppercorns) of an evergreen vine. Different colors of peppercorns depend on when the fruit is plucked. Found in the spice section of most groceries. To retain good flavor and potency, it is best to use dried spices within one year.

Pineapple, Slices or Chunks (can)—a very juicy fruit with a tangy, sweet taste. Available in rings, chunks, and crushed. For all recipes we prefer rings or chunks. We prefer to buy pineapple in 100 percent juice, although it is also available in heavy or light syrup.

Pine Nuts (Pignoli)—soft, sweet, buttery seeds of pine trees. Pine nuts are generally found in the fresh produce section of most groceries. They can be used in both savory dishes and sweet desserts. Keep in a plastic container in the refrigerator for up to a month or in your freezer for up to three months. Pistachios make a good substitute in most dishes.

Pita Bread—flatbread made with a pocket. Found near the deli counter of most groceries. Can be frozen to extend shelf life.

Plastic Wrap—plastic film used for wrapping and preserving food. Most often it is made from PVC; however, there are now non-PVC alternatives available at larger groceries and health food stores. Found near the paper products at most groceries.

Potatoes, Russet, Sweet, or Yukon Gold (fresh)—starchy, tuberous root vegetables. Store potatoes in a cool and well-ventilated place for 2 to 4 months. Do not refrigerate or freeze raw potatoes, because their starch will turn into sugar.

> *Russets:* a great all-purpose potato for mashed, baked, scalloped, and French fried potatoes. If potatoes have a lot of large eyes, do not buy them.

> *Sweet potatoes:* a very healthy option to substitute for white potatoes. They have orange flesh and a high natural sugar content.

> *Yukon Gold:* yellow-fleshed, thin-skinned potatoes with a rich creamy flavor.

Poultry Seasoning—a dried seasoning blend generally made with sage, thyme, pepper, marjoram, and sometimes cloves. Found in the spice section of most groceries. To retain good flavor and potency, it is best to use dried spices within one year.

Puff Pastry Sheets (frozen)—light and flaky pastry sheets generally made from flour, butter, salt, and cold water. Found in the frozen food section of most groceries near the frozen pie crusts. We prefer to buy it in sheets, which adds to its versatility. Make sure the dough is chilled before baking to ensure that the pastry puffs as much as possible.

Pumpkin Pie Spice—a dried spice blend generally made with cinnamon, ginger, nutmeg, and cloves. To retain good flavor and potency, it is best to use dried spices within one year.

Raisins—dried red or yellow grapes. Available in black and golden varieties. Choose your personal preference. Because drying is a natural preservation method, in an airtight container raisins stay fresh a long time. Toss if they begin to get really hard or crystallize.

Ranch or Buttermilk Dressing—generally made with vegetable oil, buttermilk, water, sugar, garlic, onion, salt, and spices. Our only purchased salad dressing, this dressing can be used on salads or as a condiment on sandwiches, and also mixes wonderfully with salsa, Tabasco, barbecue sauce, and tomato paste for dips and dressings. Refrigerate after opening.

Raspberry Jam or Jelly—Jam is made by boiling fruit and includes pieces of the fruit. Jelly is made from fruit juice and does not have any fruit parts in it. Try to buy seedless jam, which blends more easily and you avoid those pesky little seeds. Refrigerate after opening.

Red Pepper Flakes—dried and crushed red chile peppers. We love red pepper flakes for providing heat to dishes. Generally, the longer the pepper flakes cook or stand, the hotter the dish becomes. To retain good flavor and potency, it is best to use dried spices within one year.

Relish, Sweet or Dill—finely chopped pickled cucumbers. Strictly a personal preference. Depending on which you prefer, the recipes in this book will vary significantly in taste but will still work great in their own way. Store in the refrigerator after opening. Found near pickles and olives in most groceries.

Sweet: generally made with cucumbers, sugar, vinegar, water, and salt.

Dill: generally made with cucumbers, vinegar, water, dill weed, and garlic.

Rice, Jasmine and/or Brown—grain from marshy grasses. We use these rices interchangeably in all recipes, although brown rice tends to give food a crunchier texture and requires a longer cooking time.

Jasmine: long-grained, fragrant Thai rice. Basmati can be substituted.

Brown: rice grains that retain the natural bran layer.

Roasted Red Peppers (jar)—sweet red peppers, fire-roasted and then packed in water or vinegar. Roasted red peppers are usually found in the international section of most groceries, but they might also be by canned vegetables or condiments. The peppers are packed in water or vinegar, so buy according to your taste preference, although those packed in vinegar will last longer after they are opened. Refrigerate after opening.

Salsa—*Salsa* is Spanish for "sauce." Commonly a condiment made from chopped vegetables and seasonings, salsa is generally found in the international section of most groceries; however, some fresh varieties are also found in the fresh produce section. Refrigerate after opening.

Salt—mined sodium chloride. Salt is the most necessary and basic of all seasonings and is available to buy in many different forms. We feel that table salt is the most versatile. Found in the spice section of most groceries.

Saucepan—a 2- or 3-quart long-handled pot. We prefer to have lids for all our pots and pans.

Shallots/Onions—bulbed vegetables with an outer skin. Shallots taste like a combination of onions and garlic with a mild and rich flavor. Do not buy shallots if they have already begun to sprout. If you would prefer to use onions, it's better to choose white onions, which tend to have a milder taste. Any stocked recipe can use either shallots or onions. In general, use half as much shallot as onion. Shallots should be kept in a cool, dark pantry much like garlic. Store onions in a cool, dark pantry. Do not freeze.

Shrimp, Raw (frozen)—crustacean shellfish. We buy uncooked shrimp for their versatility. We also prefer to buy the shrimp peeled and deveined, to ease their preparation tremendously.

Skewers, Wooden—often made from bamboo. We love to keep these around for shish kebabs. Make sure to soak them in water before grilling to keep them from igniting. Found in the housewares or kitchen gadget sections of most groceries.

Sour Cream or Plain Yogurt—We like having the choice of using either sour cream or plain yogurt interchangeably. Although the tastes may be slightly different, your personal preference should dictate your choice. If using as a condiment on tacos or burritos, we suggest using sour cream. Both are found in the refrigerated dairy section of most groceries.

Sour cream: a cultured cream that is allowed to sour.

Yogurt: bacterially fermented milk.

Soy Sauce (Soya Sauce)—a fermented sauce made from soybeans, roasted grain, water, and salt. Low-sodium versions are completely acceptable to use for all recipes. We use soy sauce at the dinner table as a seasoning for rice and vegetables. Found in the Asian area of the international section of most groceries.

Spinach (frozen)—dark green leafy vegetable found in the frozen foods section of most groceries. We much prefer to buy it chopped and in a bag rather than in a box, so we can thaw only what we need. Great in soups, stews, dips, and pastas. See the package for cooking directions.

Springform Pan—metal baking pan whose sides can be unhinged and removed from the bottom once the dish is completed.

Stockpot—large, 6-quart (or more) pot with small handles on two sides. We prefer to have lids for all our pots and pans.

Storage Bags, Resealable Gallon—bags made from thin, flexible plastic film, with a zippered top to allow them to be repeatedly opened and closed. We love to use these bags to marinate our meats. Found near the paper products section of most groceries.

Sugar, Brown—white sugar combined with molasses. The darker the sugar, the higher the content of molasses. Brown sugar can be used as a sweetener on cereals and fruits, and in beverages. It is also good to have around for baking because of its added flavor and moisture content. Keeping a slice of bread in your airtight container of brown sugar can aid in keeping it soft. Found in the baking section of most groceries.

Sugar, Confectioners' (Powdered Sugar)—a finely ground form of highly refined beet or cane sugar, generally mixed with cornstarch. Great as a dusting for cakes and brownies. Also used in frostings, candies, and icings. Found in the baking section of most groceries.

Sugar, Granulated—white sugar granules from highly refined beet or cane sugar. The basic sugar in your cupboard. Found in the baking section of most groceries.

Tabasco/Hot Sauce—generally made from hot peppers, vinegar, and salt, and then aged. Tabasco is generally found by the ketchup and mustards at most groceries. Tabasco can be substituted for cayenne pepper, although Tabasco will add a vinegar taste to the dish. To substitute: for every ¼ teaspoon cayenne pepper, substitute 6 to 8 drops Tabasco. The flavor stays better in the refrigerator. If it changes to a dark color, it is probably best to toss it.

Tomatoes (fresh)—soft, usually red, fruit. It is best to store tomatoes on a countertop, out of the refrigerator, to prevent them from becoming mealy. There are many varieties of fresh tomatoes, but we generally choose:

> *Beefsteak:* large, sweet, and juicy, used for sauces and great sliced for sandwiches or cut up for salads.

> *Roma:* oval or pear-shaped tomato known for having less juice and fewer seeds. Great for dips and salsas.

For every 1½ cups chopped fresh tomatoes, you can substitute one drained 15-ounce can diced tomatoes.

Tomatoes, Diced (can)—tomatoes that have been diced and packed in water and salt. Found in most groceries in the canned tomato section. We love the ease of use and versatility of diced tomatoes.

One 15-ounce can diced tomatoes, drained, can generally be substituted for every 1½ cups of chopped fresh tomatoes.

Tomato Paste (can or tube)—made from tomatoes whose skins and seeds have been removed. They are cooked and pureed until a thick paste has formed. Tomato paste provides richness to sauces, soups, and chili. Although it is sometimes hard to find, we love the paste in a tube because we waste less. Refrigerate after opening.

Tomato Sauce (can)—a puree of tomatoes. Tomato sauce is a wonderful, easy way to make tomato-based sauces, soups, stews, and chilis.

Toothpicks—small sticks, usually made from wood, with pointed ends. We prefer the noncolored toothpicks to avoid having the color run into our food. Found in the paper products or kitchen gadget section of most groceries.

Tortilla Chips—baked or fried chips made from corn or flour tortillas. Tortilla chips are available in many shapes and sizes. They are also available in blue corn. Found in the salty snack section of most groceries.

Tortillas, Flour—unleavened flat bread made of wheat flour. Keep in the refrigerator or freeze to extend shelf life. To soften, microwave for 15 to 30 seconds.

Vanilla Ice Cream—frozen dessert generally made from milk, cream, sugar, and vanilla, and sometimes eggs. Low-fat and low-sugar versions are acceptable substitutions.

Vinegar, Balsamic—oxidized, unfermented juice of a grape, aged in wooden barrels. Look for vinegar from Modena, a region of Italy. The longer the vinegar has been allowed to age, the sweeter the flavor. Balsamic vinegar can be used in dressings and savory sauces and is sweet enough to pour over fruit as a dessert. Found near salad dressings in most groceries.

Vinegar, Red Wine—made by oxidation of the alcohol in red wine. A very basic vinegar, great in dressings and marinades. Found near salad dressings in most groceries.

Vinegar, White Wine—made by oxidation of the alcohol in white wine. Used in salad dressings and many other recipes. Use as a substitute for rice vinegar and cider vinegar. Found near salad dressings in most groceries.

Worcestershire Sauce—made of aged vinegars, tamarind, anchovies, spices, and sugars. This sauce has a rich and savory flavor. Anytime a recipe calls for fish sauce, you can substitute half Worcestershire sauce and half soy sauce. Found near condiments like steak sauce in most groceries.

recipes

appetizers

These quick individual bites are dedicated to Sarah's husband, Larry, and his absolute love of bacon! Enjoy these as appetizers or as delicious salad toppers.

bacon-wrapped artichoke hearts

Makes 30

5 slices bacon

30 marinated artichoke hearts, drained

1. Preheat the oven to 425°F. Line a jelly roll pan with aluminum foil and top with a cooling rack.
2. Cut the slices of bacon into thirds and cut the thirds in half lengthwise. Wrap the artichoke hearts with pieces of bacon and secure with toothpicks.
3. Lay on the cooling rack. Bake for 20 minutes or until the bacon is crispy.
4. Serve immediately.

---

bacon cooking tip

This is absolutely the easiest, cleanest, and least stinky way to cook bacon.

1. Preheat the oven to 425°F.
2. Line a jelly roll pan with aluminum foil and top with a cooling rack.
3. Lay the bacon flat on the cooling rack, being careful not to overlap.
4. Bake for 15 to 20 minutes or until desired crispness. Dab with a paper towel to remove excess grease.
5. Serve immediately or wrap and refrigerate.

bacon-wrapped pineapple

Makes 30

5 slices bacon
30 pineapple chunks,
    drained
¼ cup brown sugar

1. Preheat the oven to 425°F. Line a jelly roll pan with aluminum foil and top with a cooling rack.
2. Cut the slices of bacon into thirds and cut the thirds in half lengthwise. Wrap the pineapple chunks with pieces of bacon and secure with toothpicks. Dip into brown sugar.
3. Lay on the jelly roll pan. Bake for 20 minutes or until the bacon is crispy.
4. Serve immediately.

bacon-wrapped ranch chicken

Makes 24

4 boneless, skinless
    chicken breasts or
    6 thighs, uncooked,
    cubed into 24 pieces
¼ cup ranch dressing
2 tablespoons grill
    seasoning
4 slices bacon

1. Preheat the oven to 425°F. Line a jelly roll pan with aluminum foil and top with a cooling rack.
2. Soak the chicken cubes in ranch dressing for a few minutes, making sure to completely submerge each piece.
3. Drain off the ranch dressing and toss the chicken with the grill seasoning.
4. Cut the slices of bacon into thirds and cut the thirds in half lengthwise. Wrap the chicken chunks with pieces of bacon and secure with toothpicks.
5. Lay on the jelly roll pan. Bake for 20 minutes or until the bacon is crispy.
6. Serve immediately.

bacon-wrapped shrimp ▬

Makes 30

5 slices bacon

30 raw shrimp, thawed,
    peeled completely, and
    deveined

¼ cup barbecue sauce

1. Preheat the oven to 425°F. Line a jelly roll pan with aluminum foil and top with a cooling rack.
2. Cut the slices of bacon into thirds and cut the thirds in half lengthwise. Wrap the shrimp with pieces of bacon and secure with toothpicks.
3. Lay on the cooling rack and baste with barbecue sauce. Bake for 20 minutes or until the bacon is crispy.
4. Serve immediately.

These dips are full of flavor and extremely fast and easy to make. We love them with the Pita Chips and Garlic Toast on the following pages.

hummus ▬

Serves 6 to 8

Two 15-ounce cans Great Northern or cannellini beans, drained and rinsed

⅓ cup warm water

¼ cup peanut butter

¼ cup lemon juice

¼ cup olive oil

2 cloves garlic, minced

1 teaspoon cumin

1 teaspoon salt

Pita Chips (page 58) or Garlic Toast (page 57), for serving

1. Combine all the ingredients (except chips) in a blender or food processor and pulse until smooth. Chill.
2. Serve with Pita Chips or Garlic Toast.

roasted red pepper dip

Serves 6

4 roasted red peppers,
   drained and coarsely
   chopped
¼ cup roughly chopped
   fresh basil
1 tablespoon balsamic
   vinegar
2 tablespoons olive oil
½ cup crumbled feta cheese
Pita Chips (page 58) or
   Garlic Toast (page 57),
   for serving

1. Combine all the ingredients (except chips) in a blender
   or food processor and pulse until smooth. Chill.
2. Serve with Pita Chips or Garlic Toast.

sweet pea pesto dip

Serves 6

2 cups frozen peas, thawed
   and drained
2 cloves garlic, minced
¼ cup olive oil
¼ cup grated Parmesan
   cheese
¼ cup chopped fresh basil
¼ cup water
Pita Chips (page 58) or
   Garlic Toast (page 57),
   for serving

1. Combine all the ingredients (except chips) in a blender
   or food processor and pulse until smooth. Chill.
2. Serve with Pita Chips or Garlic Toast.

garlic toast

Serves 6

2 tablespoons unsalted butter, melted
¼ teaspoon garlic powder
6 slices bread, crusts removed

1. Preheat the oven to 400°F. Cover a jelly roll pan with parchment paper.
2. Mix the butter and garlic powder and brush over the bread. Cut each slice into eight triangles.
3. Bake for 12 minutes or until golden brown.

---

different guests, different tastes

Everyone we have tested these dips on has really liked at least one of them. Because they are so simple to make and can be made ahead of time, we like to make all three when entertaining. They look beautiful displayed together and have enough variety of flavors that everyone will find at least one favorite!

pita chips

Serves 6 to 8

4 pita breads

1. Preheat the oven to 400°F. Cover a jelly roll pan with parchment paper.
2. Cut each pita into eight triangles.
3. Bake for 8 minutes or until golden brown.

seasoned pita chips

Serves 6 to 8

¼ teaspoon garlic powder
½ teaspoon salt
2 tablespoons olive oil
4 pita breads

1. Preheat the oven to 400°F. Cover a jelly roll pan with parchment paper.
2. Mix the garlic powder and salt. Brush the oil over the pita. Sprinkle with the salt mixture. Cut each pita into eight triangles.
3. Bake for 8 minutes or until golden brown.

---

parchment paper

Parchment paper–topped jelly roll pans make these dippers' cleanup effortless! Parchment paper makes pans truly nonstick. Do not confuse parchment paper with wax paper, which can leave a wax residue when used in baking.

Cheese balls are wonderful make-ahead appetizers. Kids will love the Caramel Apple Cheese Ball!

blue cheese–cranberry cheese ball

Serves 6 to 8

One 8-ounce package cream cheese, softened

½ cup dried cranberries, chopped

½ cup shredded Cheddar cheese

¼ cup crumbled blue or Gorgonzola cheese

¼ cup finely chopped pecans

Crackers and/or celery sticks, for serving

1. Mix together the cream cheese, cranberries, and cheeses. Place the mixture on aluminum foil or plastic wrap and form into a ball. Refrigerate for at least 30 minutes.
2. Roll in the pecans right before serving. Serve with crackers and/or celery sticks.

caramel apple cheese ball ▬

Serves 6 to 8

One 8-ounce package cream cheese, softened

2 tablespoons peanut butter

½ cup brown sugar

1 teaspoon vanilla extract

¼ cup chopped peanuts

Apple slices, for serving

Lemon or lime juice

1. Mix the cream cheese, peanut butter, brown sugar, and vanilla extract with an electric hand mixer. Place the mixture on aluminum foil or plastic wrap and form into a ball. Refrigerate for at least 30 minutes.
2. Roll in the peanuts right before serving. Toss the apple slices with lemon or lime juice to prevent the apples from turning brown, and serve with the cheese ball.

pesto cheese ball

Serves 6 to 8

2 cups roughly chopped
  fresh basil
3 tablespoons pine nuts
¼ cup grated Parmesan
  cheese
2 cloves garlic
1 tablespoon olive oil
¼ teaspoon black pepper
One 8-ounce package
  cream cheese, softened
1 cup shredded mozzarella
  cheese
½ cup drained and finely
  chopped roasted red
  pepper
Crackers, Pita Chips
  (page 58), or crudités,
  for serving

1. In a blender or food processor, blend the basil, pine nuts, Parmesan, garlic, olive oil, and black pepper until smooth. Mix in the cream cheese, mozzarella, and red pepper. Place the mixture on aluminum foil or plastic wrap and form into a ball. Refrigerate for at least 30 minutes.

2. Serve with crackers, Pita Chips, or crudités.

have dip, will travel

For those times when we are asked to bring a dish to pass, we love these cheese balls because they travel well. We bring along a platter and assemble the cheese ball and accompaniment when we arrive at our destination. The Pesto Cheese Ball in particular is a festive choice for the holidays because of its green and red coloring.

These are great recipes to have in your back pocket. They are perfect with cut-up vegetables, including carrots, celery, bell peppers, and cucumbers.

cajun aioli ▬

Serves 4 to 6

1 cup mayonnaise
12 drops Tabasco or hot
 sauce
½ teaspoon garlic powder
1 tablespoon chili powder
½ teaspoon dried minced
 onion
¼ teaspoon nutmeg
½ teaspoon black pepper
Crudités, for serving

Mix all the ingredients together (except crudités) and chill for at least 1 hour. Serve with crudités.

dill dip

Serves 6 to 8

1 cup mayonnaise
1 cup sour cream or plain
 yogurt
1 tablespoon dried minced
 onion
½ teaspoon herbes de
 Provence
1 tablespoon dill weed
¼ teaspoon salt
Crudités, for serving

Mix all the ingredients together (except crudités) and chill for at least 1 hour. Serve with crudités.

spinach dip

Serves 6 to 8

2 cups frozen spinach, thawed and squeezed dry

1 cup sour cream or plain yogurt

1 cup mayonnaise

2 tablespoons dried minced onion

½ cup pine nuts

¼ teaspoon garlic powder

½ teaspoon herbes de Provence

1 tablespoon lemon juice

¼ teaspoon black pepper

1 teaspoon salt

Crudités or Pita Chips (page 58), for serving

Mix all the ingredients together well (except crudités or chips) and chill for at least 1 hour. Serve with crudités or Pita Chips.

how to drain spinach

Frozen spinach retains an enormous amount of water when thawed and must be squeezed dry. We like using a clean kitchen towel or sturdy paper towel to wrap around the spinach and squeeze out excess water. A small colander also works well: we can push the water out through the bottom.

These cream cheese–based layered dips are simple and flavorful.
They are perfect as a meal starter or a dish to pass.

black bean layered dip

Serves 6 to 8

One 15-ounce can black beans, drained and rinsed

One 8-ounce package cream cheese, softened

1 cup salsa

1 cup finely chopped lettuce

1 cup shredded Cheddar cheese

3 green onions, chopped

One 4-ounce can sliced black olives, drained

Tortilla chips, for serving

1. Mash the black beans and mix with the cream cheese and salsa until well blended.
2. Spread over the bottom of a pie plate. Layer with the lettuce, Cheddar, green onions, and olives.
3. Serve with tortilla chips.

crab cocktail layered dip ▰

Serves 6 to 8

One 8-ounce package cream cheese, softened

COCKTAIL SAUCE

½ cup ketchup

2 tablespoons prepared horseradish

1 tablespoon lemon juice

One 6-ounce can crabmeat, drained, or one 8-ounce package imitation crabmeat, finely chopped

Butter crackers, for serving

1. Spread the cream cheese over the bottom of a pie plate. Mix the cocktail sauce ingredients and spread over the cream cheese. Sprinkle with the crab. Chill.
2. Serve with butter crackers.

olive puree layered dip

Serves 6 to 8

One 8-ounce package cream cheese, softened

¼ cup almonds

2 tablespoons lemon juice

1 cup pitted green or Kalamata olives

1 tablespoon Worcestershire sauce

¼ cup olive oil

1 tablespoon herbes de Provence

¼ teaspoon black pepper

Butter crackers or carrot sticks, for serving

1. Spread the cream cheese over the bottom of a pie plate.
2. In a food processor, combine the almonds, lemon juice, olives, Worcestershire, olive oil, herbes de Provence, and pepper and pulse until a paste forms. Spread over the cream cheese.
3. Serve with butter crackers or carrot sticks.

pineapple-apricot layered dip

Serves 6 to 8

One 8-ounce package
  cream cheese, softened
½ cup apricot preserves
½ cup drained chopped
  pineapple
1 tablespoon prepared
  horseradish
1 tablespoon Dijon mustard
Butter crackers, for serving

1. Spread the cream cheese over the bottom of a pie plate.
2. In a saucepan over medium heat, combine the preserves, pineapple, horseradish, and mustard and stir until the mixture bubbles.
3. Pour over the cream cheese. Serve with butter crackers.

salsa layered dip

Serves 6 to 8

One 8-ounce package
  cream cheese, softened
1 cup salsa
Tortilla chips, for serving

1. Spread the cream cheese over the bottom of a pie plate. Pour the salsa over the top of the cream cheese.
2. Either chill or heat in the microwave for about 45 seconds.
3. Serve with tortilla chips.

---

hot or cold?

This is a great appetizer all year round. In the summer we like to keep it cold, but in the winter we heat it up in the microwave and serve it warm. Either way, it is delicious and about as simple as it gets!

Deviled eggs are a great tradition for summer backyard barbecues, but these are anything but old-fashioned. Enjoy at any season, anytime!

deviled eggs

Serves 12

12 eggs
½ cup mayonnaise
1 tablespoon dried minced
    onion
1 teaspoon yellow mustard
¼ teaspoon dill weed
¼ teaspoon chili powder
⅛ teaspoon salt

1. Place the eggs in a stockpot and cover with water by at least 1 inch. Over high heat, bring the water to a rolling boil. Remove from the heat, cover, and allow to sit in the hot water for 18 minutes.

2. Drain off the water and cover the eggs with ice cubes or very cold tap water. Allow to sit for a few minutes, drain, and refill with ice or cold tap water. Allow to sit until the eggs are cold.

3. Peel the eggs and cut them in half lengthwise. Remove the yolks and combine them with the remaining ingredients.

4. Scoop 1 teaspoon of the mixture back into each egg white half. Serve.

---

peeling eggs

Hard-boiled eggs can be maddening to peel when the shell clings to the egg like it's its job. The above cooking method seems to help with this problem. We also tap both ends of the egg and then gently roll the side of the egg on the kitchen counter to create many little cracks in the shell before we peel.

These warm, hearty dips are always a hit. To make them ahead of time, cover and place in the refrigerator, then bake just prior to serving.

hot black bean dip

Serves 6 to 8

One 15-ounce can black
beans, drained and
rinsed

1 tablespoon cumin

1 tablespoon chili powder

½ teaspoon salt

⅓ cup salsa

½ cup shredded Cheddar
cheese

¼ cup chopped green or
black olives

Tortilla chips, for serving

1. Preheat the oven to 400°F.
2. Mix together the beans, cumin, chili powder, salt, and salsa. Transfer to a pie plate or 8-inch square baking dish and top with the cheese and olives. Bake for 10 minutes.
3. Serve hot with tortilla chips.

hot crab dip

Serves 6 to 8

One 8-ounce package
    cream cheese, softened
⅓ cup mayonnaise
2 teaspoons lemon juice
1 tablespoon water
2 green onions, thinly
    sliced
1 tablespoon herbes de
    Provence
1 tablespoon prepared
    horseradish
¼ teaspoon Worcestershire
    sauce
8 drops Tabasco or hot
    sauce
½ cup chopped almonds
One 6-ounce can crabmeat,
    drained, or one 8-ounce
    package imitation
    crabmeat, chopped
Butter crackers, for serving

1. Preheat the oven to 400°F.
2. Mix all the ingredients together (except the crackers) and spread out into a pie plate or 8-inch square baking dish. Bake for 20 minutes.
3. Serve hot with butter crackers.

hot spinach-artichoke dip ▬

Serves 6 to 8

1 cup mayonnaise

One 12-ounce jar marinated
artichoke hearts, drained

1 cup frozen spinach, thawed
and squeezed dry

1 cup shredded mozzarella
cheese

⅓ cup grated Parmesan
cheese

Tortilla chips or Pita Chips
(page 58), for serving

1. Preheat the oven to 400°F.

2. Mix all the ingredients together (except the chips) and
spread out into a pie plate or 8-inch square baking dish.
Bake for 20 minutes.

3. Serve hot with tortilla chips or Pita Chips.

hot stuffed mushroom dip

Serves 6 to 8

Two 4-ounce cans sliced
mushrooms, drained
and chopped

½ cup mayonnaise

One 6-ounce can crabmeat,
drained, or one 8-ounce
package imitation
crabmeat, chopped

2 tablespoons thinly sliced
green onion

¼ cup milk

1 teaspoon Dijon mustard

¼ cup plain bread crumbs

1 teaspoon herbes de Provence

½ cup shredded mozzarella
cheese

¼ cup grated Parmesan
cheese

Butter crackers, for serving

1. Preheat the oven to 400°F.

2. Mix all the ingredients together (except the crackers) and
spread out into a pie plate or 8-inch square baking dish.
Bake for 20 minutes.

3. Serve hot with butter crackers.

Lettuce wraps make a great starter or main dish. Any of these mixtures are tasty wrapped in tortillas, too!

asian lettuce wraps

Serves 6 to 8

1 pound ground beef
One 4-ounce can
    mushrooms, drained
    and chopped
¼ cup sliced green onion
1 cup cabbage and carrot
    mix
¼ teaspoon garlic powder
¼ cup soy sauce
¼ cup packed brown sugar
1 teaspoon white wine
    vinegar
Lettuce leaves, for serving

1. In a fry pan, cook the ground beef thoroughly. Drain off the grease.
2. Add the mushrooms, green onion, cabbage mix, and garlic powder. Cook over medium heat, stirring occasionally, until the vegetables begin to soften.
3. Mix together the soy sauce, brown sugar, and vinegar. Pour over the meat mixture and cook until heated through.
4. Serve hot with lettuce leaves for wrapping.

lettuces for lettuce wraps

Our preferences for lettuce wraps are iceberg, Boston, or Bibb lettuce. Iceberg is easily found and inexpensive. We cut the iceberg head into quarters and serve.

Boston and Bibb are small and the leaves are already the perfect size for wrapping. Be sure to clean them thoroughly before serving. (Don't mistake mini cabbages for these lettuces.)

chophouse lettuce wraps

Serves 6 to 8

DIPPING SAUCE

3 tablespoons ketchup

1 tablespoon
Worcestershire sauce

2 tablespoons maple syrup

1 tablespoon chili powder

1 teaspoon prepared
horseradish

1 tablespoon unsalted
butter

1 shallot or 1 medium
onion, thinly sliced

One 4-ounce can
mushrooms, drained
and chopped

1 pound flank steak, sliced
thin against the grain

1 tablespoon grill seasoning

½ cup crumbled blue or
Gorgonzola cheese

Lettuce leaves, for serving

1. Mix together all the dipping sauce ingredients and set aside.

2. In a large fry pan over medium-high heat, melt the butter. Add the shallot and mushrooms and cook until the shallot is softened. Scoop into a bowl and set aside.

3. Add the steak to the emptied pan, sprinkle with the grill seasoning, and cook until the steak is cooked to desired doneness.

4. Return the mushroom and onion mixture to the pan. Toss the entire mixture with the cheese.

5. Serve hot with lettuce leaves for wrapping and the dipping sauce.

sweet and tangy lettuce wraps

Serves 6 to 8

GLAZE

¼ cup applesauce

2 tablespoons apricot
   preserves

1½ teaspoons honey

¼ cup white wine vinegar

2 tablespoons pureed ginger

1 tablespoon
   Worcestershire sauce

3 tablespoons soy sauce

12 ounces to 1 pound
   boneless, skinless
   chicken, chopped in
   1-inch pieces, or raw
   shrimp, thawed, peeled
   completely, deveined,
   and diced

2 tablespoons vegetable oil

½ teaspoon garlic powder

1 bell pepper, thinly sliced

3 green onions, thinly
   sliced

1 cup cabbage and carrot
   mixture

½ cup finely chopped fresh
   basil

Lettuce leaves, for serving

1. Mix together all the glaze ingredients and set aside.

2. In a fry pan over high heat, cook the chicken in the oil
   until done. Stir in the garlic powder, bell pepper, green
   onions, and cabbage mix and cook for 2 to 3 minutes
   more. Pour the glaze over the chicken and vegetables,
   sprinkle with basil, and toss to coat.

3. Serve hot with lettuce leaves for wrapping.

use the fillings as a meal

If you don't have a head of lettuce
lying around, these lettuce wrap fillings are also delicious over rice or
wrapped in a tortilla.

These individual appetizers are all delicious and impressive. Add variety by using one mini muffin pan for two different recipes. Just make sure to cut the filling recipes in half.

antipasto bites ▬

Makes 24

1 sheet puff pastry, thawed

¼ cup chopped pitted green or Kalamata olives

½ cup drained and chopped marinated artichoke hearts

1 roasted red pepper, drained and diced

½ cup shredded mozzarella cheese

1. Preheat the oven to 400°F.
2. Roll out the pastry on a floured surface to approximately 11 by 14 inches. With a pizza cutter, cut the pastry into 24 pieces (4 rows, 6 columns). Stretch the pastry pieces slightly and lay in the cups of a mini muffin pan.
3. Mix together the olives, artichoke hearts, and roasted red pepper. Fill each cup with 2 teaspoons of the mixture and top with the mozzarella.
4. Bake for 12 to 15 minutes, until the corners begin to brown. Serve immediately.

using puff pastry

Puff pastry may seem intimidating. However, it is really easy to use and very forgiving. To thaw, remove from the wrapper and set it out on the counter. If thawing two sheets, be sure to separate them and lay them on the counter side by side. A sheet takes 30 to 40 minutes to thaw. Puff pastry works best when it is still cold before baking. (This allows the fat to stay solid and melt only while baking, causing little pockets of air or what we experience as puffed flakiness.) If while working with the dough it has become warm, place in the fridge while you mix the filling.

crab rangoon with sweet-and-sour sauce

Makes 24

1 sheet puff pastry, thawed
1 tablespoon sour cream
Half an 8-ounce package
    cream cheese, softened
Half a 6-ounce can
    crabmeat, drained, or
    half an 8-ounce package
    imitation crabmeat,
    chopped
1 green onion, thinly sliced
⅛ teaspoon garlic powder
1 teaspoon pureed ginger
1 teaspoon soy sauce
⅓ cup confectioners' sugar
Sweet-and-Sour Sauce
    (recipe below)

1. Preheat the oven to 400°F.
2. Roll out the pastry on a floured surface to approximately 11 by 14 inches. With a pizza cutter, cut the pastry into 24 pieces (4 rows, 6 columns). Stretch the pastry pieces slightly and lay in the cups of a mini muffin pan.
3. Mix together the remaining ingredients (except the Sweet-and-Sour Sauce). Fill each cup with 2 teaspoons of the mixture.
4. Bake for 12 to 15 minutes, until the corners begin to brown. Serve immediately with Sweet-and-Sour Sauce.

sweet-and-sour sauce

Makes about ½ cup

3 tablespoons apricot
    preserves
2 tablespoons ketchup
2 tablespoons brown sugar
2 tablespoons soy sauce

Mix all the ingredients together and chill.

egg rolls with sweet-and sour-sauce

Makes 24

1 sheet puff pastry, thawed
1 tablespoon vegetable oil
1 tablespoon pureed ginger
½ teaspoon garlic powder
One 4-ounce can mushroom
    stems and pieces,
    drained
1 cup cabbage and carrot
    mix
1 green onion, finely
    chopped
1 tablespoon soy sauce
⅛ teaspoon black pepper
1 egg white, lightly beaten
Sweet-and-Sour Sauce
    (see recipe opposite)

1. Preheat the oven to 400°F.

2. Roll out the pastry on a floured surface to approximately 11 by 14 inches. With a pizza cutter, cut the pastry into 24 pieces (4 rows, 6 columns). Stretch the pastry squares slightly and lay in the cups of a mini muffin pan.

3. In a fry pan, heat the oil over medium heat. Mix in the ginger, garlic powder, mushrooms, cabbage mix, and green onion. Cook for 2 to 3 minutes, until the vegetables soften. Mix in the soy sauce, black pepper, and egg white until the egg is scrambled.

4. Fill each cup with 2 teaspoons of the mixture.

5. Bake for 12 to 15 minutes, until the corners begin to brown. Serve immediately with Sweet-and-Sour Sauce.

empanadas with cajun aioli ▬

Makes 24

1 sheet puff pastry, thawed
¼ pound bulk breakfast
    sausage
1½ teaspoons dried
    minced onion
¼ teaspoon garlic powder
¼ teaspoon cumin
¼ teaspoon pumpkin pie
    spice
2 tablespoons chopped
    pitted green or
    Kalamata olives
2 tablespoons raisins,
    chopped
Cajun Aioli (recipe
    below)

1. Preheat the oven to 400°F.
2. Roll out the pastry on a floured surface to approximately 11 by 14 inches. With a pizza cutter, cut the pastry into 24 pieces (4 rows, 6 columns). Stretch the pastry pieces slightly and lay in the cups of a mini muffin pan.
3. In a fry pan over medium heat, cook the sausage thoroughly. Drain off the grease. Add the minced onion, garlic powder, cumin, and pumpkin pie spice to the sausage. Cook for 4 minutes. Remove from the heat and stir in the olives and raisins.
4. Fill each cup with 1 teaspoon of the mixture and pinch the corners of the pastry closed.
5. Bake for 12 to 15 minutes, until the tops begin to brown. Serve immediately with Cajun Aioli.

cajun aioli

Makes about 1 cup

1 cup mayonnaise
12 drops Tabasco or hot
    sauce
½ teaspoon garlic powder
1 tablespoon chili powder
1½ teaspoons dried minced
    onion
¼ teaspoon nutmeg
½ teaspoon black pepper

Mix all the ingredients together and chill.

ham and cheese bites ▬

Makes 24

1 sheet puff pastry, thawed

¼ cup chopped ham, cut into small cubes

¼ cup shredded Cheddar cheese

1. Preheat the oven to 400°F.
2. Roll out the pastry on a floured surface to approximately 11 by 14 inches. With a pizza cutter, cut the pastry into 24 pieces (4 rows, 6 columns). Stretch the pastry pieces slightly and lay in the cups of a mini muffin pan. Fill each cup with ½ teaspoon of the ham and top evenly with the cheese.
3. Bake for 12 to 15 minutes, until the corners begin to brown. Serve immediately.

spinach and feta bites ▬

Makes 24

1 sheet puff pastry, thawed

1 tablespoon olive oil

1 tablespoon dried minced onion

½ cup frozen spinach, thawed and squeezed dry

Salt

⅛ teaspoon black pepper, or to taste

¼ cup crumbled feta cheese

1. Preheat the oven to 400°F.
2. Roll out the pastry on a floured surface to approximately 11 by 14 inches. With a pizza cutter, cut the pastry into 24 pieces (4 rows, 6 columns). Stretch the pastry pieces slightly and lay in the cups of mini muffin pan.
3. Mix together the oil, minced onion, and spinach. Add salt and black pepper to taste. Fill each cup with 1 teaspoon of the mixture and top evenly with the cheese.
4. Bake for 12 to 15 minutes, until the corners begin to brown. Serve immediately.

Delicious and healthy, these salsas make a perfect starter with tortilla chips. Also, try them over grilled chicken or flank steak as a fresh, tasty garnish.

black bean–mandarin orange salsa

Serves 6 to 8

One 11-ounce can mandarin orange segments, with juice

2 tablespoons balsamic vinegar

$\frac{1}{8}$ teaspoon red pepper flakes, or to taste

$\frac{1}{2}$ teaspoon salt

$\frac{1}{4}$ teaspoon black pepper

2 tablespoons olive oil

One 15-ounce can black beans, drained and rinsed

1 bell pepper, chopped

1 shallot or $\frac{1}{4}$ medium onion, diced

$\frac{1}{4}$ cup chopped fresh basil

Tortilla chips, for serving (optional)

1. Drain $\frac{1}{3}$ cup juice from the mandarin oranges. Place the juice in a bowl and discard the remaining juice. Add the vinegar, red pepper flakes, salt, and black pepper. Whisk in the olive oil until the mixture is emulsified.

2. Chop the mandarin oranges and add to the dressing with the beans, bell pepper, shallot, and basil. Mix together well. Chill for at least 1 hour. (It's even better if you chill overnight.)

3. Serve with tortilla chips or over grilled meat.

cucumber thai salsa ▬

Serves 6 to 8

1 teaspoon salt
1 tablespoon pureed
   ginger
2 tablespoons white wine
   vinegar
2 tablespoons honey
2 tablespoons vegetable oil
1 English cucumber,
   chopped
¼ cup chopped bell pepper
¼ chopped fresh basil
3 tablespoons chopped
   peanuts
Tortilla chips, for serving
   (optional)

1. Combine the salt, ginger, vinegar, and honey. Whisk in the oil well to emulsify. Stir in the cucumber, bell pepper, basil, and peanuts.

2. Chill for at least 1 hour. (It's even better if you chill overnight.)

3. Serve with tortilla chips or over grilled meat.

---

multitask your recipes

A main objective of this system is to get the most out of the ingredients you have in your home. The same philosophy applies to our recipes. We love using the same recipe in multiple ways and extending its benefits. These salsas are a perfect example. They are delicious with tortilla chips or our Garlic Toast (page 57), but also provide a fresh take on your grilled meats as a garnish. Take it a step further by marinating the meats and then topping with the salsa. Try:

Asian Marinade with Cucumber Thai Salsa
Italian Marinade with Italian Salsa/Bruschetta Topping
Honey-Lime Marinade with Pineapple-Tomato Salsa
Java Marinade with Black Bean–Mandarin Orange Salsa

italian salsa/bruschetta topping

Serves 6 to 8

1 tablespoon balsamic
    vinegar

½ teaspoon salt

¼ teaspoon black pepper

2 cloves garlic, minced

2 tablespoons olive oil

1½ cups chopped fresh
    tomatoes, or one
    15-ounce can diced
    tomatoes, drained

½ cup chopped fresh basil

Garlic Toast, for serving
    (optional; page 57)

1. Combine the vinegar, salt, pepper, and garlic. Whisk in the oil well to emulsify. Stir in the tomatoes and basil.

2. Chill for at least 1 hour. (It's even better if you chill overnight.)

3. Serve with Garlic Toast or over grilled meat.

pineapple-tomato salsa ▬

Serves 6 to 8

One 20-ounce can
  pineapple chunks
2 tablespoons lime juice
¼ teaspoon salt
½ teaspoon red pepper
  flakes, or to taste
1 tablespoon olive oil
1½ cups chopped fresh
  tomatoes, or one
  15-ounce can diced
  tomatoes, drained
¼ cup chopped bell pepper
2 tablespoons minced
  shallot or ¼ cup finely
  diced onion
¼ cup chopped fresh basil
Tortilla chips, for serving
  (optional)

1. Drain ⅓ cup juice from the pineapple. Place the juice in a bowl and discard the remaining juice. Add the lime juice, salt, and red pepper flakes. Drizzle in the olive oil while whisking to emulsify.

2. Chop the pineapple and add to the dressing with the tomatoes, bell pepper, shallot, and basil. Chill for at least 1 hour. (It's even better if you chill overnight.)

3. Serve with tortilla chips or over grilled meat.

These are wonderful bite-size starters for any occasion. Keep them warm at an event in a Crock-Pot. We dedicate this section to Stacey's husband, Craig, who not only loves these little balls of meat, but could eat the Ginger Sauce on a shoe!

sausage meatballs ▬

Makes 24

1 pound bulk breakfast
   sausage
½ cup plain bread crumbs
2 tablespoons dried
   minced onion
2 eggs

1. Preheat the oven to 375°F. Cover a jelly roll pan with aluminum foil and top with a cooling rack.
2. Combine all the ingredients. Form into 1-inch meatballs.
3. Place the meatballs on the rack. Bake for 20 to 25 minutes or until cooked through. The meatballs can be formed and baked ahead and refrigerated or frozen to serve later.

barbecue glaze

Makes 2½ cups

1½ cup barbecue sauce
1 cup water

In a saucepan over medium heat, mix the barbecue sauce and water. Add the cooked meatballs and heat thoroughly.

ginger sauce

Makes 1½ cups

1 cup apricot preserves
½ cup barbecue sauce
1 tablespoon pureed ginger

In a saucepan over medium heat, mix all the ingredients together. Add the cooked meatballs and heat thoroughly.

raspberry sauce

Makes about 1¾ cups

1 cup raspberry jam
½ cup ketchup
¼ cup packed brown sugar
2 tablespoons white wine
    vinegar
½ teaspoon pumpkin pie
    spice

In a saucepan over medium heat, mix all the ingredients together. Add the cooked meatballs and heat thoroughly.

teriyaki sauce

Makes 2 cups

One 20-ounce can
    pineapple chunks,
    drained
3 cloves garlic, minced
1 tablespoon pureed ginger
⅓ cup soy sauce
2 tablespoons white wine
    vinegar
¼ teaspoon red pepper
    flakes
¾ cup packed brown sugar

In a saucepan over medium heat, mix all the ingredients together. Add the cooked meatballs and heat thoroughly.

---

serving meatballs

Make sure to have appetizer plates and toothpicks available when serving these delicious little balls of meat. They can get rather messy without them. We always try to use real dishes instead of paper or plastic. They create a nicer presentation, stand up to heavier recipes, and cause much less waste.

These are wonderful bite-size treats. Try the same technique as below with simple PB&J for a child-friendly snack!

greek tortilla roll-ups

Makes 40

½ cup finely chopped pitted green or Kalamata olives

1 tablespoon lemon juice

¾ cup finely diced English cucumber

1 cup sour cream or plain yogurt

1½ cups crumbled feta cheese

One 8-ounce package cream cheese, softened

2 tablespoons dried minced onion

1 teaspoon dill weed

½ teaspoon garlic powder

8 flour tortillas (8-inch or fajita size)

1. Mix all the ingredients (except tortillas). Spread about ½ cup of the filling over the top of a tortilla up to the edges. Roll up the tortilla tightly. Repeat with the remaining tortillas and filling.

2. Wrap each tortilla individually in plastic wrap and refrigerate for 1 to 24 hours.

3. Cut each tortilla into 1½-inch slices.

ham and relish tortilla roll-ups

Makes 40

¼ cup sour cream or plain yogurt

One 8-ounce package cream cheese, softened

1 cup finely diced ham

½ cup sweet or dill relish

8 flour tortillas (8-inch or fajita size)

1. Mix all ingredients (except tortillas). Spread about one-eighth of the filling over the top of a tortilla up to the edges. Roll up the tortilla tightly. Repeat with the remaining tortillas and filling.

2. Wrap each tortilla individually in plastic wrap and refrigerate for 1 to 24 hours.

3. Cut each tortilla into 1½-inch slices.

vegetable tortilla roll-ups

Makes 40

½ cup finely chopped pitted black olives

¾ cup finely diced bell pepper

1 cup sour cream or plain yogurt

1 cup shredded Cheddar cheese

One 8-ounce package cream cheese, softened

2 green onions, thinly sliced

8 flour tortillas (8-inch or fajita size)

1. Mix all the ingredients (except tortillas). Spread about ½ cup of the filling over the top of a tortilla up to the edges. Roll up the tortilla tightly. Repeat with the remaining tortillas and filling.

2. Wrap each tortilla individually in plastic wrap and refrigerate for 1 to 24 hours.

3. Cut each tortilla into 1½-inch slices.

Black Bean Layered Dip *(page 63)*

Cucumber Thai Salsa *(page 79)*

Blended Chilled Dips *(page 55)*

Bacon Wraps *(page 52)*

Vegetable Tortilla Roll-Ups *(page 86)*

Savory Puff Pastry Bites *(page 73)*

Tangy Pear Vinaigrette Salad *(page 101)*

Chili-Lime Coleslaw *(page 102)*

Parmesan Crisps *(page 98)*

Apricot Chicken Salad *(page 110)*

Carrot and Raisin Salad *(page 104)*

Mediterranean Rice Salad *(page 108)*

Carrot Autumn Spice Soup *(page 116)*

Vichyssoise *(page 129)*

Gazpacho *(page 120)*

Italian Stew *(page 122)*

Ham, Potato, and Corn Chowder *(page 121)*

Cheesy Chicken Chili *(page 117)*

Veggie Pizza *(page 159)*

Tomato-Artichoke Pasta with Shrimp *(page 150)*

Peanut Noodles *(page 143)*

Margherita Pizza *(page 156)*

Chicken BBQ Pizza *(page 155)*

Stovetop Mac and Cheese *(page 148)*

salads

One of the best parts of this system is the ability to make what you need when you need it. These salad dressings are a wonderful example of this. Eat what you want and make only what you need!

balsamic vinaigrette salad

Serves 4

DRESSING
¼ cup balsamic vinegar
1 tablespoon diced shallot
    or onion
1 teaspoon Dijon mustard
¼ cup olive oil

SALAD
Lettuce or mixed greens
Tomatoes, diced
Green onions, thinly sliced
Pine nuts, toasted
Parmesan cheese, grated

Grilled chicken, flank
    steak, or shrimp, for
    serving (optional)

1. Whisk together the vinegar, shallot, and Dijon mustard. Drizzle in the oil while whisking to emulsify.
2. On four plates, layer the salad ingredients. Drizzle with the dressing.
3. Try topped with grilled chicken, grilled flank steak, or grilled or sautéed shrimp.

basil vinaigrette salad

Serves 4

DRESSING
¼ cup lemon juice
2 tablespoons Dijon
    mustard
½ teaspoon salt
¼ teaspoon black pepper
⅓ cup olive oil
1½ cups finely chopped
    fresh basil

SALAD
Lettuce or mixed greens
Marinated artichoke hearts
Green onions, thinly sliced
Green or Kalamata olives,
    chopped
Hard-boiled eggs, sliced or
    chopped
Parmesan cheese, grated

Grilled chicken, flank
    steak, or shrimp, for
    serving (optional)

1. Whisk together the lemon juice, mustard, salt, and pepper. Drizzle in the oil while whisking to emulsify. Stir in the basil.

2. On four plates, layer the salad ingredients. Drizzle with the dressing.

3. Try topped with grilled chicken, grilled flank steak, or grilled or sautéed shrimp.

---

toasting nuts

Toasting nuts adds a tremendous amount of flavor to them because their natural oils are released. We like to toast nuts the following ways.

Stovetop: In a dry fry pan over medium heat, heat the nuts until they are golden brown.

Oven: Preheat the oven to 350°F. On a parchment paper–covered jelly roll pan, heat the nuts for about 10 minutes, or until golden brown.

The aroma of toasted nuts will let you know when they are done.

bbq vinaigrette salad

Serves 4

DRESSING
¼ cup red wine vinegar
¼ cup barbecue sauce
¼ cup olive oil

SALAD
Lettuce or mixed greens
Tomatoes, sliced or diced
Green onions, thinly sliced
Blue or Gorgonzola cheese, crumbled
Bell pepper, diced

Grilled chicken, flank steak, or shrimp, for serving (optional)

1. Whisk together the vinegar and barbecue sauce. Drizzle in the oil while whisking to emulsify.
2. On four plates, layer the salad ingredients. Drizzle with the dressing.
3. Try topped with grilled chicken, grilled flank steak, or grilled or sautéed shrimp.

caesar salad

Serves 4

DRESSING
½ cup mayonnaise
½ cup milk
1 tablespoon lemon juice
1 teaspoon Worcestershire
  sauce
2 cloves garlic, minced
¼ teaspoon salt
¼ teaspoon black pepper
½ cup grated Parmesan
  cheese

SALAD
Lettuce or mixed greens
Tomatoes, sliced or diced
Croutons (recipe below)

Grilled chicken, flank
  steak, or shrimp, or
  diced ham, for serving
  (optional)

1. Whisk together all the dressing ingredients. If the dressing is too thick, add milk until it is the right consistency.
2. On four plates, layer the salad ingredients. Drizzle with the dressing.
3. Try topped with grilled chicken, grilled flank steak, grilled or sautéed shrimp, or diced ham.

croutons ▬

Makes 40

2 slices bread, cubed
  (extra bread from
  baked frozen bread
  dough works great)
1 tablespoon olive oil
¼ teaspoon garlic powder
  (optional)

1. Preheat the oven to 400°F.
2. Place the cubed bread in a mixing bowl. Drizzle with the olive oil and sprinkle with garlic powder if desired. Toss together.
3. On a jelly roll pan, lay out the cubed bread in a single layer and bake for 10 minutes or until crisp on the outside.
4. Serve warm or at room temperature on salads.

catalina salad

Serves 4

DRESSING

½ cup ketchup

2 tablespoons sugar

2 tablespoons white wine vinegar

½ teaspoon salt

2 tablespoons dried minced onion

⅓ cup vegetable oil

SALAD

Lettuce or mixed greens

Green onions, thinly sliced

Celery, diced

Carrots, diced

Frozen peas, thawed

Corn kernels

Grilled chicken, flank steak, shrimp, diced ham, or crabmeat, for serving (optional)

1. Whisk together the ketchup, sugar, vinegar, salt, and minced onion. Drizzle in the oil while whisking to emulsify.

2. On four plates, layer the salad ingredients. Drizzle with the dressing.

3. To make this a meal, serve topped with grilled chicken, grilled flank steak, grilled or sautéed shrimp, diced ham, or crabmeat.

creamy cucumber salad

Serves 4

DRESSING

¼ cup sour cream or plain yogurt

¼ cup milk

⅓ cup finely chopped English cucumber

2 tablespoons mayonnaise

2 tablespoons thinly sliced green onion

2 tablespoons lemon juice

¼ teaspoon salt

¼ teaspoon dill weed

⅛ teaspoon black pepper

SALAD

Lettuce or mixed greens

Bacon, cooked and crumbled

Cheddar cheese, shredded

Frozen peas, thawed

Tomatoes, diced

Grilled chicken, flank steak, or shrimp, or diced ham, for serving (optional)

1. Whisk together all the dressing ingredients.
2. On four plates, layer the salad ingredients. Drizzle with the dressing.
3. Try topped with grilled chicken, grilled flank steak, grilled or sautéed shrimp, or diced ham.

ginger salad ▬

Serves 4

DRESSING

1 tablespoon pureed
  ginger
1 teaspoon dried minced
  onion
2 tablespoons white wine
  vinegar
2 tablespoons mayonnaise
1 tablespoon soy sauce
¼ cup vegetable oil

SALAD

Lettuce or mixed greens
Green onions, thinly sliced
Mandarin orange segments
Almonds, toasted
Cabbage and carrot mix

Grilled chicken, flank
  steak, or shrimp, for
  serving (optional)

1. Whisk together the ginger, minced onion, vinegar, mayonnaise, and soy sauce. Drizzle in the oil while whisking to emulsify.

2. On four plates, layer the salad ingredients. Drizzle with the dressing.

3. Try topped with grilled chicken, grilled flank steak, or grilled or sautéed shrimp.

greek salad ▬

Serves 4

DRESSING
¼ cup lemon juice
1 tablespoon Italian
    seasoning
1 clove garlic, minced
½ teaspoon salt
Black pepper
⅓ cup olive oil

SALAD
Lettuce or mixed greens
English cucumber,
    chopped
Pitted black olives
Marinated artichoke
    hearts, drained
Roasted red peppers
Feta cheese, crumbled

Grilled chicken, flank
    steak, or shrimp, for
    serving (optional)

1. Whisk together the lemon juice, Italian seasoning, garlic, salt, and pepper to taste. Drizzle in the oil while whisking to emulsify.
2. On four plates, layer the salad ingredients. Drizzle with the dressing.
3. Try topped with grilled chicken, grilled flank steak, or grilled or sautéed shrimp.

honey apricot salad

Serves 4

DRESSING
¼ cup apricot preserves
1 cup sour cream or
    plain yogurt
¼ cup honey
1 tablespoon lemon juice
¼ teaspoon cinnamon

SALAD
Lettuce or mixed greens
Frozen peas, thawed
Mandarin orange segments
Blue or Gorgonzola cheese,
    crumbled
Sugared Nuts (recipe below)

Grilled chicken, flank
    steak, or shrimp, or
    diced ham, for serving
    (optional)

1. Whisk together all the dressing ingredients.
2. On four plates, layer the salad ingredients. Drizzle with the dressing.
3. Try topped with grilled chicken, grilled flank steak, grilled or sautéed shrimp, or diced ham.

sugared nuts ▬

Makes ½ cup

¼ cup sugar
½ cup whole or chopped
    almonds, pecans, or
    peanuts

1. Over medium heat in a fry pan, stir the sugar and nuts until the sugar is melted and the nuts are coated.
2. Toss the hot nuts onto a sheet of parchment paper and allow to cool.
3. Once cool, break apart the nuts.

honey mustard salad

Serves 4

DRESSING
½ cup mayonnaise
¼ cup milk
2 tablespoons yellow
   mustard
2 tablespoons honey
1 teaspoon lemon juice

SALAD
Lettuce or mixed greens
Frozen peas, thawed
Hard-boiled eggs, chopped
Tomatoes, diced
Cheddar cheese, shredded
Bacon, cooked and chopped

Grilled chicken or flank
   steak, or diced ham, for
   serving (optional)

1. Whisk together all the dressing ingredients.
2. On four plates, layer the salad ingredients. Drizzle with the dressing.
3. Try topped with grilled chicken, grilled flank steak, or diced ham.

---

that's a wrap!

Many of these salads can also make great wraps, particularly this Honey Mustard Salad. Place the salad ingredients in a flour tortilla or pita, top with some grilled chicken, and drizzle with honey mustard dressing. Wrap like a burrito and enjoy a delicious snack or lunch.

italian vinaigrette salad

Serves 4

DRESSING
¼ cup red wine vinegar
1 tablespoon water
2 teaspoons sugar
1 teaspoon lemon juice
½ teaspoon garlic powder
½ teaspoon salt
1 teaspoon dried minced onion
¼ teaspoon black pepper
1 tablespoon Italian seasoning
¼ cup olive oil

SALAD
Lettuce or mixed greens
Tomatoes, diced
Bell pepper, diced
Pitted black olives
Green onions, thinly sliced
Parmesan Crisps (recipe
    follows)

Grilled chicken, flank steak,
    or shrimp, for serving
    (optional)

1. Whisk together the vinegar, water, sugar, lemon juice, garlic powder, salt, minced onion, black pepper, and Italian seasoning. Drizzle in the oil while whisking to emulsify.
2. On four plates, layer the salad ingredients. Drizzle with the dressing.
3. To make this a meal, serve topped with grilled chicken, grilled flank steak, or grilled or sautéed shrimp.

parmesan crisps ▬

Makes 32

2 cups grated Parmesan cheese
2 teaspoons herbes de
    Provence
¼ teaspoon black pepper

1. Preheat the oven to 350°F. Cover two jelly roll pans
   with parchment paper.
2. In a mixing bowl, mix together the cheese, herbes de
   Provence, and black pepper. Spoon tablespoons of the
   mixture onto the pans. Press mounds down flat. Keep
   approximately 4 inches between crisps.
3. Bake for 4 to 5 minutes, until just golden brown. Cool
   completely and serve.

raspberry vinaigrette salad ▬

Serves 4

DRESSING
3 tablespoons raspberry
    jam or jelly
3 tablespoons balsamic
    vinegar
1 teaspoon Dijon mustard
3 tablespoons olive oil

SALAD
Lettuce or mixed greens
Green onions, thinly sliced
Blue or Gorgonzola cheese,
    crumbled
Pears or apples, diced
Dried cranberries
Sugared Nuts (page 96)

Grilled chicken, flank
    steak, or shrimp, or
    diced ham, for serving
    (optional)

1. Whisk together the raspberry jam, vinegar, and mustard.
   Drizzle in the oil while whisking to emulsify.
2. On four plates, layer the salad ingredients. Drizzle with
   the dressing.
3. To make this a meal, serve topped with grilled chicken,
   grilled flank steak, grilled or sautéed shrimp, or diced
   ham.

salsa ranch salad

Serves 4

DRESSING
½ cup ranch dressing
¼ cup salsa

SALAD
Lettuce or mixed greens
Tomatoes, chopped
Kidney beans, drained and
    rinsed
Corn, drained
Green onions, thinly sliced
Cheddar cheese, shredded
Tortilla chips

Grilled chicken or flank
    steak, or Taco Meat
    (page 199), for serving
    (optional)

1. Whisk together the dressing ingredients.
2. On four plates, layer the salad ingredients. Drizzle with the dressing.
3. Try topped with grilled chicken, grilled flank steak, or Taco Meat.

simple blue cheese salad

Serves 4

DRESSING
½ cup ranch dressing
¼ cup crumbled blue or
    Gorgonzola cheese

SALAD
Lettuce or mixed greens
Tomatoes, chopped
Bell peppers, diced
Carrots, chopped
Green onions, thinly sliced

Grilled chicken or flank
    steak, or diced ham, for
    serving (optional)

1. Whisk together the dressing ingredients.
2. On four plates, layer the salad ingredients. Drizzle with the dressing.
3. Try topped with grilled chicken, grilled flank steak, or diced ham.

tangy pear vinaigrette salad

Serves 12

DRESSING

Half of a 15-ounce can pears, drained

½ cup white wine vinegar

1 tablespoon minced shallot or dried minced onion

¼ teaspoon garlic powder

3 tablespoons honey

¼ teaspoon salt

⅛ teaspoon black pepper

½ cup vegetable oil

1 teaspoon Dijon mustard

SALAD

Lettuce or mixed greens

Apples, peeled and chopped

Dried cranberries

Pine nuts, toasted

Bacon, cooked and chopped

Grilled chicken, flank steak, or shrimp, for serving (optional)

1. Blend together all the dressing ingredients in a blender until smooth.
2. On individual plates, layer the salad ingredients. Drizzle with the dressing.
3. To make this a meal, serve topped with grilled chicken, grilled flank steak, or grilled or sautéed shrimp.

a perfect holiday starter

This makes a lot of dressing, which makes it perfect for a large gathering. Enjoy this salad during the holidays for a wonderful alternative to the can-o'-cranberries.

These coleslaws are not only delicious, quick, and easy side dishes,
they are a wonderful way to use up cabbage and carrot mix!

asian vinaigrette coleslaw

Serves 6

¼ cup sugar
2 tablespoons soy sauce
½ cup red wine vinegar
½ cup vegetable oil
4 cups cabbage and carrot
    mix

1. Whisk together the sugar, soy sauce, vinegar, and oil in a large bowl until well combined.
2. Add the cabbage and carrot mix and toss to coat. Cover and refrigerate for at least 1 hour before serving.

chili-lime coleslaw ▬

Serves 6

¾ cup mayonnaise
¼ cup sour cream or plain
    yogurt
¼ cup milk
¼ cup lime juice
2 teaspoons chili powder
1 teaspoon cumin
1 tablespoon sugar
4 cups cabbage and carrot
    mix

1. Whisk together the mayonnaise, sour cream, milk, lime juice, chili powder, cumin, and sugar in a large bowl until well combined.
2. Add the cabbage and carrot mix and toss to coat. Cover and refrigerate for at least 1 hour before serving.

traditional/dill coleslaw

Serves 6

¾ cup mayonnaise

¾ cup milk

3 tablespoons white wine
  vinegar

3 tablespoons sugar

1 tablespoon Dijon mustard

1 teaspoon dill weed
  (optional)

4 cups cabbage and carrot
  mix

1. Whisk together the mayonnaise, milk, vinegar, sugar, mustard, and dill (if using) in a large bowl until well combined.

2. Add the cabbage and carrot mix and toss to coat. Cover and refrigerate for at least 1 hour before serving.

As this title implies, these salads are perfect for warm summer barbecues. What it doesn't imply are the little twists that make these recipes special, delicious, and perfect for any occasion.

carrot and raisin salad

Serves 6 to 8

One 20-ounce can
   pineapple chunks,
   with juice
1 tablespoon cinnamon
2 tablespoons lime juice
½ cup sour cream or plain
   yogurt
4 cups peeled and shredded
   carrots
1 cup raisins

1. Drain ¼ cup of the pineapple juice into a large bowl. Whisk in the cinnamon, lime juice, and sour cream.

2. Drain the remaining juice from the pineapple and discard. Add the carrots, raisins, and pineapple to the dressing and toss to coat. Chill for at least 1 hour before serving.

crab macaroni salad

Serves 4 to 6

⅓ cup mayonnaise

⅓ cup sour cream or plain yogurt

2 tablespoons milk

2 tablespoons sugar

¼ teaspoon nutmeg

½ teaspoon salt

⅛ teaspoon black pepper

6 to 8 ounces penne pasta, cooked, drained, and cooled

½ cup thawed frozen peas

4 hard-boiled eggs, chopped

¼ cup thinly sliced green onion

½ cup shredded carrot

One 6-ounce can crabmeat, drained, or one 8-ounce package imitation crabmeat, chopped

1. Whisk together the mayonnaise, sour cream, milk, sugar, nutmeg, salt, and pepper.
2. Toss all the remaining ingredients with the dressing. Chill for at least 1 hour before serving.

ginger pasta salad

Serves 4

1 tablespoon pureed ginger
1 teaspoon dried minced
  onion
2 tablespoons white wine
  vinegar
2 tablespoons mayonnaise
1 tablespoon soy sauce
¼ cup vegetable oil
8 ounces spaghettini, cooked,
  drained, and cooled
3 green onions, thinly sliced
One 10-ounce can mandarin
  orange segments, drained
½ cup sliced or chopped
  almonds, toasted
1 cup cabbage and carrot mix

1. Whisk together the ginger, minced onion, vinegar, mayonnaise, and soy sauce. Drizzle in the oil while whisking to emulsify.
2. Toss all the remaining ingredients with the dressing. Chill for at least 1 hour before serving.

greek pasta salad ▬

Serves 4

¼ cup lemon juice
1 tablespoon Italian seasoning
1 clove garlic, minced
½ teaspoon salt
Black pepper
⅓ cup olive oil
6 to 8 ounces penne pasta,
  cooked, drained, and cooled
1 cup chopped English
  cucumber
½ cup sliced or chopped pitted
  black olives
1 cup drained marinated
  artichoke hearts
2 roasted red peppers, chopped
¾ cup crumbled feta cheese

1. Whisk together the lemon juice, Italian seasoning, garlic, salt, and black pepper to taste. Drizzle in the oil while whisking to emulsify.
2. Toss all the remaining ingredients with the dressing. Chill for at least 1 hour before serving.

the stocked kitchen

italian pasta salad

Serves 4

¼ cup red wine vinegar
1 tablespoon water
2 teaspoons sugar
1 teaspoons lemon juice
½ teaspoon garlic powder
½ teaspoon salt
1 teaspoon dried minced onion
¼ teaspoon black pepper
1 tablespoon Italian seasoning
¼ cup olive oil
6 to 8 ounces penne pasta,
    cooked, drained, and cooled
½ bell pepper, diced
1 medium tomato, diced
2 carrots, peeled and chopped
2 stalks celery, chopped
1 cup diced English cucumber
3 green onions, thinly sliced

1. Whisk together the vinegar, water, sugar, lemon juice, garlic powder, salt, minced onion, black pepper, and Italian seasoning. Drizzle in the oil while whisking to emulsify.
2. Toss all the remaining ingredients with the dressing. Chill for at least 1 hour before serving.

mediterranean rice salad ▬

Serves 4 to 6

¼ cup lemon juice

2 cloves garlic, minced

1 teaspoon salt

¼ cup olive oil

1 cup rice, cooked

One 15-ounce can Great Northern or cannellini beans, drained and rinsed

¾ cup crumbled feta cheese

1 roasted red pepper, diced

½ cup chopped fresh basil

1 teaspoon dill weed

3 green onions, very thinly sliced

1. Whisk together the lemon juice, garlic, and salt. Drizzle in the oil while whisking to emulsify.
2. Add the rice and all the remaining ingredients to the dressing and toss to coat. Chill for at least 1 hour before serving.

salsa ranch pasta salad

Serves 4

½ cup ranch dressing

¼ cup salsa

6 to 8 ounces penne pasta, cooked, drained, and cooled

1 medium tomato, chopped

One 15-ounce can kidney beans, drained and rinsed

One 15-ounce can corn, drained

3 green onions, thinly sliced

1 cup shredded Cheddar cheese

Tortilla chips, crushed

1. Whisk together the ranch dressing and salsa. Toss the pasta, tomato, beans, corn, green onions, and cheese with the dressing. Chill for at least 1 hour before serving.
2. Sprinkle with the tortilla chips and serve.

tangy potato salad

Serves 6 to 8

5 pounds potatoes (russet or Yukon Gold), unpeeled

4 to 6 eggs

DRESSING

1 shallot or ¼ onion, finely diced

1 tablespoon sweet or dill relish

1 cup mayonnaise

2 tablespoons white wine vinegar

2 tablespoons sugar

¼ cup ketchup

2 tablespoons olive oil

½ teaspoon garlic powder

1 teaspoon Worcestershire sauce

1 teaspoon salt

½ teaspoon black pepper

1. In a stockpot, place the potatoes and eggs. Cover with water. Bring to a boil over medium-high heat. Reduce the heat and allow to simmer. Meanwhile, half-fill a large bowl with ice and water.

2. Remove the eggs after 15 minutes and place in the ice bath to cool. Remove the potatoes when they are fork-tender. Allow the potatoes and eggs to cool.

3. Peel and dice the potatoes. Peel and dice the eggs.

4. Whisk together all the dressing ingredients. Add the potatoes and eggs and toss gently. Chill for at least 3 hours before serving. (Can be made a day ahead.)

Any of these delicious salads can be served on a bed of mixed greens, in pita bread, on bread, or as a wrap in a tortilla.

apricot chicken salad ▬

Serves 4

2 tablespoons mayonnaise

2 tablespoons apricot preserves

½ teaspoon herbes de Provence

1½ teaspoons Dijon mustard

¼ teaspoon salt

⅛ teaspoon black pepper

2 cups cooked, cooled, and diced chicken

2 tablespoons slivered or chopped almonds

2 tablespoons chopped celery

1. Mix together the mayonnaise, apricot preserves, herbes de Provence, mustard, salt, and pepper.
2. Add the chicken, almonds, and celery.
3. Chill for at least 1 hour before serving.

---

the rotisserie chicken

Although a rotisserie chicken is not on our list, we like to pick one up on the day that we shop and use it for recipes that require cooked and chopped or shredded chicken. It is a great way to cut out one step.

curry chicken salad

Serves 4

½ cup mayonnaise
1 tablespoon lemon juice
2 teaspoons curry powder
½ teaspoon salt
2 cups cooked, cooled, and diced chicken
¼ cup thinly sliced green onion
½ cup raisins or dried cranberries

1. Mix together the mayonnaise, lemon juice, curry powder, and salt.
2. Add the chicken, green onion, and raisins.
3. Chill for at least 1 hour before serving.

egg salad

Serves 4

¼ cup mayonnaise
1 teaspoon dried minced onion
1 teaspoon yellow mustard
½ teaspoon salt
¼ teaspoon black pepper
6 hard-boiled eggs, chopped
2 tablespoons minced celery
1½ tablespoons sweet or dill relish

1. Mix together the mayonnaise, dried minced onion, mustard, salt, and pepper.
2. Add the eggs, celery, and relish.
3. Chill for at least 1 hour before serving.

ham salad

Serves 4

2 cups diced ham
⅓ cup mayonnaise
2 teaspoons yellow
    mustard
1 teaspoon honey
1 tablespoon sweet or dill
    relish
⅛ teaspoon black pepper

1. In a food processor, grind the ham coarsely. If a food processor is not available, finely dice the ham. Mix with the remaining ingredients.
2. Chill for at least 1 hour before serving.

ham it up!

Ham salad might, at first, sound a bit old-fashioned. We think this recipe is just the opposite. Not only is it a quick and easy lunch, it makes a wonderful dip with crackers. Try serving it topped with chopped green or black olives.

seafood salad

Serves 4

¼ cup mayonnaise
¼ cup ranch dressing
2 tablespoons lemon juice
½ teaspoon dill weed
1 cup cooked, peeled,
    deveined, and chopped
    shrimp
One 6-ounce can crabmeat,
    drained, or one 8-ounce
    package imitation
    crabmeat, chopped
¼ cup thinly sliced green
    onion
½ cup diced bell pepper

1. Mix together the mayonnaise, ranch dressing, lemon juice, and dill weed.
2. Add the shrimp, crabmeat, green onion, and bell pepper.
3. Chill for at least 1 hour before serving.

traditional chicken salad

Serves 4

⅔ cup mayonnaise

1 teaspoon sugar

½ teaspoon salt

¼ teaspoon black pepper

½ teaspoon dried minced onion

2 cups cooked, cooled, and diced chicken

1 tablespoon sweet or dill relish

1. Mix together the mayonnaise, sugar, salt, pepper, and dried minced onion.
2. Add the chicken and relish.
3. Chill for at least 1 hour before serving.

chicken salad options

We like to enhance the flavor of our Traditional Chicken Salad by mixing in the following:

¼ cup chopped, sliced, or slivered nuts

¼ cup raisins or dried cranberries

½ cup peeled and diced apple

soups, stews, chilis, and breads

Nothing is more comforting on a cold winter's day than a great-tasting soup. The cold soups, meanwhile, are perfect warm-weather options. Most freeze wonderfully!

asian black bean chili

Serves 6

2 tablespoons olive oil

1 cup chopped shallot or
   2 cups chopped onion

2 cloves garlic, minced

2 tablespoons chili powder

1 teaspoon cumin

½ teaspoon cinnamon

Three 15-ounce cans black
   beans, drained

Two 15-ounce cans diced
   tomatoes, undrained

1 cup drained mandarin
   orange segments,
   chopped

2 teaspoons salt

2 tablespoons honey

1. Heat the olive oil in a stockpot over medium heat. Add the shallot and garlic. Cook until the vegetables are softened.

2. Stir in the chili powder, cumin, and cinnamon. Stir in the black beans, tomatoes and their juices, mandarin oranges, and salt and bring to a boil. Reduce the heat to low and add the honey. Simmer, covered, for 30 minutes, stirring often, to blend the flavors and heat through.

carrot autumn spice soup

Serves 6

1 tablespoon unsalted
  butter
1 medium onion, diced
3 medium apples, peeled,
  cored, and diced
3 cups thinly sliced carrot
½ teaspoon salt
¼ teaspoon black pepper
2 teaspoons herbes de
  Provence
1 teaspoon pumpkin pie
  spice, plus more for
  serving (optional)
1 tablespoon brown sugar
One 15-ounce can chicken
  broth
2 cups water
½ cup sour cream or plain
  yogurt (optional)
Sugared Nuts (page 96),
  chopped, for serving
  (optional)

1. In a stockpot over medium heat, melt the butter. Add the onion, apples, and carrot. Cook, stirring occasionally, for approximately 3 minutes to soften the vegetables.

2. Mix in the salt, pepper, herbes de Provence, and pumpkin pie spice and cook for another minute. Add the brown sugar, broth, and water and bring to a boil. Reduce the heat, cover, and let simmer for 15 minutes.

3. Blend the soup in a blender until smooth. Stir in the sour cream, if desired, and allow it to melt into the soup before blending it in. Serve warm, at room temperature, or cold.

4. If desired, garnish with a sprinkle of pumpkin pie spice, chopped Sugared Nuts, or a dollop of sour cream.

cheese soup ▬

Serves 6

One 15-ounce can or
    2 cups chicken broth
½ cup shredded carrot
¼ cup shredded celery
¼ cup shredded onion or
    1 tablespoon dried
    minced onion
1¾ cups milk
⅓ cup flour
½ teaspoon salt
Pinch black pepper
1½ cups shredded Cheddar
    cheese

1. In a medium saucepan, combine the chicken broth, carrot, celery, and onion. Bring to a boil. Reduce the heat and simmer for 8 minutes or until the vegetables are tender.

2. In a bowl, whisk together the milk, flour, salt, and pepper until smooth. Stir into the chicken broth and cook, stirring, until thick and bubbly.

3. Add the cheese and stir until completely melted. Serve immediately.

cheesy chicken chili

Serves 6

1½ pounds boneless,
    skinless chicken
2 tablespoons olive oil
Four 15-ounce cans white or
    cannellini beans
One 15-ounce can or
    2 cups chicken broth
2 cups salsa
1 teaspoon cumin
2 cups shredded Cheddar
    cheese, plus more for
    serving (optional)
Sour cream or plain
    yogurt, for serving
    (optional)
Tortilla chips, for serving
    (optional)

1. Cut the chicken into 1-inch cubes. In a stockpot over medium heat, cook the chicken in the olive oil until no longer pink inside.

2. Stir in the beans, chicken broth, salsa, and cumin. Bring to a boil. Reduce the heat and simmer for 30 minutes, stirring occasionally.

3. Add the cheese and stir until completely melted.

4. Serve immediately. If desired, top with Cheddar cheese and sour cream and serve with tortilla chips.

chicken noodle soup

Serves 6

1 tablespoon olive oil

½ cup chopped onion or
    2 tablespoons dried
    minced onion

½ cup chopped celery

½ cup chopped carrot

Two 15-ounce cans or
    4 cups chicken broth

4 cups hot water

½ teaspoon salt

¼ teaspoon black pepper

1 cup egg noodles

1 pound boneless, skinless
    chicken, cut into 1-inch
    cubes

½ cup frozen peas

1. In a stockpot, heat the oil over medium heat. Add the onion and cook for 5 minutes.
2. Add the celery, carrot, chicken broth, water, salt, and pepper. Cover and bring to a boil over high heat. Add the egg noodles. Cover and cook for 3 minutes.
3. Stir in the chicken and peas. Cover and bring to a boil again. Reduce the heat and simmer for 10 minutes. Serve.

creamy broccoli soup

Serves 6

3 tablespoons olive oil

1 cup chopped carrot

1 cup chopped celery

¾ cup chopped onion or
    2 tablespoons dried
    minced onion

Two 15-ounce cans or
    4 cups chicken broth

½ teaspoon black pepper

4½ cups chopped broccoli

½ cup white rice

2 cups milk

¼ cup grated Parmesan
    cheese

1. Heat the olive oil in a large saucepan. Add the carrot, celery, and onion and cook for 5 minutes.
2. Add the chicken broth and pepper. Stir and bring to a boil.
3. Stir in the broccoli and rice. Reduce the heat and simmer for 30 minutes.
4. In 1-cup increments, pour the soup into a blender or food processor and blend until pureed.
5. Return to a clean saucepan. Stir in the milk and cheese. Cook over low heat until heated through. Serve immediately.

curry tomato and rice soup

Serves 6

2 tablespoons unsalted
butter

½ cup diced onion

2 teaspoons curry powder

Two 15-ounce cans diced
tomatoes, undrained

Two 15-ounce cans or 4 cups
chicken broth

½ cup rice

½ cup sour cream, plus
more for serving

1. In a stockpot over medium heat, melt the butter and cook
the onion until soft.

2. Stir in the curry powder and cook for another minute.

3. Add the tomatoes and their juices, the chicken broth, and
the rice and bring to a boil, stirring occasionally. Cover,
reduce the heat, and simmer for about 30 minutes or until
the rice is tender.

4. Add the sour cream and allow it to melt into the soup.
Whisk the soup until the sour cream is combined.

5. Serve immediately with a dollop of sour cream.

gazpacho

Serves 6

3 medium tomatoes, diced, or one 15-ounce can diced tomatoes, undrained

One 15-ounce can tomato sauce

2 tablespoons diced shallot or ¼ cup diced onion

½ English cucumber, diced

½ bell pepper, seeded and diced

2 stalks celery, chopped

2 tablespoons chopped fresh basil

1 clove garlic, minced

1 tablespoon balsamic vinegar

1 teaspoon Worcestershire sauce

2 tablespoons olive oil

1 teaspoon salt

¼ teaspoon black pepper

1. Combine all the ingredients in a blender and pulse until blended to desired consistency.
2. Chill for 1 to 24 hours. Serve cold.

what is gazpacho?

Gazpacho is a cold Spanish soup made from tomatoes and other raw vegetables. It is delicious, easy, and completely satisfying on a hot summer's day! Try it topped with sour cream and served with Garlic Toast (page 57).

ham, potato, and corn chowder ▬

Serves 6

2 tablespoons unsalted butter

½ cup diced shallot or 1 cup diced onion

3 stalks celery, diced

2 tablespoons flour

3 cups milk

One 15-ounce can or 2 cups chicken broth

Three 15-ounce cans corn, undrained

3 pounds potatoes, peeled and cubed

1 teaspoon herbes de Provence

12 drops Tabasco or hot sauce

1 tablespoon salt

2 cups diced ham

1 cup sour cream or plain yogurt

1. In a stockpot, melt the butter over medium heat. Add the shallot and celery and cook until the vegetables are tender.

2. Sprinkle with the flour and stir until blended. Gradually stir in the milk and broth. Bring to a boil and cook for about 3 minutes or until it begins to thicken.

3. Meanwhile, blend two cans of the corn until smooth. Add the blended corn and potatoes to the soup. Return to a boil and cook for 10 minutes.

4. Drain the remaining can of corn and add the kernels along with the herbes de Provence, Tabasco, salt, and ham. Simmer for 20 minutes.

5. Serve hot, with a dollop of sour cream.

italian stew ▬

Serves 6

1 pound ground beef or bulk
   breakfast
   sausage
½ cup diced shallot or
   1 cup diced onion
1 cup chopped celery
1 cup chopped carrot
2 cloves garlic, minced
One 15-ounce can diced
   tomatoes, undrained
One 15-ounce can tomato
   sauce
One 15-ounce can kidney
   beans, undrained
One 15-ounce can or
   2 cups beef broth
1 tablespoon Italian
   seasoning
2 tablespoons chopped
   fresh basil
1 teaspoon salt
¼ teaspoon black pepper
2 cups cabbage and carrot
   mix
1 cup frozen cut green
   beans
1 cup penne pasta or egg
   noodles
Grated Parmesan cheese,
   for serving

1. In a stockpot over medium heat, cook the ground beef thoroughly. Drain off the excess grease and return the pot to the stovetop.

2. Add the shallot, celery, carrot, and garlic. Cook over medium heat until the vegetables soften.

3. Add the tomatoes, tomato sauce, kidney beans, beef broth, Italian seasoning, basil, salt, and pepper. Bring to a boil, cover, reduce the heat, and simmer for 30 minutes.

4. Add the cabbage mix, green beans, and pasta. Return to a boil and cook for 10 minutes.

5. Serve topped with Parmesan cheese.

---

a hearty, healthy meal

This stew is a wonderful make-ahead meal, and we use it as a way to sneak a lot of vegetables into our children. (Just sprinkle with Parmesan cheese!)

This stew is also a great meal for guests. Serve with Garlic-Parmesan Roll-Up Bread (page 134) for a simple and more-than-satisfying meal!

the stocked kitchen

mom's basic chili

Serves 6

1 pound ground beef

2 shallots or ½ large onion, diced

1 bell pepper, diced

Two 15-ounce cans kidney beans, undrained

One 15-ounce can tomato sauce

Two 15-ounce cans diced tomatoes, undrained

Two 15-ounce cans or 4 cups beef broth

2 tablespoons chili powder

1 tablespoon cumin

½ teaspoon Tabasco or hot sauce, or to taste

1 teaspoon garlic powder

½ teaspoon salt

½ teaspoon black pepper

Sour cream and shredded Cheddar cheese, for serving (optional)

1. In a stockpot, brown the ground beef. Drain off the excess grease and return the pot to medium heat.
2. Add the shallots and bell pepper. Cook until the vegetables are softened.
3. Add the kidney beans with their liquid, the tomato sauce, tomatoes, and beef broth. Stir in the chili powder, cumin, Tabasco, garlic powder, salt, and pepper. Bring to a boil.
4. Reduce the heat and simmer for at least 30 minutes. Simmering longer will enhance the flavors.
5. Try serving with sour cream and Cheddar cheese.

roasted red pepper bisque

Serves 6

1 tablespoon olive oil

2 shallots, chopped, or
  ½ cup chopped onion

Two 15-ounce cans diced
  tomatoes, undrained,
  or 4 cups diced fresh
  tomatoes

3 roasted red peppers,
  chopped

2 cloves garlic, minced

1 teaspoon Italian
  seasoning

1 teaspoon salt

½ teaspoon black pepper

One 15-ounce can or
  2 cups chicken broth

1 tablespoon sugar

1 tablespoon chopped
  fresh basil

¼ cup sour cream or
  plain yogurt

1. In a stockpot, heat the oil over medium heat and cook the shallots until translucent.
2. Add the tomatoes, roasted red peppers, garlic, Italian seasoning, salt, pepper, and chicken broth. Bring to a boil and simmer for 10 minutes.
3. Add the sugar and basil.
4. In batches, transfer the soup to a blender and puree until smooth.
5. Return the soup to the stockpot. Cook for 5 minutes to reheat.
6. Remove from the heat and whisk in the sour cream. Serve immediately.

make these soups vegetarian

Many of these soups are veggie based. Don't forget, however, that to make them truly vegetarian, you need to substitute vegetable broth for the chicken or beef broth. Although vegetable broth isn't on the list, it is readily available and can be substituted anytime for chicken or beef broth.

shrimp bisque

Serves 6

Two 15-ounce cans or
  4 cups chicken broth
3 tablespoons unsalted
  butter
¼ cup chopped onion, or
  1 shallot, chopped
¼ cup chopped celery
¼ cup chopped carrot
One 15-ounce can diced
  tomatoes, undrained,
  or 1½ cups diced fresh
  tomatoes
¼ cup rice
1 tablespoon olive oil
12 ounces to 1 pound raw
  shrimp, thawed, peeled
  completely, and
  deveined
1 cup heavy cream
¼ teaspoon salt
¼ teaspoon black pepper

1. Over medium heat, heat the chicken broth in a stockpot.

2. While the broth is heating, in a fry pan, melt 1 tablespoon of the butter. Add the onion, celery, and carrot and cook for 5 minutes.

3. Add the tomatoes to the vegetables and cook for another 5 minutes.

4. Add the vegetable mixture to the chicken broth. (Do not wash the fry pan.) Stir in the rice and bring to a boil. Simmer, partially covered, for 20 minutes, or until the rice is tender.

5. Heat the olive oil in the fry pan used for the vegetables. Add the shrimp and cook until pink, about 2 to 3 minutes, turning halfway through. Remove the shrimp from the fry pan and set aside.

6. When the rice is soft, puree half of the shrimp and all of the soup in a blender, in batches if necessary. Return the soup to the stockpot.

7. Whisk the remaining 2 tablespoons butter, the cream, salt, and pepper into the soup and cook for 5 minutes to reheat. Ladle the soup into bowls and top with the remaining shrimp.

shrimp chili

Serves 6

2 tablespoons unsalted
   butter
1 cup chopped shallot, or
   2 cups chopped onion
1 cup chopped carrot
1 cup chopped celery
3 cloves garlic, minced
½ cup diced drained
   roasted red pepper
1 tablespoon Italian
   seasoning
1 tablespoon chili powder
1 teaspoon cumin
Two 15-ounce cans diced
   tomatoes, undrained
Two 15-ounce cans kidney
   beans, undrained
One 15-ounce can or
   2 cups chicken broth
2 teaspoons salt
1 tablespoon
   Worcestershire sauce
Tabasco or hot sauce,
   to taste
12 ounces to 1 pound raw
   shrimp, thawed, peeled
   completely, and deveined

1. Melt the butter in a stockpot over medium heat. Add the shallot, carrot, celery, and garlic and cook until the vegetables are softened.

2. Stir in all the remaining ingredients except the shrimp and bring to a boil. Reduce the heat and simmer, uncovered, for 20 minutes, stirring occasionally.

3. Cut the shrimp in half and add to the pot. Cover and cook for 10 minutes more, until the shrimp are pink and cooked through. Serve immediately.

steak, potato, and corn chili

Serves 6

1 tablespoon vegetable oil

1 pound flank steak, pounded to tenderize and cut into ½-inch cubes

1 tablespoon flour

½ cup diced shallot, or 1 cup diced onion

1 bell pepper, diced

1 clove garlic, minced

3 tablespoons chili powder

1 teaspoon cumin

Two 15-ounce cans diced tomatoes, undrained

One 15-ounce can or 2 cups beef broth

5 medium potatoes (about 1½ pounds), peeled and cut into ½-inch cubes

One 15-ounce can corn, drained

2 teaspoons salt

1. Heat the vegetable oil in a stockpot over medium heat. Add the steak and brown. Sprinkle with the flour.

2. Add the shallot, bell pepper, and garlic and cook until the vegetables are softened.

3. Stir in the chili powder, cumin, tomatoes, beef broth, potatoes, corn, and salt.

4. Bring to a boil, reduce the heat, and simmer, covered, for 30 minutes, stirring occasionally.

game on!

This chili is a hearty and delicious game day option because it is a departure from a traditional chili recipe. When you serve it in a Bread Bowl (page 131) made with frozen bread dough, you are sure to have a winner.

sweet-and-sour stew

Serves 6

½ cup plus 3 tablespoons flour

1 tablespoon salt

1½ pounds flank steak, pounded to tenderize and cut into 1-inch pieces

2 tablespoons olive oil

One 15-ounce can or 2 cups beef broth

¼ cup packed brown sugar

3 tablespoons white wine vinegar

½ cup ketchup

1 cup chopped onion, or ½ cup chopped shallot

1 tablespoon Worcestershire sauce

1 cup chopped carrot

One 4-ounce can mushrooms, drained and chopped

2 cups peeled, cubed potato

1. Combine the ½ cup flour and the salt in a bowl. Add the flank steak pieces to the flour mixture, turning to coat.

2. Heat the olive oil in a fry pan over medium heat, add the flank steak pieces, and cook the meat, turning to brown all sides.

3. In a stockpot, combine 1½ cups of the water, the brown sugar, vinegar, ketchup, onion, and Worcestershire. Add the browned meat and bring to a boil.

4. Stir in the carrot, mushrooms, and potato and return to a boil, reduce the heat, cover, and simmer for an additional 45 minutes, or until the potato cubes are fork-tender.

5. Mix together the remaining ½ cup water and the 3 tablespoons flour. Stir into the stew to thicken.

vichyssoise

Serves 6

2 tablespoons unsalted butter

1 cup thinly sliced green onion, plus more for serving (optional)

2 cups peeled and cubed potato (russet or Yukon Gold)

Two 15-ounce cans or 4 cups chicken broth

1 cup milk

1½ teaspoons salt

¼ teaspoon nutmeg

1 cup sour cream or plain yogurt

1. Melt the butter over low heat in a stockpot. Add the green onion and cook until very soft but not browned.

2. Add the remaining ingredients except the sour cream. Turn up the heat to medium, cover, and bring to a boil. Cook until the potato cubes are fork-tender, 20 to 30 minutes.

3. Allow to cool. Place in a blender, in batches if necessary, and blend until smooth. Stir in the sour cream.

4. Let sit for 10 minutes. Chill if desired or serve at room temperature. Top with additional sliced green onion, if desired, before serving.

what is vichyssoise?

Vichyssoise (vee-shee-SWAHZ) is a French soup made from potatoes and onions or leeks. It is generally served chilled or at room temperature and has a lovely and light creamy texture. Try serving it with flank steak kebabs for a new twist on meat and potatoes.

white bean and ham soup

Serves 6

1 tablespoon unsalted
    butter
½ cup diced shallot, or
    1 cup diced onion
1 cup chopped celery
1 cup chopped carrot
2 cloves garlic, minced
Two 15-ounce cans Great
    Northern or cannellini
    beans, undrained
1 cup diced ham
One 15-ounce can or 2 cups
    chicken broth
1½ teaspoons herbes de
    Provence
1 teaspoon salt
½ teaspoon black pepper
Tabasco or hot sauce
    (optional)

1. Melt the butter in a stockpot over medium heat. Add the shallot, celery, carrot, and garlic and cook until the vegetables are softened.
2. Mash one can of the beans with a fork.
3. Stir all the beans, the ham, chicken broth, herbes de Provence, salt, and pepper into the vegetables. Cover and simmer for 20 minutes.
4. Add Tabasco if desired.
5. Let sit for an additional 10 minutes before serving.

We are huge fans of frozen bread dough for its versatility and fresh-baked-bread taste. Try these breads as great accompaniments to your soups, salads, or various dishes.

bread bowls

Serves 2 to 4

1 pound frozen bread dough, thawed

1. Cover a jelly roll pan with parchment paper.
2. Cut the bread dough into four pieces for small bowls or two pieces for larger bowls. Roll the pieces into balls. Place on the jelly roll pan about 3 inches apart. Cover with greased plastic wrap, set on a counter, and allow to double in size (about 3 hours).
3. Preheat the oven to 350°F.
4. Remove the plastic wrap and bake for 20 minutes or until golden brown.
5. Allow to cool on the pan.
6. To make bread bowls, hollow out by slicing into the top of the bread at an angle.

---

frozen bread dough quick-thaw methods

These quick-thaw methods save you a lot of time when making any of the dishes that use frozen bread dough.

Oven: Preheat the oven to 325°F. Wrap a piece of frozen bread dough in a sheet of parchment paper like a burrito. Place seam side down in a loaf pan. Place in the oven for approximately 12 minutes.

Microwave: Spray a microwave-safe loaf pan or bowl with nonstick spray. Place the frozen bread dough in the pan. Cover with plastic wrap. Microwave for 15 seconds on high. Uncover and flip the bread over. Re-cover and repeat until the bread is thawed.

---

breadsticks

Serves 4 to 6

1 pound frozen bread dough, thawed

2 tablespoons unsalted butter, melted

1½ teaspoons garlic powder

½ cup grated Parmesan cheese

1. Cover a jelly roll pan with parchment paper.
2. Cut the bread dough into eight pieces. Roll the pieces into 6- to 8-inch-long ropes. Place on the jelly roll pan 1 inch apart. Cover with greased plastic wrap, set on a counter, and allow to double in size (2 to 4 hours).
3. Preheat the oven to 350°F.
4. Brush the breadsticks with the melted butter. Sprinkle with the garlic powder and Parmesan cheese.
5. Bake for 20 minutes or until golden brown.

cheddar-chili roll-up bread

Serves 4 to 6

1 pound frozen bread dough, thawed

⅔ cup shredded Cheddar cheese

2 tablespoons grated Parmesan cheese

1 tablespoon chili powder

1. Gently stretch the dough into a 9 by 11-inch rectangle and lay flat. Sprinkle the stretched dough with the cheeses and chili powder. Roll up, starting with one shorter end, and place in a greased loaf pan, seam side down. Cover with greased plastic wrap and place on a counter for 2 hours or until the dough has risen to the top of the pan.
2. Preheat the oven to 350°F.
3. Bake for 20 to 25 minutes, until golden brown. Remove from the pan and allow to cool for about 10 minutes. Slice and serve.

cheesy ranch roll-up bread

Serves 4 to 6

1 pound frozen bread
   dough, thawed

¼ cup ranch dressing

¼ cup shredded mozzarella
   or Cheddar cheese

1. Gently stretch the dough into a 9 by 11-inch rectangle and lay flat. Spread the stretched dough with the ranch dressing. Sprinkle with the cheese. Roll up, starting with one shorter end, and place in a greased loaf pan, seam side down. Cover with greased plastic wrap and place on a counter for 2 hours or until the dough has risen to the top of the pan.

2. Preheat the oven to 350°F.

3. Bake for 20 to 25 minutes, until golden brown. Remove from the pan and allow to cool for about 10 minutes. Slice and serve.

again . . . frozen bread dough quick-thaw methods

These quick-thaw methods save you a lot of time when making any of the dishes that use frozen bread dough.

Oven: Preheat the oven to 325°F. Wrap a piece of frozen bread dough in a sheet of parchment paper like a burrito. Place seam side down in a loaf pan. Place in the oven for approximately 12 minutes.

Microwave: Spray a microwave-safe loaf pan or bowl with nonstick spray. Place the frozen bread dough in the pan. Cover with plastic wrap. Microwave for 15 seconds on high. Uncover and flip the bread over. Re-cover and repeat until the bread is thawed.

cinnamon raisin roll-up bread

Serves 4 to 6

1 pound frozen bread
   dough, thawed
¼ cup sugar
1 teaspoon cinnamon
2 tablespoons unsalted
   butter, melted
½ cup raisins

1. Gently stretch the dough into a 9 by 11-inch rectangle and lay flat. Mix together the sugar, cinnamon, and butter. Spread over the stretched bread dough. Sprinkle with the raisins. Roll up, starting with one shorter end, and place in a greased loaf pan, seam side down. Cover with greased plastic wrap and place on a counter for 2 hours or until the dough has risen to the top of the pan.

2. Preheat the oven to 350°F.

3. Bake for 20 to 25 minutes, until golden brown. Remove from the pan and allow to cool for about 10 minutes. Slice and serve.

garlic-parmesan roll-up bread ▬

Serves 4 to 6

1 pound frozen bread
   dough, thawed
2 tablespoons olive oil
1 clove garlic, minced
½ cup grated Parmesan
   cheese

1. Gently stretch the dough into a 9 by 11-inch rectangle and lay flat. Mix together the olive oil and garlic and spread over the stretched bread dough. Sprinkle the Parmesan on top. Roll up, starting with one shorter end, and place in a greased loaf pan, seam side down. Cover with greased plastic wrap and place on a counter for 2 hours or until the dough has risen to the top of the pan.

2. Preheat the oven to 350°F.

3. Bake for 20 to 25 minutes, until golden brown. Remove from the pan and allow to cool for about 10 minutes. Slice and serve.

grilled flatbread

Serves 4 to 6

1 pound frozen bread
    dough, thawed
2 tablespoons olive oil
¼ teaspoon garlic powder,
    or to taste

1. Preheat a grill to medium.
2. Cut the bread dough into four even pieces. Roll out each piece into a round, flat disk 5 to 6 inches in diameter. Brush the olive oil on both sides. Sprinkle with garlic powder.
3. Place directly on the grill rack for about 5 minutes. Flip and grill for another 5 minutes, or until golden brown on both sides.
4. Serve cut in wedges or serve as a "plate" for a salad.

---

grilled bread?

Although this is an unconventional recipe, the results are outstanding. We love this bread's crisp outside and chewy inside. Experiment with different spices and flavorings. Larger herbs might need to be rolled into the bread dough before grilling.

hamburger buns

Makes 6 buns

1 pound frozen bread dough, thawed

1. Cover a jelly roll pan with parchment paper.
2. Cut the bread dough into six pieces. Roll the pieces into balls. Place on the jelly roll pan. Cover with greased plastic wrap and allow to double in size. (This takes 2 to 4 hours.)
3. Preheat the oven to 350°F.
4. Remove the plastic wrap and bake for 20 minutes or until golden brown.

pastas and pizzas

These pastas are our go-to recipes for busy weekday dinners. We always salt our pasta water to make our pasta much more flavorful. A good rule of thumb is 1½ teaspoons of salt per quart of water.

baked penne

Serves 8

1 pound penne pasta

1 pound ground beef or bulk breakfast sausage

2 tablespoons Italian seasoning

1 shallot or ½ onion, diced

2 cloves garlic, minced

1 bell pepper, finely chopped

One 4-ounce can mushrooms, drained and chopped

Two 15-ounce cans diced tomatoes

One 15-ounce can tomato sauce

¼ cup minced fresh basil

2 tablespoons brown sugar

2 cup shredded mozzarella cheese

½ cup grated Parmesan cheese

1. Preheat the oven to 350°F. Bring a stockpot of salted water to a boil.
2. Cook the pasta according to the package directions. Drain and set aside.
3. In a large fry pan or stockpot, brown the meat. Drain off the excess grease.
4. Add the Italian seasoning, shallot, garlic, and bell pepper and cook over medium heat until the vegetables are tender.
5. Mix in the mushrooms, tomatoes, tomato sauce, basil, and brown sugar. Combine with the cooked penne and pour into a 9 by 13-inch baking dish. Top with the cheeses.
6. Bake for 30 minutes or until the cheeses begin to brown.

make, then bake

This dish is perfect for serving when another family comes to dinner. We make it a few hours ahead and refrigerate. Then just before our guests arrive, we stick it in the oven. It is cheesy and delicious and very child friendly. Best of all, we are able to enjoy our guests!

lemon-dill seafood pasta

Serves 4 to 6

6 to 8 ounces pasta of your choice

2 tablespoons unsalted butter

3 cloves garlic, minced

2 tablespoons flour

1½ cups milk

½ cup sour cream or plain yogurt

¼ cup grated Parmesan cheese

½ teaspoon salt

¼ teaspoon black pepper

⅛ teaspoon nutmeg

12 ounces to 1 pound raw shrimp, thawed, peeled completely, and deveined

One 6-ounce can crabmeat, drained, or one 8-ounce package imitation crabmeat, chopped

¼ cup thinly sliced green onion

1 teaspoon dill weed

2 tablespoons lemon juice

1. Cook the pasta according to the package directions. Drain and keep warm.

2. In a saucepan over medium heat, melt the butter. Mix in the garlic and cook until softened. (Do not let the garlic brown.)

3. Add the flour and whisk together, creating a roux. Cook the roux, stirring constantly, for about 1 minute, or until it bubbles and smooths.

4. Slowly whisk in the milk, ½ cup at a time, until smooth. Cook until thickened.

5. Once the mixture is thickened and bubbling, mix in the sour cream, Parmesan, salt, pepper, and nutmeg. Allow the sauce to heat through.

6. Add the shrimp and crab. Cook over medium heat until the shrimp are pink and done.

7. Stir in the green onion, dill, and lemon juice. Toss with the pasta and serve immediately.

thick and creamy without the cream

In our Alfredo-type sauces we use a roux, which is a thickening agent made up of equal parts flour and fat. We generally use butter. Roux are fairly simple; however, it is important to whisk the sauce smooth, and make sure the flour is completely incorporated to avoid lumps.

mediterranean pasta ▬

Serves 4 to 6

6 to 8 ounces pasta of
   your choice
¼ cup olive oil
1 clove garlic, minced
¼ cup diced shallot, or
   ½ cup diced onion
½ cup diced drained
   roasted red pepper
¼ cup sliced black olives
2 cups frozen spinach,
   thawed
½ teaspoon salt
¼ teaspoon black pepper
1 tablespoon lemon juice
¾ cup crumbled feta cheese
½ cup toasted pine nuts
Grilled chicken, flank
   steak, or shrimp, for
   serving (optional)

1. Cook the pasta according to the package directions. Drain and keep warm.

2. Heat 2 tablespoons of the olive oil in a fry pan over medium heat. Add the garlic and shallot and cook until softened.

3. Add the red pepper, olives, spinach, salt, and black pepper and cook until heated through.

4. Toss with the pasta, the remaining 2 tablespoons olive oil, the lemon juice, feta, and pine nuts. Serve immediately.

5. Try topped with grilled chicken, grilled flank steak, or sautéed or grilled shrimp.

pasta carbonara

Serves 4 to 6

2 cloves garlic, peeled
2 teaspoons salt
6 to 8 ounces pasta of your choice
3 slices bacon, cut into ¼-inch pieces
¾ cup milk
3 egg yolks
½ cup grated Parmesan cheese, plus more for serving
¾ cup frozen peas, thawed
Grilled chicken, flank steak, or shrimp, or cooked crabmeat, for serving (optional)

1. Bring a stockpot of water with the garlic and 1 teaspoon of the salt to a boil. Add the pasta and cook according to the package directions.
2. In a fry pan, cook the bacon until crispy.
3. Drain off the excess grease. Reduce the heat to low and whisk in the milk, egg yolks, Parmesan, and the remaining 1 teaspoon salt. Whisk continuously until the mixture begins to thicken.
4. When the pasta is done, drain it in a colander, remove the garlic, and set the pasta aside. Cut off the ends of the garlic and mash the rest with the side of a large knife.
5. Toss the sauce with the mashed garlic, pasta, and peas. Serve with extra Parmesan cheese.
6. Try topped with grilled chicken, grilled flank steak, sautéed or grilled shrimp, or crabmeat.

separating eggs

The best way to separate egg yolks from the whites is to crack the eggs in half and pour the egg yolk from one shell half to the other, allowing the egg whites to fall out of the shell.

pasta primavera

Serves 4 to 6

6 to 8 ounces pasta of your choice

2 tablespoons unsalted butter

3 cloves garlic, minced

¼ cup thinly sliced shallot, or ½ cup thinly sliced onion

1 bell pepper, finely diced

1 carrot, peeled and finely diced

2 tablespoons flour

1½ cups milk

½ cup sour cream or plain yogurt

¼ cup grated Parmesan cheese

1½ teaspoons salt

¼ teaspoon black pepper

⅛ teaspoon nutmeg

2 cups frozen chopped broccoli, thawed

1 tablespoon Italian seasoning

12 ounces to 1 pound raw shrimp, thawed, peeled completely, and deveined (optional)

Grilled chicken or flank steak, or cooked crabmeat, for serving (optional)

1. Cook the pasta according to the package directions. Drain and keep warm.

2. In a saucepan over medium heat, melt the butter. Mix in the garlic, shallot, bell pepper, and carrot. Cook until softened. (Do not let the garlic brown.)

3. Add the flour and whisk together, creating a roux. Cook the roux, stirring constantly, for about 1 minute, or until it bubbles and smooths.

4. Slowly whisk in the milk, ½ cup at a time, and cook until thickened and bubbling.

5. Stir in the sour cream, Parmesan, salt, black pepper, nutmeg, broccoli, and Italian seasoning. If adding the shrimp, add them here. Allow the mixture to heat through, or cook until the shrimp are pink.

6. Toss the sauce with the pasta.

7. If you don't like shrimp, try topping the pasta with grilled chicken, grilled flank steak, or crabmeat.

peanut noodles ▬

Serves 8

1 pound spaghettini
(thin spaghetti)

PEANUT SAUCE
¾ cup peanut butter
⅓ cup soy sauce
¼ cup honey
1½ tablespoons lemon
juice
1 tablespoon pureed
ginger
1 clove garlic, minced
¼ teaspoon Tabasco or hot
sauce, or to taste

½ cup warm water
½ cup milk
3 green onions, sliced
½ bell pepper, cut into thin
strips
½ English cucumber, diced
Grilled chicken, flank
steak, or shrimp, for
serving (optional)

1. Cook the pasta according to the package directions.
Drain and keep warm.

2. In a bowl, thoroughly combine the peanut sauce
ingredients. Stir in the water and milk.

3. Place the cooked pasta in a serving bowl and pour the
peanut sauce over the top. Toss to coat.

4. Sprinkle the green onions, bell pepper, and cucumber
over the pasta. Serve at room temperature.

5. Try topped with grilled chicken, grilled flank steak, or
grilled shrimp.

peanut sauce uses

To serve four, try making this peanut sauce recipe and then mix half
of the sauce with half of the water,
milk, and pasta, and use only half
of the garnish. Use the remainder of the peanut sauce
as a marinade or on top of a Thai Peanut Pizza
(page 158). This sauce is exceptional and versatile.

pink pasta alfredo

Serves 4 to 6

6 to 8 ounces pasta of your choice

2 tablespoons unsalted butter

3 cloves garlic, minced

2 tablespoons flour

1½ cups milk

½ cup sour cream or plain yogurt

¼ cup grated Parmesan cheese

1½ teaspoons salt

¼ teaspoon black pepper

⅛ teaspoon nutmeg

One 15-ounce can diced tomatoes, undrained

¼ teaspoon red pepper flakes

12 ounces to 1 pound raw shrimp, thawed, peeled completely, and deveined (optional)

Grilled chicken or flank steaks, or cooked crabmeat, for serving (optional)

1. Cook the pasta according to the package directions. Drain and keep warm.

2. In a saucepan over medium heat, melt the butter. Add the garlic and cook until softened. (Do not let the garlic brown.)

3. Add the flour and whisk together, creating a roux. Cook the roux, stirring constantly, for about 1 minute, until it bubbles and smooths.

4. Slowly whisk in the milk, ½ cup at a time, until smooth. Cook until thickened and bubbling.

5. Stir in the sour cream, Parmesan, salt, black pepper, nutmeg, tomatoes, and red pepper flakes. If adding the shrimp, add them here. Allow the mixture to heat through, or cook until the shrimp are pink.

6. Toss the sauce with the pasta.

7. If you don't like shrimp, try topping the pasta with grilled chicken, grilled flank steak, or crabmeat.

quick marinara and meatballs ▬

Serves 4 to 6

MARINARA

1 tablespoon olive oil

¼ cup diced shallot, or
   ½ cup diced onion

2 cloves garlic, minced

½ bell pepper, minced

¼ cup tomato paste

Two 15-ounce cans diced
   tomatoes, undrained

One 15-ounce can or
   2 cups beef broth

2 tablespoons sugar

¼ cup chopped fresh basil

2 tablespoons Italian
   seasoning

1 tablespoon aniseed or
   fennel seed

MEATBALLS

1 pound ground beef

½ cup plain bread crumbs

1 tablespoon Italian
   seasoning

2 eggs, lightly beaten

2 tablespoons dried minced
   onion

1 teaspoon salt

¼ teaspoon black pepper

6 to 8 ounces pasta of your
   choice

1. In a stockpot over medium heat, warm the olive oil. Add the shallot, garlic, and bell pepper and cook until the vegetables soften.

2. Add the tomato paste and cook, stirring, for a couple of minutes to reduce its bitterness.

3. Add the remaining marinara ingredients (make sure to crush the aniseed in your hand before adding). Bring to a boil.

4. Mix all the ingredients for the meatballs with your hands and roll into 2-inch balls. Add to the sauce. Cook for 30 minutes or until the meatballs are cooked through.

5. Cook the pasta according to the package directions. Drain and serve topped with meatballs and sauce.

---

toss it in

My grandmother and mother taught me the concept of "use what you have," and this sauce is a perfect example. When this sauce gets to a rolling boil, we throw in not only the meatballs, but also pieces of chicken, and will even crack in eggs for a meatless dish. Boil for 30 minutes or until the chicken is cooked through or the eggs are hard-boiled.

southwest pasta

Serves 4 to 6

6 to 8 ounces pasta of your choice

¼ cup cream cheese

1 cup salsa

1 cup shredded Cheddar cheese

2 teaspoons cumin

1 tablespoon chili powder

One 15-ounce can kidney beans, drained and rinsed

One 15-ounce can corn, drained

Grilled chicken or flank steak, or browned and drained breakfast sausage meat or ground beef, for serving (optional)

1. Cook the pasta according to the package directions. Drain and keep warm.
2. In a saucepan over medium heat, stir together the cream cheese, salsa, Cheddar, cumin, and chili powder until melted and smooth.
3. Stir in the beans and corn and heat through.
4. Toss with the pasta and serve.
5. Try topped with grilled chicken, grilled flank steak, breakfast sausage meat, or ground beef.

spicy tolerance

All of these recipes will taste different based on the ingredients that you choose. This recipe, for instance, can go from very mild to super spicy based on the type of salsa. If it is still not spicy enough for you, add some Tabasco to really pack in the heat.

stocked pasta alfredo

Serves 4 to 6

6 to 8 ounces pasta of your choice

2 tablespoons unsalted butter

3 cloves garlic, minced

2 tablespoons flour

1½ cups milk

½ cup sour cream or plain yogurt

¼ cup grated Parmesan cheese

½ teaspoon salt

¼ teaspoon black pepper

⅛ teaspoon nutmeg

12 ounces to 1 pound raw shrimp, thawed, peeled completely, and deveined (optional)

Grilled chicken or flank steak, or cooked crabmeat, for serving (optional)

1. Cook the pasta according to the package directions. Drain and keep warm.

2. In a saucepan over medium heat, melt the butter. Add the garlic and cook until softened. (Do not let the garlic brown.)

3. Add the flour and whisk together, creating a roux. Cook the roux, stirring constantly, for about 1 minute, until it bubbles and smooths.

4. Slowly whisk in the milk, ½ cup at a time, until smooth. Cook until thickened and bubbling.

5. Stir in the sour cream, Parmesan, salt, pepper, and nutmeg. If adding the shrimp, add them here. Allow the mixture to heat through, or cook until the shrimp are pink.

6. Toss the sauce with the pasta.

7. If you don't like shrimp, try topping the pasta with grilled chicken, grilled flank steak, or crabmeat.

alfredo pizza sauce

This Alfredo sauce also makes an amazing pizza sauce. We like to spread it over pizza dough and top with mozzarella, shrimp, broccoli, or any stocked topping.

stovetop mac and cheese ▬

Serves 4 to 6

4 cups egg noodles, or
    6 ounces penne pasta

1 tablespoon unsalted
    butter

1 egg

¾ cup sour cream or plain
    yogurt

¼ cup milk

1 teaspoon salt

Black pepper

1½ cups shredded Cheddar
    cheese

Diced ham or Sloppy Joes
    (page 197), for serving
    (optional)

1. Cook the noodles according to the package directions. Drain and return to the saucepan.

2. Over low heat, add the butter and stir until melted.

3. In a bowl, whisk together the egg, sour cream, milk, salt, and pepper to taste. Add to the noodles along with the cheese.

4. Cook over low heat, stirring until smooth.

5. Try topped with ham or Sloppy Joe mixture.

a more child-friendly option

This recipe tastes different from (and as far as we are concerned, much better than) the boxes. Your children might prefer a mild Cheddar cheese. Try using only ¾ cup Cheddar and ¾ cup shredded mozzarella to give it an even smoother taste.

stroganoff

Serves 4 to 6

4 cups egg noodles, or
    6 ounces penne pasta

1½ tablespoons unsalted
    butter

¼ cup sliced shallot or
    ½ cup thinly sliced
    onion

One 4-ounce can
    mushrooms, drained

1½ tablespoons flour

¼ teaspoon garlic powder

1 teaspoon salt

⅛ teaspoon black pepper

1 cup beef broth

1½ teaspoons
    Worcestershire sauce

½ teaspoon dill weed

½ cup sour cream or plain
    yogurt

Grilled flank steak,
    browned ground beef,
    or baked Meatballs
    (page 195), for serving
    (optional)

1. Cook the noodles according to the package directions. Drain and keep warm.

2. In a fry pan, melt the butter over medium heat. Add the shallot and mushrooms and cook for 5 to 6 minutes, until the vegetables soften.

3. Stir in the flour, garlic powder, salt, and pepper and cook for 2 to 3 minutes more. Whisk in the beef broth gradually and bring to a boil, stirring occasionally, until thickened, approximately 8 minutes.

4. Stir in the Worcestershire, dill weed, and sour cream.

5. Reduce the heat and simmer for 5 to 6 more minutes.

6. Toss with the pasta and serve.

7. Try topped with grilled flank steak, ground beef, or Meatballs.

tomato-artichoke pasta

Serves 4 to 6

6 to 8 ounces pasta of your
  choice
¼ cup olive oil
2 cloves garlic, minced
1 cup drained marinated
  artichoke hearts
1 cup diced fresh tomato, or
  one 15-ounce can diced
  tomatoes, undrained
¼ cup chopped fresh basil
1 tablespoon Italian
  seasoning
½ teaspoon salt, or to taste
Black pepper to taste
12 ounces to 1 pound raw
  shrimp, thawed, peeled
  completely, and
  deveined (optional)
Grated Parmesan cheese,
  for serving
Grilled chicken or flank
  steak, or cooked
  crabmeat, for serving
  (optional)

1. Cook the pasta according to the package directions.
   Drain and keep warm.

2. In a fry pan over medium heat, heat 2 tablespoons of the
   olive oil and the garlic. Allow the garlic to soften but not
   burn.

3. Add the artichoke hearts, tomatoes, basil, Italian
   seasoning, salt, pepper, and shrimp, if using, and cook
   for 5 minutes.

4. Toss with the pasta and the remaining 2 tablespoons
   olive oil. Serve with Parmesan cheese.

5. If you don't like shrimp, try topping the pasta with
   grilled chicken, grilled flank steak, or crabmeat.

*"Always be a guest at your
own party!"*

We are big proponents of enjoying our
get-togethers and dinner parties just
as much as our guests. This recipe
is perfect for that because it is fast, easy, and impressive. Best of all, you aren't stuck in the kitchen all
night. Serve with our Italian Vinaigrette Salad
(page 98) and freshly baked bread, and enjoy!

These pizzas not only taste great, they are a fun activity to do as a family. We love having friends over for "make your own pizza" night.

pizza crust

Serves 4

1 pound frozen bread dough, thawed
2 tablespoons olive oil
Pizza Sauce and Pizza Toppings (page 154), as needed

1. Preheat the oven to 400°F.
2. Spread the bread dough on a greased deep-dish pizza pan or jelly roll pan. Drizzle the olive oil over the dough, covering it.
3. Build your own pizza with Pizza Sauce and Pizza Toppings.
4. Bake for 10 to 15 minutes, until the bottom is golden brown and the crust is crispy.
5. This crust also works great for any of the specialty pizzas in this section.

the pizza dough grip

Don't be delicate with this dough. Show it who's boss! We cover our hands with olive oil, mold the dough into a ball, and then grip it like a steering wheel with the palms of our hands facing away and our fingers tucked into the back side of the dough. We grip it and turn it until it starts to release. Keep turning it until it becomes shaped more like a crust, lay it on the pan, and push it to the desired thickness and shape.

individual pizza crusts

Serves 4

1 pound frozen bread
    dough, thawed
2 tablespoons olive oil
Pizza Sauce and Pizza
    Toppings (page 154),
    as needed

1. Preheat the oven to 400°F.
2. Cut the bread dough into four balls. Pull each of the balls of dough into a 6- or 7-inch-diameter round. Lay on a greased pizza pan or jelly roll pan and drizzle olive oil over the dough, covering it.
3. Build your own pizza with Pizza Sauce and Pizza Toppings.
4. Bake for 10 to 15 minutes, until the bottom is golden brown and the crust is crispy.
5. This crust also works great for any of the specialty pizzas in this section.

---

don't forget . . . frozen bread dough quick-thaw methods

These quick-thaw methods save you a lot of time when making any of the dishes that use frozen bread dough.

Oven: Preheat the oven to 325°F. Wrap a piece of frozen bread dough in a sheet of parchment paper like a burrito. Place seam side down in a loaf pan. Place in the oven for approximately 12 minutes.

Microwave: Spray a microwave-safe loaf pan or bowl with nonstick spray. Place the frozen bread dough in the pan. Cover with plastic wrap. Microwave for 15 seconds on high. Uncover and flip the bread over. Re-cover and repeat until the bread is thawed.

pita pizza crusts

Serves 4

4 pita breads
Pizza Sauce and Pizza Toppings (page 154), as needed

1. Preheat the oven to 400°F. Cover a jelly roll pan with parchment paper.
2. Lay out the pita breads on the pan.
3. Build your own pizza with Pizza Sauce and Pizza Toppings.
4. Bake for 10 to 12 minutes, until the cheese is melted and beginning to brown.
5. This crust also works great for any of the specialty pizzas in this section.

---

pizza party

The individual pizza crusts and pita pizza crusts are fun for both children and adults. We like to set out sauce and toppings and then let everyone put his or her own concoction together. It's a great activity and everyone has a meal to enjoy.

pizza sauce ▬

Makes enough for 2 large or 8 individual pizzas

One 15-ounce can tomato
  sauce
¼ cup tomato paste
¼ teaspoon garlic powder
2 tablespoons Italian
  seasoning
3 tablespoons brown sugar

Mix all the ingredients together. Use immediately or refrigerate for later use. Making it at least 1 hour ahead helps the flavors to meld.

pizza toppings

Mozzarella cheese, shredded
  or sliced
Cheddar cheese, shredded
  or sliced
Feta cheese, crumbled
Blue or Gorgonzola cheese,
  crumbled
Parmesan cheese, grated or
  shredded
Ham, diced
Breakfast sausage, cooked and
  drained
Ground beef, cooked and drained
Bacon, cooked and crumbled
Chicken, cooked and cubed

Shrimp, cooked
Mushrooms
Spinach
Bell pepper, diced or sliced
Shallots or onions, diced or thinly
  sliced
Marinated artichoke hearts,
  drained
Pineapple
Roasted red peppers, diced or sliced
Pitted black olives, sliced
Pitted green or Kalamata olives,
  sliced
Tomatoes, diced or sliced

chicken bbq pizza

Serves 4

1 cup barbecue sauce

1 tablespoon honey

Pizza Crust (page 151), Individual Pizza Crusts (page 152), or Pita Pizza Crusts (page 153)

1 cup cubed cooked chicken

3 slices bacon, cooked and chopped

½ bell pepper, thinly sliced

¼ cup diced shallot or onion

1½ cups shredded mozzarella or Cheddar cheese

1. Preheat the oven to 400°F.

2. Mix together the barbecue sauce and honey. Spread over the crust(s).

3. Top with the remaining ingredients in order.

4. Bake according to the crust directions.

margherita pizza

Serves 4

1 medium tomato, very
thinly sliced

Pizza Crust (page 151),
Individual Pizza Crusts
(page 152), or Pita Pizza
Crusts (page 153)

2 tablespoons olive oil

2 cloves garlic, minced

½ teaspoon salt

¼ teaspoon black pepper

1 cup shredded mozzarella
cheese

½ cup loosely packed fresh
basil leaves

½ cup grated Parmesan
cheese

1. Preheat the oven to 400°F.
2. Lay the tomato slices over the crust(s). Mix together
   the oil and garlic. Spread the mixture evenly over the
   tomato. Sprinkle with the salt and pepper.
3. Top with the mozzarella, basil, and Parmesan.
4. Bake according to the crust directions.

the stocked kitchen

pesto spinach pizza ▬

Serves 4

PESTO SAUCE

1 cup roughly chopped fresh basil

3 tablespoons pine nuts

¼ cup grated Parmesan cheese

2 cloves garlic, peeled

¼ cup olive oil

½ teaspoon salt

¼ teaspoon black pepper

Pizza Crust (page 151), Individual Pizza Crusts (page 152), or Pita Pizza Crusts (page 153)

1 cup frozen spinach, thawed and squeezed dry

1 cup shredded mozzarella cheese

½ cup crumbled feta or grated Parmesan cheese

1 roasted red pepper, chopped

1 shallot or onion, thinly sliced

1. Preheat the oven to 400°F.

2. Place all the pesto sauce ingredients in a food processor or blender and blend until smooth. Spread over the crust(s).

3. Top with the spinach, mozzarella, feta, roasted red pepper, and shallot.

4. Bake according to the crust directions.

pesto sauce

Try this pesto sauce as a delicious pasta sauce by adding ½ cup chicken broth. It is also delicious as a dipping sauce for Breadsticks (page 132).

thai peanut pizza

Serves 4

PEANUT SAUCE

⅓ cup peanut butter

2 tablespoons soy sauce

2 tablespoons honey

2 teaspoons lemon juice

1 tablespoon pureed
   ginger

1 clove garlic, minced

¼ teaspoon Tabasco or
   hot sauce, or to taste

Pizza Crust (page 151),
   Individual Pizza Crusts
   (page 152), or Pita Pizza
   Crusts (page 153)

¼ pound cooked and thinly
   sliced boneless, skinless
   chicken

1 carrot, thinly sliced with
   a peeler

1½ cups shredded
   mozzarella cheese

2 green onions, thinly
   sliced

1. Preheat the oven to 400°F.

2. Combine all the peanut sauce ingredients and spread over the crust(s).

3. Top with the chicken, carrot, mozzarella, and green onions.

4. Bake according to the crust directions.

veggie pizza

Serves 4

One 8-ounce package
   cream cheese, softened
Pizza Crust (page 151),
   Individual Pizza Crusts
   (page 152), or Pita Pizza
   Crusts (page 153)
1 cup ranch dressing
1½ cups shredded Cheddar
   or mozzarella cheese
1 cup thawed, drained, and
   finely chopped frozen
   broccoli
One 4-ounce can
   mushrooms, well
   drained and sliced or
   chopped
¼ cup well-drained sliced
   or chopped pitted black
   olives

1. Preheat the oven to 400°F.
2. Spread the cream cheese evenly over the crust(s). Top evenly with the ranch dressing. Top with the cheese and the remaining ingredients.
3. Bake according to the crust directions.

---

softening cream cheese or butter

The best way to soften an item like cream cheese or butter is to let it sit out until it naturally becomes soft. We suggest using your microwave only if you have a "soften" setting on it. Otherwise you can wind up with a soupy recipe!

chicken, meat,

and seafood

These marinades can be used for flank steak, chicken, shrimp, or fresh vegetables. Make sure not to cross-contaminate, or transfer bacteria from meats to other meats or vegetables; marinate meat, seafood, and vegetables separately. Consuming raw or undercooked meats or seafood may increase your risk of foodborne illness.

1. Mix all of the ingredients for your chosen marinade in a gallon-size resealable storage bag and shake to combine.
2. Add the meat, chicken, and seafood, and refrigerate for 2 to 24 hours. (Do not use the Honey-Lime, Lemon-Pepper, or Moroccan marinades for longer than 2 hours.)
3. Drain off and discard the marinade. Pat dry with paper towels.
4. Cook according to the basic directions at the start of the following sections.

asian marinade

Makes about 1 cup

⅓ cup olive oil

2 cloves garlic, minced

2 tablespoons white wine vinegar

⅓ cup soy sauce

¼ cup honey

½ teaspoon black pepper

⅛ teaspoon red pepper flakes

greek marinade

Makes about ½ cup

¼ cup olive oil

¼ cup lemon juice

1 tablespoon grated lemon zest (optional)

1 tablespoon Italian seasoning

3 cloves garlic, minced

1 tablespoon dried minced onion

1 teaspoon salt

¼ teaspoon black pepper

honey-lime marinade

Makes about ½ cup

¼ cup honey

2 tablespoons vegetable oil

¼ cup lime juice

½ teaspoon salt

½ teaspoon Tabasco or hot sauce, or to taste

italian marinade

Makes about ½ cup

2 tablespoons extra virgin olive oil

⅓ cup red wine vinegar

1 teaspoon salt

1 teaspoon sugar

1 tablespoon Italian seasoning

1 clove garlic, minced

1 tablespoon Dijon mustard

1 teaspoon dried minced onion

java marinade

Makes about 1¼ cups

3 tablespoons Worcestershire sauce

½ cup cooled strong brewed coffee

¼ cup vegetable oil

3 tablespoons balsamic vinegar

3 tablespoons brown sugar

2 teaspoons salt

½ teaspoon black pepper

1 clove garlic, minced

1 tablespoon pureed ginger

lemon-pepper marinade

Makes about 1 cup

½ cup lemon juice

¼ cup Dijon mustard

1 tablespoon olive oil

1 tablespoon sugar

1 tablespoon coarsely ground black pepper

1 teaspoon salt

moroccan marinade

Makes about 1 cup

½ cup olive oil
2 teaspoons cumin
2 tablespoons pureed ginger
1 teaspoon cinnamon

¼ cup lemon juice
1 tablespoon dried minced onion
½ teaspoon salt
¼ teaspoon black pepper

thai peanut marinade

Makes about 1¼ cups

¾ cup peanut butter
⅓ cup soy sauce
¼ cup honey
1½ tablespoons lemon juice

1 tablespoon pureed ginger
1 clove garlic, minced
¼ teaspoon Tabasco or hot sauce, or to taste

Adding cooked chicken to a salad, pasta, or rice is an easy trick to creating a complete meal. Here are a few ways to get the job done.

to poach

1. In a stockpot, place 4 chicken breasts, 2 cloves garlic, and 10 peppercorns (optional).
2. Cover with one 15-ounce can or 2 cups chicken broth and, over medium-high heat, bring to a boil.
3. Reduce the heat and simmer for 20 minutes. Remove the garlic and peppercorns before using the chicken.
4. Use the remaining broth for another recipe or discard.

to pan-fry

1. Heat a fry pan over medium heat. Drizzle about 1 tablespoon olive oil or melted butter into the skillet for 4 chicken breasts or 6 chicken thighs.
2. Cook until the meat is white on the bottom. Turn over and cook the other side until white.
3. Reduce the heat to medium-low, cover, and cook for about 5 more minutes or until cooked through.
4. To cook faster, cut into strips or chunks before cooking.

to bake

1. Preheat the oven to 425°F. Lay out a large piece of parchment paper.
2. Place 4 chicken breasts or 6 chicken thighs on the paper and sprinkle with grill seasoning or salt and pepper.
3. Wrap the chicken in the parchment paper like a burrito. Be sure not to wrap too tightly, leaving room for steam.
4. Place the package seam side down in an 8-inch square baking dish. Bake for 25 to 30 minutes.
5. If using frozen chicken, bake for 40 to 45 minutes, or until the juices run clear.

apricot chicken ▬

Serves 4

1 pound boneless, skinless chicken
½ teaspoon salt
½ teaspoon black pepper
1 tablespoon vegetable oil
1 shallot or ½ onion, thinly sliced
One 15-ounce can diced tomatoes, undrained
1 cup apricot preserves

1. Season both sides of the chicken with the salt and pepper.
2. In a fry pan, heat the oil. Cook the shallot over medium heat until soft.
3. Add the chicken. Top with the tomatoes and their juices, and the apricot preserves. Cook, uncovered, until the chicken is done, approximately 20 minutes.

blue cheese and pear chicken

Serves 4

1 pound boneless, skinless chicken
1 teaspoon salt
1 teaspoon herbes de Provence
1 cup crumbled blue or Gorgonzola cheese
One 15-ounce can pears, drained and chopped
¼ cup balsamic vinegar
2 tablespoons olive oil

1. Preheat the oven to 375°F. Spray an 8-inch square baking dish with nonstick spray.
2. Lay the chicken in the baking dish and sprinkle with the salt and herbes de Provence. Sprinkle the tops with the blue cheese and pears.
3. Whisk together the balsamic vinegar and olive oil and drizzle over the pears.
4. Cover with aluminum foil and bake for 35 to 40 minutes or until the chicken is fully cooked.
5. If cooking frozen chicken, bake for an additional 15 minutes.

chicken cordon bleu with rice ▬

Serves 4

3 tablespoons Dijon
   mustard

1 cup white rice

One 15-ounce can or
   2 cups chicken broth

½ cup water

1 cup frozen chopped
   broccoli or frozen peas,
   thawed

1 pound boneless, skinless
   chicken, thawed if
   frozen

4 to 6 thin slices ham

1 cup shredded mozzarella
   cheese

¼ cup grated Parmesan
   cheese

1. Preheat the oven to 375°F. Spray a 9 by 13-inch baking dish with nonstick spray.

2. Combine the mustard, rice, chicken broth, water, and broccoli. Spread on the bottom of the baking dish. Top with the chicken. Cover the chicken with the ham. Evenly sprinkle the cheeses on top.

3. Cover the pan with aluminum foil and bake for 40 to 50 minutes or until the chicken and rice are completely cooked.

quick prep

Have time to bake, but no time to prepare? This family-friendly dish allows you to put it together quickly and then bake. Perfect for a multitasking evening!

chicken enchiladas

Serves 4 to 6

2 cups salsa

One 8-ounce package, cream cheese, cubed

2 cups cubed, cooked, boneless, skinless chicken

8 flour tortillas (8-inch or fajita size)

1 cup shredded Cheddar cheese

1 cup shredded mozzarella cheese

1 cup heavy cream

1. Preheat the oven to 350°F. Spray a 9 by 13-inch baking dish with nonstick spray.
2. In a saucepan over medium heat, stir together the salsa, cream cheese, and chicken and cook, stirring occasionally, until the cream cheese melts.
3. Spoon ¼ cup of the chicken mixture down the center of each tortilla. Roll up the tortillas and place seam side down in the baking dish.
4. Combine the Cheddar and mozzarella and sprinkle evenly on top. Drizzle the cream evenly over the top.
5. Bake, uncovered, for 30 minutes, or until the cheese is completely melted and browned.

heavy cream alternative

Don't have cream on hand? Mix together ½ cup milk and ½ cup sour cream or plain yogurt. Use according to the recipe directions.

chicken fajitas

Serves 4

1 pound boneless, skinless chicken

2 tablespoons vegetable oil

2 shallots or ½ onion, thinly sliced

3 cloves garlic, minced

1 bell pepper, thinly sliced

2 teaspoons cumin

2 tablespoons chili powder

3 tablespoons lime juice

Tabasco or hot sauce

6 to 8 flour tortillas (8-inch or fajita size)

1 cup shredded Cheddar cheese

Sour cream and salsa, for serving (optional)

1. Thinly slice the chicken.
2. Heat the oil in a fry pan over high heat. Once very hot, add the shallots, garlic, and bell pepper. Stir occasionally until the vegetables begin to get tender, approximately 5 minutes.
3. Stir in the cumin and chili powder, and then add the chicken. Add the lime juice and Tabasco to taste. Stir occasionally until the chicken is cooked thoroughly, about 5 minutes.
4. Serve with the flour tortillas and Cheddar cheese. Garnish with sour cream and salsa, if desired.

chicken potpie

Serves 4

2 tablespoons unsalted
   butter

1 pound boneless, skinless
   chicken, cut into 1-inch
   cubes

¼ cup flour

One 15-ounce can or
   2 cups chicken broth

¼ cup dried minced onion

½ teaspoon salt

Tabasco or hot sauce

¼ teaspoon black pepper

1 teaspoon poultry
   seasoning

One 15-ounce can corn,
   drained

1 cup thawed and drained
   frozen peas, cut green
   beans, or chopped
   broccoli

½ cup shredded mozzarella
   cheese

½ cup shredded Cheddar
   cheese

1 sheet puff pastry, thawed

1. Preheat the oven to 400°F.

2. In a stockpot over medium heat, melt the butter. Toss the chicken with the flour. Pour the mixture into the stockpot and sauté until the chicken is completely cooked, about 8 minutes.

3. Stir in the chicken broth and continue to stir until the mixture thickens.

4. Add the minced onion, salt, Tabasco to taste, the pepper, and poultry seasoning. Stir in the corn and vegetables and remove from the heat.

5. Sprinkle the mozzarella and Cheddar in the bottom of an 8-inch square baking dish. Pour in the chicken mixture. Lay the puff pastry sheet over the top of the baking dish.

6. Bake for 40 minutes or until the puff pastry is puffed and golden brown. Let sit for a few minutes before serving.

chicken florentine ▬

Serves 8

8 boneless, skinless chicken breasts, thawed if frozen

1 teaspoon salt

½ teaspoon black pepper

2 cups frozen spinach, thawed and squeezed dry

½ cup shredded mozzarella cheese

½ cup grated Parmesan cheese

2 cloves garlic, minced

¼ cup olive oil

⅓ cup chicken broth

1. Preheat the oven to 375°F.
2. Place the chicken between two pieces of plastic wrap. Pound the chicken with a mallet or rolling pin until ¼ inch thick. Salt and pepper both sides of the chicken pieces.
3. Combine the spinach, cheeses, and garlic.
4. Spread one-eighth of the spinach mixture on each chicken breast. Roll up, starting with a short end, and secure with a toothpick.
5. Place the chicken bundles in 9 by 13-inch baking dish. Drizzle with the olive oil and chicken broth. Bake, uncovered, for 40 minutes or until cooked through.

avoid chicken or steak jerky!

You will notice that when we bake chicken or flank steak, we often drizzle the meat with olive oil and/or broth. Boneless, skinless chicken and lean flank steak need additional fat and liquid to protect them from the dry heat of the oven. Adding olive oil or broth helps keep them tender and juicy.

chicken satay

Serves 4

1 pound boneless, skinless chicken breasts

THAI PEANUT MARINADE
¾ cup peanut butter
⅓ cup soy sauce
¼ cup honey
1½ tablespoons lemon juice
1 tablespoon pureed ginger
1 clove garlic, minced
¼ teaspoon Tabasco or hot sauce, or to taste
11-inch wooden skewers

1. Cut the chicken lengthwise into 1- to 2-inch-wide strips.
2. Whisk together the marinade ingredients. Pour into a resealable storage bag. Add the chicken and refrigerate. Allow to marinate for 1 to 4 hours.
3. In the meantime, soak wooden skewers in water for 20 to 30 minutes to keep them from catching fire while grilling. Preheat a grill to medium-high.
4. Thread pieces of chicken lengthwise onto the skewers. Discard any leftover marinade.
5. Grill the skewers, flipping once, until the chicken is cooked through, about 5 minutes per side.

not authentic, but delicious

We would never claim that our recipes are completely authentic. It is more important to us to create great-tasting recipes with the essence of the ethnicity, using the ingredients we already have stocked. This Chicken Satay is wonderful with our Peanut Noodles (page 143). They both use versions of the same sauce, which saves you a step. Add our Ginger Salad (page 94) and you have a delicious Asian-flavored meal.

chicken strips

Serves 6

½ cup milk

2 teaspoons lemon juice

8 drops Tabasco or hot sauce

1 pound boneless, skinless chicken breasts, cut lengthwise into 1- to 2-inch-wide strips

1 sleeve or 32 butter crackers

½ cup plain bread crumbs

1 teaspoon grill seasoning

HONEY MUSTARD DIPPING SAUCE

½ cup mayonnaise

2 tablespoons yellow mustard

2 tablespoons honey

1 teaspoon lemon juice

1. Preheat the oven to 425°F. Cover a jelly roll pan with parchment paper.
2. Whisk together the milk, lemon juice, and Tabasco in a large bowl. Add the chicken and stir until the chicken is coated.
3. Place the crackers in a resealable storage bag, and seal the bag. Finely crush the crackers with a rolling pin. Add the bread crumbs and grill seasoning to the crackers.
4. Remove the chicken from the milk mixture with a slotted spoon and place the chicken in the bag with the crumbs. (Discard the remaining milk mixture.) Reseal the bag and shake to coat the chicken.
5. Place the chicken on the jelly roll pan in a single layer.
6. Bake for 20 minutes, or until the center of the thickest piece of chicken is cooked through.
7. Mix together the dipping sauce ingredients and serve with the chicken strips.

grown-up chicken strips

Chicken strips are often found on the kids' menu, but these flavorful strips are great for everyone! To give them a more adult presentation, use them to top a salad or wrap them in a flour tortilla with lettuce, tomato slices, and a drizzle of honey mustard dipping sauce.

curry-rubbed chicken

Serves 6

2 tablespoons lime juice
1 tablespoon curry powder
1 teaspoon salt
1 teaspoon black pepper
1 tablespoon vegetable oil
2 pounds boneless, skinless
   chicken

1. Combine the lime juice, curry powder, salt, pepper, and oil. Rub the chicken with the mixture. Set aside, covered.
2. Preheat a grill to medium-high.
3. Grill the chicken until cooked through, turning once.
4. This rub is also great on 2 pounds flank steak. Grill until cooked to desired doneness.

feta chicken

Serves 4

2 cups frozen chopped
   spinach, thawed and
   squeezed dry
1½ pounds boneless,
   skinless chicken
Grill seasoning
1 cup crumbled feta cheese
1 roasted red pepper or bell
   pepper, diced
3 tablespoons lemon juice

1. Preheat the oven to 350°F. Spray a 9 by 13-inch baking dish with nonstick spray.
2. Spread the spinach on the bottom of the baking dish. Sprinkle each side of the chicken pieces with grill seasoning. Lay over the spinach. Top with the feta cheese and red pepper and drizzle with the lemon juice.
3. Bake, uncovered, for 35 to 40 minutes, until the chicken is fully cooked.

ginger broccoli stir-fry

Serves 4

1 tablespoon pureed
　ginger
1 tablespoon soy sauce
½ cup chicken broth
1 tablespoon vegetable oil
1 pound boneless, skinless
　chicken, cut into thin
　strips
2 cloves garlic, minced
One 16-ounce package
　frozen broccoli, thawed
¼ cup chopped peanuts
Cooked rice, for serving

1. Mix together the ginger, soy sauce, and chicken broth and set aside.
2. In a fry pan, heat the oil on high until very hot. Add the chicken. Add the garlic and stir-fry until the meat is cooked through, about 8 minutes.
3. Add the broccoli and reduce the heat to medium-low. Stir in the soy sauce mixture and cook until the broccoli is heated through, 5 to 10 minutes. Sprinkle with the peanuts and serve with cooked rice.

and a side of egg noodles

Pasta and egg noodles can be an excellent side dish without a recipe. Cook them according to the package directions. Drain and stir in 1 to 2 tablespoons unsalted butter or olive oil. Sprinkle with Parmesan, feta, or blue cheese and serve. Olive oil and feta cheese are delicious with this recipe.

mexican chicken

Serves 4

1 pound boneless, skinless chicken
½ cup salsa
¼ cup sour cream or plain yogurt
½ cup crushed tortilla chips
½ cup shredded Cheddar cheese
¼ cup chopped or sliced pitted black olives

1. Preheat the oven to 375°F. Spray an 8-inch square baking dish with nonstick spray.
2. Lay the chicken in the baking dish. Score the chicken pieces three times across the top to open them up and allow the flavors to penetrate.
3. Mix together the salsa and sour cream. Spread the chicken with the salsa mixture. Sprinkle with the tortilla chips.
4. Bake, uncovered, for 20 minutes. Remove from the oven, sprinkle with the cheese and olives, and bake for another 10 minutes or until the chicken is cooked through.

nutty chicken

Serves 4

1 pound boneless, skinless chicken
1 teaspoon salt
½ teaspoon black pepper
2 tablespoons mayonnaise
2 tablespoons Dijon mustard
½ cup finely chopped almonds, pecans, or pine nuts

1. Preheat the oven to 375°F. Spray an 8-inch square baking dish with nonstick spray.
2. Lay the chicken in the baking dish and sprinkle with the salt and pepper.
3. Mix the mayonnaise and mustard until blended. Spread on top of the chicken. Sprinkle with the nuts.
4. Bake, uncovered, for 20 to 25 minutes, or until the chicken is cooked through.

southwest chicken and rice ▬

Serves 4

1 cup rice

One 15-ounce can black beans, drained and rinsed

One 15-ounce can corn, drained

One 15-ounce can diced tomatoes, undrained

2 cups water

2 tablespoons dried minced onion

1½ teaspoons salt

1 tablespoon chili powder

½ teaspoon garlic powder

1 pound boneless, skinless chicken

1 cup shredded Cheddar cheese

1. Preheat the oven to 375°F. Spray a 9 by 13-inch baking dish with nonstick spray.

2. Combine the rice, beans, corn, tomatoes, water, minced onion, salt, chili powder, and garlic powder. Spread in the bottom of the baking dish. Top with the chicken. Cover the chicken with the cheese.

3. Cover the baking dish with aluminum foil or a lid. Bake for 40 to 45 minutes, or until the chicken and rice are completely cooked.

baked dishes for guests

These chicken bakes are ideal for guests. They taste great and since they're baked, you can actually enjoy your guests' company before dinner. Use one chicken breast or two chicken thighs per guest and increase the recipe accordingly.

sweet-and-sour stir-fry

Serves 4

2 tablespoons soy sauce

2 tablespoons balsamic vinegar

1 tablespoon brown sugar

¼ teaspoon red pepper flakes, or to taste

2 tablespoons vegetable oil

1 pound boneless, skinless chicken, thinly sliced

1 bell pepper, cut into 1-inch chunks

½ cup diced shallot or onion

One 15-ounce can pineapple chunks, drained

Cooked rice or flour tortillas, for serving

1. Mix together the soy sauce, balsamic vinegar, brown sugar, and red pepper flakes and set aside.
2. Heat a fry pan over high heat. Add the oil and heat until very hot. Add the chicken, bell pepper, and shallot and cook until the chicken is cooked through and the vegetables are soft.
3. Add the pineapple and the sauce mixture and stir to coat and warm through.
4. Serve with cooked rice or flour tortillas.

These are cost-effective and lean cuts of steak. The following cooking methods are all great with marinated meat. (See our marinade recipes on pages 162 through 164.) When marinating the meat, make sure to score or cut the meat about ⅛ inch deep, against the grain, across the entire piece. It is best if meat is at room temperature before cooking. A 1½-pound flank steak will generally serve four to six. These steaks are best when cut in thin slices against the grain. Try serving them topped with our homemade salsas.

to broil

1. If you don't have a broiling pan, cover a jelly roll pan with aluminum foil and top with a cooling rack.
2. Season the steak on both sides with grill seasoning.
3. Preheat the broiler if necessary. Broil the steak for about 7 minutes on each side for medium, or to desired doneness.

to grill

1. Season the steak with grill seasoning and place on a preheated grill at medium heat.
2. Grill for approximately 7 minutes on each side for medium, or to desired doneness.

to braise

1. In a large fry pan over medium-high heat, place about 1 tablespoon olive oil.
2. Season the meat on both sides with grill seasoning.
3. Lightly brown both sides of the steak.
4. Add 1 cup beef broth, reduce the heat, cover, and simmer for approximately 1½ hours, until fork-tender.
5. If the steak is marinated, just put the steak and marinade in the fry pan and simmer, covered, for 1½ hours.

black-and-blue roll-up ▰

Serves 4 to 6

1½ pounds flank steak
   or skirt steak
1 tablespoon grill seasoning
½ cup crumbled blue or
   Gorgonzola cheese
½ cup cream cheese
1 tablespoon dried
   minced onion
3 tablespoons prepared
   horseradish
1 tablespoon olive oil
½ cup beef broth

1. Preheat the oven to 375°F.

2. Pound the steak to tenderize it. Season both sides lightly with the grill seasoning.

3. Mix together the blue cheese, cream cheese, minced onion, and horseradish. Spread over the steak. Roll up the steak starting with a short end, and secure with toothpicks.

4. Lay in an 8-inch square baking dish. Drizzle the olive oil over the top and pour the beef broth into the baking dish. Cover with aluminum foil.

5. Bake for 1 hour or until cooked to desired doneness. Let sit for a couple of minutes before slicing.

marinated black-and-blue roll-up

Try marinating the tenderized meat in the Italian Marinade (page 163) first. Instead of topping it with olive oil and beef broth, simply pour the remaining marinade over the top of the rolled-up steak. Then season with the grill seasoning. Bake according to the directions above.

braised provençal steak

Serves 4 to 6

6 tablespoons flour

1 teaspoon salt

¼ teaspoon black pepper

1½ to 2 pounds flank steak, cubed

2 tablespoons olive oil

2 cloves garlic, minced

¼ cup diced shallot, or ½ cup diced onion

1 cup chopped carrot

1 cup chopped celery

One 15-ounce can diced tomatoes, undrained

One 15-ounce can or 2 cups beef broth

¼ cup balsamic vinegar

1 teaspoon salt

1 tablespoon herbes de Provence

½ cup cold water

Cooked egg noodles or mashed potatoes, for serving

1. Mix together 2 tablespoons of the flour, the salt, and pepper in a resealable storage bag. Toss in the flank steak, seal the bag, and shake to coat.

2. Heat the olive oil in a stockpot over medium heat. Remove the steak from the bag and brown on all sides for 2 to 3 minutes.

3. Add the garlic, shallot, carrot, celery, tomatoes, broth, vinegar, salt, and herbes de Provence. Cook on medium-high heat for 10 minutes.

4. Reduce the heat to low and simmer, covered, for 1½ hours.

5. Mix the remaining ¼ cup flour with the cold water and stir until combined. Slowly stir the flour mixture into the juices in the pot, cooking over low heat until the gravy is the desired thickness.

6. Serve over egg noodles or mashed potatoes.

7. To make Provençal Chicken, substitute whole boneless, skinless chicken breasts for the flank steak and chicken broth for the beef broth. Proceed as above, but remove the chicken from the pot before adding the flour mixture. Arrange the chicken on plates and scoop the gravy and vegetable mix over the chicken.

greek roll-up ▬

Serves 4 to 6

1½ pounds flank steak
  or skirt steak
2 tablespoons grill
  seasoning
1 clove garlic, minced
¼ teaspoon salt
¼ cup finely diced shallot,
  or ½ cup finely diced
  onion
¼ cup plain bread crumbs
2 cups frozen spinach,
  thawed and squeezed dry
¼ cup crumbled feta
  cheese
1 tablespoon olive oil
½ cup beef broth

1. Preheat the oven to 375°F.
2. Pound the steak to tenderize it. Season both sides lightly with the grill seasoning.
3. Mix together the garlic, salt, shallot, bread crumbs, spinach, and feta. Spread over the steak. Roll up the steak starting with a short end, and secure with toothpicks.
4. Lay in an 8-inch square baking dish. Drizzle the olive oil over the top and pour the beef broth into the baking dish. Cover with aluminum foil.
5. Bake for 1 hour or until cooked to desired doneness. Let sit for a couple of minutes before slicing.

---

marinated greek roll-up

Try marinating the tenderized meat in the Greek Marinade (page 162) first. Instead of topping it with olive oil and beef broth, simply pour the remaining marinade over the top of the rolled-up steak. Then season with the grill seasoning. Bake according to the directions above.

the stocked kitchen

Chicken Florentine *(page 171)*

Chicken Strips *(page 173)*

Black-and-Blue Roll-Up *(page 180)*

Mock Shrimp Ceviche *(page 205)*

Crab Enchiladas *(page 202)*

Oven Chips and Oven Fries *(pages 220 and 221)*

Black Bean Burger *(page 212)*

Kidney Bean–Tortilla Lasagna *(page 213)*

Glazed Carrots *(page 231)*

Tomatoes Provençal *(page 235)*

Stocked Paella *(page 227)*

PB&J Ice Cream Sandwiches *(page 251)*

Chocolate Truffles *(page 248)*

Lemon Bars *(page 253)*

Mandarin Orange Cream Tart *(page 272)*

Rice Pudding *(page 264)*

Traditional Cheesecake *(page 246)*

Aniseed and Pine Nut Biscotti *(page 276)*

Eggs Benedict *(page 287)*

Mushroom–Red Pepper Quiche *(page 302)*

Cinnamon Roll Loaf *(page 282)*

Cheddar-Herb Scones *(page 304)*

Turtle Pancakes *(page 298)*

jerk-rubbed steak

Serves 4 to 6

1½ pounds flank steak
　or skirt steak
2 tablespoons olive oil
2 tablespoons dried
　minced onion
2 teaspoons poultry
　seasoning
2 teaspoons brown sugar
2 teaspoons salt
1 teaspoon pumpkin pie
　spice
1 teaspoon black pepper
¼ teaspoon Tabasco or
　hot sauce, or to taste

1. Preheat a grill to medium-low.
2. Pound the meat thoroughly to tenderize it. With a sharp knife, make ¼-inch-deep cuts every inch across the grain of the meat.
3. Mix the remaining ingredients into a paste. Rub over both sides of the steak.
4. Grill for 7 minutes on each side or until cooked to desired doneness.

rubs

Rubs are a combination of seasonings and herbs that are literally rubbed over raw meat before cooking. They provide a lot of taste and texture to your grilled steak. It is best to grill at a lower temperature when using rubs so that the meat is cooked more slowly for more tenderness and so that the sugars in the rubs are not scorched.

moroccan roll-up ▬

Serves 4 to 6

1½ pounds flank steak
    or skirt steak
1 tablespoon grill seasoning
4 cloves garlic, peeled
½ cup pitted green or
    Kalamata olives
½ cup raisins
2 tablespoons herbes de
    Provence
2 tablespoons lemon juice
3 tablespoons olive oil
¼ teaspoon salt
¼ teaspoon black pepper,
    or to taste
½ cup beef broth

1. Preheat the oven to 375°F.
2. Pound the steak to tenderize it. Season both sides lightly with the grill seasoning.
3. In a blender or food processor, blend together the garlic, olives, raisins, herbes de Provence, lemon juice, 2 tablespoons of the olive oil, the salt, and pepper. Spread over the steak. Roll up the steak, starting with a short end, and secure with toothpicks.
4. Lay in an 8-inch square baking dish. Drizzle the remaining 1 tablespoon olive oil over the top and pour the beef broth into the baking dish. Cover with aluminum foil.
5. Bake for 1 hour or until cooked to desired doneness. Let sit for a couple of minutes before slicing.

marinated moroccan roll-up

Try marinating the tenderized meat in the Moroccan Marinade (page 164) first. Instead of topping it with olive oil and beef broth, simply pour the remaining marinade over the top of the rolled-up steak. Then season with the grill seasoning. Bake according to the directions above.

pepper and fennel–rubbed steak

Serves 4 to 6

1½ pounds flank steak
or skirt steak
1 tablespoon olive oil
1 teaspoon black pepper
1 tablespoon salt
1 tablespoon aniseed or
fennel seed, crushed
½ teaspoon garlic powder

1. Preheat a grill to medium-low.
2. Pound the meat thoroughly to tenderize it. With a sharp knife, make ¼-inch-deep cuts every inch across the grain of the meat.
3. Mix the remaining ingredients into a paste. Rub over both sides of the steak.
4. Grill for 7 minutes on each side or until cooked to desired doneness.

pepper steak

Serves 4 to 6

1½ pounds flank steak
  or skirt steak
Salt and black pepper
2 tablespoons flour
1 tablespoon water
1 cup beef broth
2 tablespoons white wine
  vinegar
3 tablespoons vegetable oil
4 cloves garlic, minced
2 tablespoons pureed ginger
One 4-ounce can
  mushrooms, drained
  and chopped
1 bell pepper, sliced into
  strips
½ cup thinly sliced shallot
  or onion
¼ cup chopped almonds
Cooked rice, egg noodles,
  or mashed potatoes, for
  serving

1. Pound the meat thoroughly to tenderize it. Season both sides with salt and pepper. Broil or grill to desired doneness. Set aside and keep warm.

2. Whisk together the flour and water. Whisk in the beef broth, 1 teaspoon salt, and the vinegar and set aside.

3. In a large fry pan, heat the oil over medium-low heat. Add the garlic, ginger, mushrooms, bell pepper, and shallot. Cook until just tender, about 3 minutes. Add the almonds and the broth mixture. Cook until thickened.

4. Slice the steak diagonally across the grain into very thin slices and place on a platter.

5. Pour the pepper mixture over the top. Serve with cooked rice, egg noodles, or mashed potatoes.

pesto roll-up ▬

Serves 4 to 6

1½ pounds flank steak
   or skirt steak
1 tablespoon grill seasoning
1 cup coarsely chopped
   fresh basil
3 tablespoons pine nuts
¼ cup grated Parmesan
   cheese
2 cloves garlic, peeled
¼ cup olive oil
¼ teaspoon salt
⅛ teaspoon black pepper,
   or to taste
1 tablespoon olive oil
½ cup beef broth

1. Preheat the oven to 375°F.

2. Pound the steak to help tenderize it. Season both sides lightly with the grill seasoning.

3. In a blender or food processor, blend the basil, pine nuts, Parmesan, garlic, olive oil, salt, and pepper to a paste. Spread over the steak. Roll up the steak, starting with a short end, and secure with toothpicks.

4. Lay in an 8-inch square baking dish. Drizzle the olive oil over the top and pour the beef broth into the baking dish. Cover with aluminum foil.

5. Bake for 1 hour or until cooked to desired doneness. Let sit for a couple of minutes before slicing.

---

marinated pesto roll-up

Try marinating the tenderized meat in our Italian Marinade (page 163) first. Instead of topping it with olive oil and beef broth, simply pour the remaining marinade over the top of the rolled-up steak. Then season with the grill seasoning. Bake according to the directions above.

steak fajitas

Serves 4

1 pound flank steak or
    skirt steak

2 tablespoons vegetable oil

2 shallots or ½ onion,
    thinly sliced

3 cloves garlic, minced

1 bell pepper, thinly sliced

2 teaspoons cumin

2 tablespoons chili powder

3 tablespoons lime juice

Tabasco or hot sauce

6 to 8 flour tortillas (8-inch
    or fajita size)

1 cup shredded Cheddar
    cheese

Sour cream and salsa, for
    serving (optional)

1. Thinly slice the steak against the grain.

2. Heat the oil in a fry pan. Once very hot, add the shallots, garlic, and bell pepper. Stir occasionally until the vegetables begin to get tender, approximately 5 minutes.

3. Stir in the cumin and chili powder. Add the steak, lime juice, and Tabasco to taste. Stir occasionally until the steak is cooked to desired doneness.

4. Serve with the flour tortillas and Cheddar cheese. Garnish with sour cream and salsa, if desired.

fiesta!

These fajitas are also delicious with chicken or shrimp. (See pages 169 and 209 for recipes.) Make it a complete meal with Spanish Rice (page 226) and Catalina Salad (page 92).

steak and potato shish kebab

Serves 4 to 6

2 medium potatoes,
  scrubbed well

JAVA MARINADE

3 tablespoons
  Worcestershire sauce
½ cup cooled strong brewed
  coffee
¼ cup vegetable oil
3 tablespoons balsamic
  vinegar
3 tablespoons brown sugar
2 teaspoons salt
½ teaspoon black pepper
1 clove garlic, minced
1 tablespoon pureed ginger

1½ pounds flank steak,
  cut into 1-inch cubes
1 bell pepper, cut into
  1½-inch chunks
2 shallots or 1 onion, cut
  into 1½-inch chunks
11-inch wooden skewers

1. Place the potatoes in a stockpot and cover with water. Bring to a boil and cook for 3 to 5 minutes, until they just begin to become tender. Drain and cool slightly. Cut into 1½-inch chunks.

2. Whisk together the marinade ingredients. Split between two resealable storage bags. Add the steak to one bag and the potatoes, bell pepper, and shallots to the other. Marinate for at least 1 hour.

3. In the meantime, soak the skewers in water for 20 to 30 minutes to keep them from catching fire while grilling. Preheat a grill to medium-high.

4. Skewer pieces of steak, potato, bell pepper, and shallot in the desired pattern. Discard the remaining marinade.

5. Grill the skewers for 5 minutes or until the steak is cooked to desired doneness.

---

parboiling potatoes

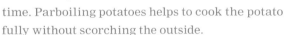

Parboiling is a technique in which the ingredient is partially cooked, and cooking is finished at a later time. Parboiling potatoes helps to cook the potato fully without scorching the outside.

steak wellington

Serves 4 to 6

1½ pounds flank steak
    or skirt steak
1 tablespoon grill seasoning
One 4-ounce can
    mushrooms, well
    drained and finely
    chopped
¼ cup dried minced
    onion
1 tablespoon
    Worcestershire sauce
1 cup crumbled blue or
    Gorgonzola cheese
1 sheet puff pastry,
    thawed

STEAK SAUCE
3 tablespoons ketchup
3 tablespoons
    Worcestershire sauce
1 tablespoon maple syrup
1 tablespoon chili powder
1 teaspoon prepared
    horseradish

1. Preheat the oven to 425°F. Preheat a grill or broiler.

2. Pound the meat thoroughly to tenderize it. Sprinkle both sides with the grill seasoning. Grill or broil for approximately 4 minutes per side or until medium-rare.

3. Mix together the mushrooms, minced onion, Worcestershire, and blue cheese.

4. Roll out the puff pastry into a 10 by 14-inch rectangle. Spread half of the mushroom mixture over the center of the puff pastry, leaving approximately 3 inches around the edges clear.

5. Slice the meat against the grain into very thin slices. Lay half of the steak slices over the mushroom mixture. Top with the remaining mushroom mixture and the remaining steak.

6. Fold up the short ends of the puff pastry, then fold in the sides, one at a time, so that the mushroom mixture and steak are completely contained.

7. Bake for 25 minutes or until the pastry is golden brown. Let sit for a few minutes.

8. Mix together the sauce ingredients and serve with slices of the Steak Wellington.

All of these recipes work great with ground beef, turkey, or chicken.

beef enchiladas ▬

Serves 4 to 6

TACO MEAT

1 pound ground beef

2 tablespoons flour

1 tablespoon chili powder

1 teaspoon salt

1 teaspoon dried minced
   onion

½ teaspoon garlic powder

½ teaspoon cumin

½ cup water

ENCHILADA SAUCE

3 tablespoons chili powder

3 tablespoons flour

1 teaspoon cocoa powder

½ teaspoon garlic powder

½ teaspoon salt

1 teaspoon cumin

2 cups water

One 15-ounce can tomato
   sauce

8 flour tortillas (8-inch or
   fajita size)

2 cups shredded Cheddar
   cheese

½ cup chopped olives

½ cup sliced green onions

1. Preheat the oven to 350°F. Spray a 9 by 13-inch baking dish with nonstick spray.

2. Brown the ground beef. Drain off the excess grease. In a saucepan, combine with the remaining taco meat ingredients. Stir over low heat for a few minutes until mixed well. Set aside.

3. For the enchilada sauce, combine the chili powder, flour, cocoa, garlic powder, salt, and cumin with a couple of tablespoons of water to make a paste. Scoop the mixture into a saucepan and stir in the remaining water. Cook over medium heat, stirring occasionally, until the mixture thickens, about 5 minutes. Remove from the heat and stir in the tomato sauce. Spread about ½ cup of the enchilada sauce on the bottom of the baking dish.

4. Fill each tortilla with taco meat and fold up like a burrito. Place the filled tortillas, seam side down, in the baking dish. Cover with the remaining enchilada sauce. Sprinkle on the cheese, olives, and green onions.

5. Bake for 30 minutes or until the cheese is completely melted.

beef nachos

Serves 4 to 6

1 pound ground beef
2 tablespoons flour
1 tablespoon chili powder
1 teaspoon salt
1 teaspoon dried minced
   onion
½ teaspoon garlic powder
½ teaspoon cumin
½ cup water
30 to 35 tortilla chips
1 cup drained and rinsed
   canned black beans
2 cups shredded Cheddar
   cheese
1 medium tomato, diced
Salsa and sour cream, for
   serving (optional)

1. Preheat the oven to 350°F. Cover a jelly roll pan with aluminum foil.

2. In a fry pan, brown the meat thoroughly. Drain off the excess grease.

3. Combine the flour, chili powder, salt, minced onion, garlic powder, and cumin and stir into the beef along with the water. Simmer for a few minutes until mixed well.

4. Arrange the tortilla chips on the jelly roll pan. Top with the beef mixture, black beans, cheese, and tomato.

5. Bake for 15 to 20 minutes, until the cheese is melted and beginning to brown.

6. Serve with salsa and sour cream, if desired.

greek burger

Serves 4

1 pound ground beef
1 clove garlic, minced
1 teaspoon herbes de
Provence
1 tablespoon dried minced
onion
1 teaspoon salt
¼ teaspoon cinnamon
2 tablespoons sour cream
or plain yogurt
2 pita breads
½ cup crumbled feta cheese
1 medium tomato, diced

CUCUMBER SAUCE
½ English cucumber, finely
diced
¾ cup sour cream or plain
yogurt
⅛ teaspoon garlic powder
½ teaspoon dill weed
¼ teaspoon salt

1. Mix together the ground beef, garlic, herbes de Provence, minced onion, salt, cinnamon, and sour cream. Form into four patties. Pan-fry or grill to desired doneness.
2. Cut the pitas in half and stuff each half with a cooked burger patty, feta cheese, and tomato.
3. Mix together the cucumber sauce ingredients. Spoon over the burgers and serve.

italian burger

Serves 4

Hamburger Buns (page 136) or store-bought

1 pound ground beef

1 clove garlic, minced

1 tablespoon unsalted butter, melted

1 teaspoon salt

½ teaspoon black pepper

1 tablespoon Italian seasoning

1 teaspoon dried minced onion

½ cup shredded mozzarella cheese

PESTO MAYONNAISE

½ cup coarsely chopped fresh basil

2 tablespoons pine nuts

¼ cup grated Parmesan cheese

1 clove garlic, coarsely chopped

¼ cup mayonnaise

Lettuce

Sliced tomato

1. Make the Hamburger Buns.

2. Mix together the ground beef, garlic, butter, salt, pepper, Italian seasoning, and minced onion. Form into four patties. Begin to pan-fry or grill. When the burgers are just about cooked through, top with the cheese and allow the cheese to melt.

3. In a food processor or blender, pulse the pesto mayonnaise ingredients together until smooth.

4. Serve the burgers on buns, topped with the pesto mayonnaise, lettuce, and tomato slices.

meatballs

Serves 4

1 pound ground beef
½ cup plain bread crumbs
1 tablespoon Italian
  seasoning
2 eggs, lightly beaten
2 tablespoons dried minced
  onion
1 teaspoon salt
¼ teaspoon black pepper

1. Use your hands to mix all the ingredients. Roll into 2-inch balls.
2. Cook in boiling sauce, such as marinara sauce (page 145), for 30 minutes. You can also bake at 375°F for 20 to 25 minutes on a foil-lined jelly roll pan topped with a cooling rack.

have them on hand

Doubling or tripling this recipe doesn't add much, if any, extra effort. We at least double the recipe and then freeze the cooked meatballs in a re-sealable freezer bag. We can then toss them into any of our meatball sauces for a quick meal or appetizer. Just take out as many as you need.

meat loaf

Serves 4

¼ cup milk
3 slices bread
1 pound ground beef
¾ cup ketchup
1 teaspoon Worcestershire
  sauce
2 teaspoons Dijon
  mustard
1 egg, lightly beaten
1 tablespoon dried
  minced onion
½ teaspoon salt
¼ teaspoon pepper
¼ cup brown sugar
1 teaspoon yellow
  mustard

1. Preheat the oven to 400°F. Spray a loaf pan with nonstick spray.
2. Pour the milk into a mixing bowl. Add the bread and allow it to absorb the milk. Add the ground beef, ¼ cup of the ketchup, the Worcestershire, Dijon mustard, egg, minced onion, salt, and pepper and mix together well. (It is easiest to use your hands.) Press the mixture into the loaf pan.
3. Combine the brown sugar, yellow mustard, and the remaining ½ cup ketchup. Spread over the top of the meat loaf.
4. Bake for 35 to 45 minutes or until the juices run clear and the meat loaf is browned on top.
5. Remove from the pan and drain off any fat. Slice and serve.

comfort food

Meat loaf is comfort food at its best.
Serve this with mashed potatoes
(pages 219 and 223) or Corn Casserole
(page 229) for a hearty, delicious meal.

sloppy joes ▬

Serves 4

Bread, pita breads, or
  Hamburger Buns
  (page 136), for serving

1 pound ground beef,
  turkey, or chicken

1 tablespoon dried minced
  onion

¾ teaspoon salt

1 tablespoon
  Worcestershire sauce

⅔ cup ketchup

¼ cup brown sugar

1 tablespoon yellow
  mustard

1 tablespoon barbecue
  sauce

1. If using Hamburger Buns, make them.

2. In a fry pan, cook the ground meat thoroughly. Drain off the excess grease. Mix in the remaining ingredients and simmer, stirring often, for 20 minutes. Serve.

southwest burger

Serves 4

1 pound ground beef
1 tablespoon chili powder
1 teaspoon salt
1 teaspoon dried minced
  onion
½ teaspoon garlic powder
½ teaspoon cumin
2 tablespoons sour cream
  or plain yogurt, plus
  more for serving
½ cup shredded Cheddar
  cheese
4 flour tortillas (8-inch or
  fajita size)
Lettuce
Sliced tomato
Black olives, sliced or
  chopped
Salsa
Sour cream

1. Mix together the ground beef, chili powder, salt, minced onion, garlic powder, cumin, and sour cream. Form four patties and begin to panfry or grill. When the burgers are just about cooked through, top with cheese and allow the cheese to melt.
2. Serve the burgers on flour tortillas, topped with lettuce, tomato slices, olives, salsa, and sour cream.

like a zestier burger?

For an even zestier version, try the Southwest Burger topped with Cajun Aioli (page 61) instead of sour cream and salsa.

taco meat ▬

Serves 4

1 pound ground beef
2 tablespoons flour
1 tablespoon chili powder
1 teaspoon salt
1 teaspoon dried minced
   onion
½ teaspoon garlic powder
½ teaspoon cumin
½ cup water
Flour tortillas or tortilla
   chips, for serving

1. In a fry pan, brown the meat thoroughly. Drain off the excess grease.
2. Stir in the remaining ingredients and simmer for a few minutes.
3. Serve on flour tortillas or over tortilla chips.

---

take your taco meat further

We love to add a can of black beans—drained and rinsed—to our Taco Meat to inexpensively double the recipe without adding any extra fat. This is also one of our go-to recipes when we need dinner quickly. We make a taco salad by topping lettuce with Taco Meat, drained corn, drained and rinsed black beans, cheese, black olives, and Salsa Ranch Salad dressing (page 100). Our children get Taco Meat with flour tortillas and cheese. It is healthy and economical "fast food."

Our seafood options make great meals. We toss crabmeat and shrimp into salads, pastas, or rice. For pasta dishes, we add shrimp to the sauce toward the end and save the step of cooking them separately. For an appetizer, we leave the tails on our shrimp; for entrées, we generally remove the tails before cooking. Do not overcook shrimp! Cook only until pink, or they become very tough.

to boil:

1. Into a stockpot filled halfway with water, toss 1 peeled clove garlic and 10 peppercorns.
2. Bring to a boil. Add the shrimp and cook for 2 minutes or until all the shrimp are just pink. Drain, remove the peppercorns and garlic, and serve.

to grill:

1. Soak wooden skewers in water for 20 to 30 minutes to keep them from catching fire while grilling.
2. Marinate 1 pound shrimp in a resealable storage bag for 1 to 2 hours in the refrigerator, if desired.
3. Skewer 4 to 6 shrimp (depending on size). If you haven't marinated the shrimp, baste with a little olive oil and sprinkle with grill seasoning.
4. Place shrimp skewers on a hot grill for 1 to 2 minutes. Turn to the other side for about 30 seconds. The shrimp will be done when pink.

to sauté:

1. Melt 1 to 2 tablespoons unsalted butter in a fry pan. Toss in the shrimp and cook until pink.
2. Try marinating the shrimp before cooking.

crab cakes ▬

Serves 4

Two 8-ounce packages imitation crabmeat, chopped, or two 6-ounce cans lump crabmeat, drained

⅔ cup plain bread crumbs

3 green onions, minced

3 tablespoons milk

3 tablespoons mayonnaise

½ teaspoon salt

¼ teaspoon black pepper

2 tablespoons unsalted butter

2 to 3 tablespoons flour

TARTAR SAUCE

1 cup mayonnaise

1 tablespoon sweet or dill relish

1 tablespoon dried minced onion

2 tablespoons lemon juice

1. Combine the crabmeat, bread crumbs, green onions, milk, mayonnaise, salt, and pepper in a mixing bowl. Form into small round patties with your hands, and place on a plate. Cover with plastic wrap and refrigerate for about 1 hour.

2. Heat a fry pan over medium heat and melt the butter. Pour the flour onto a plate and dip both sides of the crab cakes in the flour.

3. Place the crab cakes in the fry pan and cook until golden brown, 4 to 5 minutes on each side.

4. Mix the tartar sauce ingredients together and serve with the warm crab cakes.

crab enchiladas

Serves 4 to 6

2 cups salsa

One 8-ounce package cream
cheese, cubed

1 teaspoon dill weed

Two 8-ounce packages
imitation crabmeat,
chopped, or two
6-ounce cans lump
crabmeat, drained

8 flour tortillas (8-inch
or fajita size)

1 cup shredded Cheddar
cheese

1 cup shredded mozzarella
cheese

1 cup heavy cream

1. Preheat the oven to 350°F. Spray a 9 by 13-inch baking
   dish with nonstick spray.

2. In a saucepan over medium heat, combine the salsa,
   cream cheese, dill, and crabmeat and cook, stirring, until
   the cream cheese melts.

3. Spoon 2 to 3 tablespoons of the crab mixture down the
   center of each tortilla. Roll up the tortillas and place
   seam side down in the baking dish.

4. Sprinkle with the cheeses and drizzle the cream evenly
   over the top.

5. Bake for 30 minutes or until the cheese is completely
   melted.

heavy cream alternative

Don't have cream on hand? Mix
together ½ cup milk and ½ cup
sour cream or plain yogurt. Use
according to the recipe directions.

crab noodle casserole

Serves 4

3 cups egg noodles

½ cup mayonnaise

½ cup grated Parmesan cheese

1 tablespoon Dijon mustard

1 cup milk

½ teaspoon salt

¼ teaspoon black pepper

2 tablespoons dried minced onion

One 4-ounce can mushrooms, drained and chopped

1 cup frozen peas, thawed

One 8-ounce package imitation crabmeat, chopped, or one 6-ounce can lump crabmeat, drained

½ cup smashed butter crackers

1. Preheat the oven to 375°F. Spray an 8-inch square baking dish with nonstick spray.

2. In a saucepan, cook the noodles according to the package directions. Drain and keep warm.

3. In a mixing bowl, whisk together the mayonnaise, Parmesan, mustard, milk, salt, and pepper. Mix in the minced onion and mushrooms.

4. Add the noodles to the milk mixture. Stir in the peas and crabmeat. Pour into the baking dish. Sprinkle with the cracker crumbs.

5. Bake for 25 to 30 minutes, until golden brown and bubbling.

curry shrimp

Serves 4

2 tablespoons vegetable oil
1 medium onion, diced
1 teaspoon minced ginger
1 clove garlic, minced
½ teaspoon salt
1½ teaspoons curry
   powder
1 medium tomato, diced
¼ teaspoon red pepper
   flakes
1 pound raw shrimp,
   thawed, peeled
   completely, and deveined
¼ cup water
Cooked rice, for serving

1. In a fry pan over medium-high heat, warm the oil. Add the onion, ginger, garlic, salt, and curry powder and cook, stirring, for about 1 minute.
2. Mix in the tomato, red pepper flakes, shrimp, and water. Reduce the heat to medium and cook for about 7 minutes, until the shrimp are opaque and pink. Serve over rice.

lemon-pepper shrimp

Serves 4

1 lemon
8 tablespoons (1 stick)
   unsalted butter, melted
2 teaspoons black pepper
½ teaspoon herbes de
   Provence
½ teaspoon Tabasco or
   hot sauce
½ teaspoon salt
1 clove garlic, minced
12 ounces to 1 pound raw
   shrimp, thawed, peeled
   completely, and deveined
Cooked rice, for serving
Bread, for serving

1. Preheat the oven to 400°F.
2. Cut the lemon in half. Slice one half and set aside. Squeeze the juice from the other half into a mixing bowl. Stir in the butter, pepper, herbes de Provence, Tabasco, salt, and garlic.
3. Pour ¼ cup of the sauce into the bottom of an 8-inch square baking dish. Arrange the shrimp over the top of the sauce and top the shrimp with the lemon slices. Pour the remaining sauce over the top.
4. Bake for about 20 minutes or until all the shrimp have turned pink.
5. Great served over rice and with fresh, warm bread.

mock shrimp ceviche ▬

Serves 4

12 ounces to 1 pound raw shrimp, thawed, peeled completely, and deveined

½ cup salsa

1½ teaspoons chili powder

½ teaspoon salt

½ cup lime juice

1 clove garlic, minced

1 green onion, chopped

One 15-ounce can black beans, drained and rinsed

½ English cucumber, diced

1. Bring a stockpot filled halfway with water to a boil. Cook the shrimp for 2 minutes or until pink. Remove from the heat, drain, and set aside.

2. Whisk together the salsa, chili powder, salt, and lime juice. Stir in the shrimp and the remaining ingredients. Chill for about 1 hour. Serve in individual glasses or bowls.

---

mock shrimp martini

Wow your guests by serving this wonderful ceviche (se-vē-chā) in martini glasses, garnished with tortilla chips or cucumber slices. It is a refreshing salad course or appetizer. Although ceviches are technically seafood "cooked" in the acid of lemon or lime juice, this stocked version provides all the flavor with fully cooked shrimp.

moo shoo shrimp stir-fry

Serves 4

¼ cup soy sauce

1 tablespoon peanut
butter

1 tablespoon honey

2 teaspoons white wine
vinegar

⅛ teaspoon garlic powder

10 drops Tabasco or hot
sauce

Black pepper

2 tablespoons pureed
ginger

3 eggs

Salt

2 tablespoons vegetable
oil

12 ounces to 1 pound raw
shrimp, thawed, peeled
completely, and deveined

1 clove garlic, minced

One 4-ounce can
mushrooms, drained
and chopped

3 cups cabbage and carrot
mix

3 green onions, thinly
sliced on an angle

Cooked rice or flour
tortillas, for serving

1. Mix together the soy sauce, peanut butter, honey, vinegar, garlic powder, Tabasco, ⅛ teaspoon pepper, and the ginger and set aside.

2. Beat the eggs with salt and pepper and set aside.

3. Heat a fry pan over high heat. Add the oil and heat until very hot. Add the shrimp and cook until pink.

4. Add the egg mixture and scramble for about 2 minutes.

5. Add the garlic, mushrooms, cabbage mix, and green onions and cook until the green onions are tender.

6. Toss with the soy sauce mixture to coat. Serve with cooked rice or flour tortillas.

pancake-batter fried shrimp ▬

Serves 4

1½ cups pancake mix
1 egg yolk
½ cup milk
1 teaspoon chili powder
½ teaspoon pumpkin pie spice
12 ounces to 1 pound raw shrimp, thawed, peeled completely, and deveined
Vegetable oil, for frying

TARTAR SAUCE
1 cup mayonnaise
1 tablespoon sweet or dill relish
1 tablespoon dried minced onion
2 tablespoons lemon juice

1. Combine 1 cup of the pancake mix with the egg yolk and milk. Add the chili powder and pumpkin pie spice and set aside.

2. Place the remaining ½ cup pancake mix in a mixing bowl and toss the shrimp around in it until coated.

3. Heat ½ inch of oil in a fry pan over high heat until very hot. Dip the shrimp in the batter and transfer them to the hot oil. Cook for 1 to 2 minutes on each side, until golden. (The tails will turn pink.)

4. Drain the shrimp on paper towels.

5. Mix the tartar sauce ingredients together and serve with the warm or room-temperature shrimp.

seafood nachos

Serves 4

One 8-ounce package
  imitation crabmeat,
  chopped, or one
  6-ounce can lump
  crabmeat, drained
¼ cup sour cream or
  plain yogurt, plus
  more for serving
  (optional)
¼ cup mayonnaise
2 tablespoons dried
  minced onion
¼ teaspoon dill weed
30 to 35 tortilla chips
2 cups shredded Cheddar
  cheese
1 medium tomato, diced
Salsa, for serving (optional)

1. Preheat the oven to 350°F. Cover a jelly roll pan with aluminum foil.
2. In a mixing bowl, combine the crab, sour cream, mayonnaise, minced onion, and dill weed.
3. Arrange the tortilla chips on the jelly roll pan. Top with the crab mixture, Cheddar, and tomato.
4. Bake for 15 to 20 minutes, until the cheese is melted and beginning to brown.
5. Serve with salsa and more sour cream, if desired.

shrimp cocktail

Serves 4

3 cloves garlic, peeled
10 peppercorns
12 ounces to 1 pound
  raw shrimp, thawed,
  peeled completely, and
  deveined

COCKTAIL SAUCE
½ cup ketchup
2 tablespoons prepared
  horseradish
1 tablespoon lemon juice

1. In a stockpot filled halfway with water, add the garlic and peppercorns. Bring to a boil.
2. Add the shrimp and cook for 2 minutes or until all the shrimp are just pink. Drain and chill the shrimp.
3. Mix together the cocktail sauce ingredients and chill.
4. Serve the shrimp over ice with the cocktail sauce.

shrimp fajitas

Serves 4

2 tablespoons vegetable oil

2 shallots or ½ onion, thinly sliced

3 cloves garlic, minced

1 bell pepper, thinly sliced

12 ounces to 1 pound raw shrimp, thawed, peeled completely, and deveined

2 teaspoons cumin

2 tablespoons chili powder

3 tablespoons lime juice

Tabasco or hot sauce

6 to 8 flour tortillas (8-inch or fajita size)

1 cup shredded Cheddar cheese

Sour cream and salsa, for serving (optional)

1. Heat the oil in a fry pan. Once very hot, add the shallots, garlic, and bell pepper. Stir occasionally until the vegetables begin to get tender, approximately 5 minutes.

2. Stir in the shrimp, cumin, and chili powder. Add the lime juice and Tabasco to taste and stir occasionally until the shrimp are cooked thoroughly and pink.

3. Serve on flour tortillas with the cheese. Garnish with sour cream and salsa, if desired.

shrimp-pineapple shish kebab

Serves 4

HONEY-LIME MARINADE
¼ cup honey
2 tablespoons vegetable oil
¼ cup lime juice
¼ teaspoon salt
¼ teaspoon Tabasco or
  hot sauce, or to taste

12 ounces to 1 pound raw
  shrimp, thawed, peeled
  completely, and deveined
One 15-ounce can
  pineapple chunks,
  drained
1 bell pepper, cut into
  1-inch pieces
11-inch wooden skewers

1. Whisk together the marinade ingredients. Pour the marinade into two resealable storage bags. Add the shrimp to one bag and the pineapple and bell pepper to the other. Refrigerate. Allow to marinate for 1 to 4 hours.
2. In the meantime, soak the skewers in water for 20 to 30 minutes to keep them from catching fire while grilling. Preheat a grill to medium-high.
3. Skewer pieces of shrimp, pineapple, and bell pepper on the skewers. Grill the skewers, flipping once, until the shrimp are cooked through and pink.

shrimp scampi

Serves 4

4 tablespoons (½ stick)
  unsalted butter
2 cloves garlic, minced
12 ounces to 1 pound raw
  shrimp, thawed, peeled
  completely, and deveined
½ teaspoon salt
¼ teaspoon black pepper
1 tablespoon lemon juice
Bread or rice, for serving

1. Melt the butter over medium heat in a fry pan. Add the garlic and cook until slightly softened but not brown.
2. Add the shrimp. Cook until pink. Sprinkle with the salt and pepper.
3. Remove from the heat and toss with the lemon juice. Serve immediately with freshly baked bread or rice.

beans, potatoes, rice, and veggies

We love beans because they are inexpensive, easy to use, and very nutritious.

black bean burger ▬

Serves 4

One 15-ounce can black beans, drained and rinsed

¼ cup diced shallot or onion

¼ cup plain bread crumbs

2 tablespoons salsa

¼ cup drained corn kernels

½ cup grated Cheddar cheese

1 teaspoon cumin

8 drops Tabasco or hot sauce

1 teaspoon salt

¼ teaspoon black pepper, or to taste

1 tablespoon olive oil

Cooked rice or Hamburger Buns (page 136), for serving

1. Using a potato masher, mash the beans in a mixing bowl. Mix in the shallot, bread crumbs, salsa, corn, cheese, cumin, Tabasco, salt, and pepper. Using moistened hands, shape the bean mixture into 3-inch patties. Refrigerate for 15 minutes to set.

2. In a fry pan, heat the olive oil over medium heat. Fry the patties until golden brown, approximately 3 minutes on each side.

3. Serve with rice or on Hamburger Buns.

kidney bean–tortilla lasagna ▬

Serves 8

Two 15-ounce cans tomato sauce

2 tablespoons chili powder

1 teaspoon salt

2 tablespoons dried minced onion

1 teaspoon garlic powder

1 teaspoon cumin

Two 15-ounce cans kidney beans, drained and rinsed

One 4-ounce can chopped black olives, drained

One 4-ounce can mushrooms, drained and sliced or chopped

One 15-ounce can corn, drained

6 flour tortillas (8-inch or fajita size)

2 cups grated Cheddar cheese

1. Preheat the oven to 350°F. Spray a 9 by 13-inch baking dish with nonstick spray.

2. In a mixing bowl, stir together the tomato sauce, chili powder, salt, minced onion, garlic powder, and cumin. Add the beans, olives, mushrooms, and corn. Spread 1 cup of the mixture on the bottom of the baking dish.

3. Lay two tortillas over the mixture. Spread one-third of the remaining bean mixture over the tortillas and sprinkle with one-third of the cheese. Repeat this step twice.

4. Cover with aluminum foil and bake for 25 minutes.

5. Remove the foil and bake for 15 more minutes or until the cheese becomes golden brown.

maple-ginger baked beans ▬

Serves 8

½ cup diced shallot, or
   1 cup diced onion
1 tablespoon olive oil
2 tablespoons Dijon
   mustard
¼ cup maple syrup
¼ cup ketchup
¼ cup brown sugar
1 tablespoon pureed
   ginger
Three 15-ounce cans
   kidney beans, 1 can
   drained and 2 cans
   undrained
½ teaspoon Tabasco or
   hot sauce
½ teaspoon salt
¼ teaspoon black pepper

1. Preheat the oven to 350°F.
2. In a large saucepan over medium heat, cook the shallot in the oil until softened.
3. Add the mustard, maple syrup, ketchup, brown sugar, and ginger and bring to a boil. Reduce the heat and simmer for 10 minutes to blend the flavors.
4. Stir in the beans with their liquid, the Tabasco, salt, and pepper. Pour into a 9 by 13-inch baking dish. Bake, uncovered, for 1 hour, until bubbly and beginning to brown on top.
5. Let sit for 5 to 10 minutes before serving.

teriyaki pork and beans

Serves 8

½ cup diced shallot, or
    1 cup diced onion
1 tablespoon olive oil
2 tablespoons yellow
    mustard
One 15-ounce can
    pineapple, drained
    and chopped
1 cup brown sugar
¼ cup soy sauce
1 tablespoon white wine
    vinegar
Three 15-ounce cans Great
    Northern or cannellini
    beans, 1 can drained
    and 2 cans undrained
1 cup diced ham or cooked
    crumbled bacon

1. Preheat the oven to 350°F.
2. In a large saucepan over medium heat, cook the shallot in the oil until softened.
3. Add the mustard, pineapple, brown sugar, soy sauce, and vinegar and bring to a boil. Reduce the heat and simmer for 5 to 10 minutes, to blend the flavors.
4. Stir in the beans with their liquid and the meat. Pour into a 9 by 13-inch baking dish. Bake, uncovered, for 1 hour.
5. Let sit for 5 to 10 minutes before serving.

tuscan baked cannellini beans

Serves 8

½ cup diced shallot, or
    1 cup diced onion

1 tablespoon olive oil

One 12-ounce jar marinated
    artichoke hearts,
    undrained

2 cloves garlic, minced

One 15-ounce can diced
    tomatoes, undrained

2 tablespoons sugar

¼ cup chopped fresh basil
    leaves

1 tablespoon Dijon
    mustard

Three 15-ounce cans Great
    Northern or cannellini
    beans, 1 can drained
    and 2 cans undrained

½ cup grated Parmesan
    cheese

1. Preheat the oven to 350°F.

2. In a large saucepan over medium heat, cook the shallot in the oil until softened.

3. Add the artichokes and their marinade, the garlic, tomatoes with their juice, the sugar, and basil and bring to a boil. Reduce the heat and simmer for 5 to 10 minutes to blend the flavors.

4. Stir in the mustard, the beans with their liquid, and the cheese. Pour into a 9 by 13-inch baking dish. Bake, uncovered, for 1 hour.

5. Let sit for 5 to 10 minutes before serving.

Potatoes are versatile and delicious. They also stay fresh in your pantry for a long time. Choose from russet, sweet, or Yukon Gold for most recipes.

baked potatoes

Serves 6

6 to 8 potatoes

1. Preheat the oven to 400°F. Scrub the potatoes under cold running water. Prick the potatoes with a fork many times to prevent them from bursting and to shorten the baking time.
2. Place directly on the oven rack. Bake for 30 minutes.
3. Flip the potatoes and continue to bake for 30 more minutes or until soft when squeezed.
4. When the potatoes are done, cut a cross in the top of each potato and squeeze gently to open up.
5. If desired, fill with your favorite toppings, such as butter, sour cream or plain yogurt, Cheddar cheese, broccoli, or cooked bacon.

to wrap or not to wrap?

By baking potatoes without wrapping them in aluminum foil, you produce a delicious, crisp-skinned potato. The skin of an aluminum foil–wrapped potato is much softer because you are actually steaming it. We love the crispy skin, but it is necessary to pierce the potatoes deeply with a fork quite a few times—otherwise, CABOOM! Big mess in your oven. But if you would prefer, wrap them up and bake according to the directions above.

baked-twice potatoes ▬

Serves 6

6 to 8 potatoes

4 tablespoons (½ stick)
   unsalted butter,
   melted

½ cup sour cream or
   plain yogurt

2 tablespoons cream
   cheese, softened

1 teaspoon salt

½ teaspoon black pepper

½ cup shredded Cheddar
   cheese

1. Preheat the oven to 400°F. Scrub the potatoes under cold running water. Prick the potatoes with a fork many times to prevent them from bursting and to shorten the baking time.

2. Place directly on the oven rack. Bake for 30 minutes.

3. Flip the potatoes and continue to bake for 30 more minutes or until soft when squeezed.

4. When the potatoes are done, cut in half lengthwise with a sharp knife. Spoon out the soft potato, leaving a thin layer of potato against the skin to create a sturdier shell. Place the potato skins on a parchment paper–covered jelly roll pan, open side up.

5. Place the scooped-out potato in a mixing bowl and, using an electric hand mixer, beat in the remaining ingredients. Fill each skin with the potato mixture.

6. Bake at 400°F for 15 to 20 minutes, until heated through.

---

make-ahead holiday meal

We like to prepare as much as possible ahead of time when serving a large holiday meal. These Baked-Twice Potatoes are perfect for that. After filling the shells with the potato mixture, freeze them. When you are ready to serve, bake the frozen potatoes at 350°F for 45 minutes or until heated through. If you choose to refrigerate, bake according to the directions above.

cheddar mashed potatoes

Serves 4 to 6

2 pounds potatoes
(4 to 6 russet, 6 to 8
Yukon Gold)

2 teaspoons salt, or to
taste

2 tablespoons unsalted
butter, softened

½ cup milk, plus more
if needed

¼ teaspoon black pepper

1 cup grated Cheddar
cheese

1. Peel the potatoes and cut into 2-inch chunks. Place in a stockpot. Add cold water to cover and add ½ teaspoon salt.
2. Bring to a boil, reduce the heat to a simmer, cover, and cook for 15 to 20 minutes, until fork-tender.
3. Drain the potatoes and return to the pot.
4. Mash the potatoes with a potato masher. Mix in the remaining 1½ teaspoons salt and all the other ingredients. (Mix in more milk, little by little, until the desired consistency is reached.)

garlic mashed potatoes

Serves 4 to 6

2 pounds potatoes
(4 to 6 russet, 6 to 8
Yukon Gold)

2 teaspoons salt, or to
taste

Half of an 8-ounce package
cream cheese, cubed

⅔ cup milk, plus more if
needed

1 clove garlic, minced

Black pepper

1. Peel the potatoes and cut into 2-inch chunks. Place in a stockpot. Add cold water to cover and add ½ teaspoon salt.
2. Bring to a boil, reduce the heat to a simmer, cover, and cook for 15 to 20 minutes, until fork-tender.
3. Drain the potatoes and return to the pot.
4. Mash the potatoes with a potato masher. Mix in the remaining 1½ teaspoons salt, the cream cheese, milk, garlic, and pepper to taste. (Mix in more milk, little by little, until the desired consistency is reached.)

mashed sweet potatoes

Serves 4 to 6

2 pounds sweet potatoes
    (2 or 3 large)
½ teaspoon salt
2 tablespoons unsalted
    butter, softened
½ teaspoon pumpkin pie
    spice
2 tablespoons brown sugar
½ cup milk, plus more if
    needed

1. Peel the potatoes and cut into 2-inch chunks. Place in a stockpot. Add cold water to cover and add the salt.
2. Bring to a boil, reduce the heat to a simmer, cover, and cook for 15 to 20 minutes, until fork-tender.
3. Drain the potatoes and return to the pot.
4. Mash the potatoes with a potato masher. Mix in the remaining ingredients. (Mix in more milk, little by little, until the desired consistency is reached.)

oven chips

Serves 4

2 pounds potatoes
    (4 to 6 russet, 6 to 8
    Yukon Gold, 2 or 3
    sweet potatoes), peeled
    or unpeeled
1 tablespoon olive oil
2 tablespoons grill
    seasoning

1. Preheat the oven to 425°F. Cover a jelly roll pan with aluminum foil.
2. Slice the potatoes into ⅛-inch chips. Place in a stockpot and add cold water to cover. Bring to a boil and parboil for approximately 3 minutes or until just fork-tender.
3. Drain the potatoes thoroughly and return to the pot.
4. Toss with the oil. Lay in a single layer on the jelly roll pan. Sprinkle with the grill seasoning.
5. Bake for 15 minutes, then broil for 5 minutes or until crispy.

the stocked kitchen

oven fries

Serves 4

2 pounds potatoes
(4 to 6 russet, 6 to 8
Yukon Gold, 2 or 3
sweet potatoes), peeled
or unpeeled
1 tablespoon olive oil
2 tablespoons grill
seasoning

1. Preheat the oven to 425°F. Cover a jelly roll pan with aluminum foil.
2. Slice the potatoes in half lengthwise and then slice each half into four lengthwise slices. Place in a stockpot and add cold water to cover. Bring to a boil and parboil for approximately 3 minutes or until just fork-tender.
3. Drain the potatoes thoroughly and return to the pot.
4. Toss with the oil. Lay in a single layer on the jelly roll pan. Sprinkle with the grill seasoning.
5. Bake for 15 minutes, then broil for 5 minutes or until crispy.

parboiling potatoes

Parboiling is a technique in which the ingredient is partially cooked, and cooking is finished at a later time. Parboiling potatoes helps to cook the potato fully without scorching the outside.

potatoes au gratin

Serves 4

4 cups peeled and thinly sliced russet or Yukon Gold potatoes

1 cup milk

½ cup sour cream or plain yogurt

½ teaspoon garlic powder

2 tablespoons chopped fresh basil

¼ teaspoon salt

⅛ teaspoon black pepper

6 drops Tabasco or hot sauce

1 cup shredded mozzarella cheese

1 cup diced ham (optional)

⅓ cup grated Parmesan cheese

1. Preheat the oven to 375°F. Spray an 8-inch square baking dish with nonstick spray.

2. Place the potatoes in a stockpot and add cold water to cover. Bring to a boil and parboil for 3 minutes, or just until the potatoes start to become tender.

3. Drain the potatoes and return to the pot.

4. In a mixing bowl, whisk together the milk, sour cream, garlic powder, basil, salt, pepper, and Tabasco. Pour over the potatoes and gently toss.

5. Spoon half of the potato mixture into the baking dish. Top with half of the mozzarella and ham, if using. Repeat with the remaining potatoes, cheese, and ham. Sprinkle the top with the Parmesan.

6. Cover and bake for 30 minutes.

7. Uncover and bake for 15 additional minutes. Let sit for 10 minutes before serving.

meat and potatoes at its best!

Serve this as a delicious side dish, or add the ham for a complete family-friendly meal. Also, try substituting ½ cup Cheddar cheese for mozzarella to give the dish added zip.

sour cream and onion mashed potatoes

Serves 4 to 6

2 pounds potatoes (4 to 6 russet, 6 to 8 Yukon Gold)

2 teaspoons salt, or to taste

⅓ cup milk, plus more if needed

¼ cup sour cream or plain yogurt

2 tablespoons thinly sliced green onions

1. Peel the potatoes and cut into 2-inch chunks. Place in a stockpot. Add cold water to cover and add ½ teaspoon salt.

2. Bring to a boil, reduce the heat to a simmer, cover, and cook for 15 to 20 minutes, until fork-tender.

3. Drain the potatoes and return to the pot.

4. Mash the potatoes with a potato masher. Mix in the remaining 1½ teaspoons salt and all the other ingredients. (Mix in more milk, little by little, until the desired consistency is reached.)

We love these rice recipes, not only because they are delicious, but because they are just about as easy as the packets we used to buy. We now cook healthier meals without sacrificing convenience.

black beans and rice

Serves 4 to 6

1 tablespoon vegetable oil

1 shallot or ½ onion, finely diced

1 clove garlic, minced

½ bell pepper, finely diced

1 cup rice

One 15-ounce can or 2 cups chicken broth

One 20-ounce can pineapple chunks, chopped, with juice

One 15-ounce can black beans, drained and rinsed

½ teaspoon salt

¼ teaspoon red pepper flakes, or to taste

1. In a fry pan over medium heat, heat the oil. Cook the shallot, garlic, and bell pepper until tender. (Do not burn the garlic!)

2. Add the rice, chicken broth, juice from the pineapple, the beans, salt, and red pepper flakes. Bring to a boil. Reduce the heat to a simmer, cover, and cook for 30 minutes or until the liquid is absorbed.

3. Add the pineapple and heat thoroughly.

curry rice

Serves 4 to 6

1 tablespoon unsalted
  butter
1 tablespoon curry powder
1 cup rice
1 cup peas (frozen are fine)
1 cup diced carrot
1 teaspoon salt
One 15-ounce can or
  2 cups chicken broth

1. Melt the butter in a saucepan over medium heat. Add the curry powder and rice, and cook for a couple of minutes, stirring occasionally, until the rice toasts slightly.
2. Stir in the remaining ingredients and bring to a boil. Cover and reduce the heat. Simmer for 30 minutes or until the liquid is absorbed.

ginger rice ▬

Serves 4

1 tablespoon pureed ginger
1 cup rice
One 15-ounce can or
  2 cups chicken broth
1 teaspoon salt
¼ cup thinly sliced green
  onion
¼ cup chopped almonds

1. In a saucepan over medium heat, stir together the ginger, rice, chicken broth, and salt. Bring to a boil. Reduce the heat, cover, and simmer for 30 minutes.
2. When the rice is tender and all the liquid is absorbed, fluff with a fork. Fold in the green onion and almonds.

lemon-dill rice

Serves 4

1 cup rice
1 teaspoon dill weed
2 tablespoons lemon juice
1 teaspoon grated lemon
  zest
One 15-ounce can or
  2 cups chicken broth
1 teaspoon salt

In a saucepan, stir together all the ingredients. Bring to a boil. Cover, reduce the heat, and simmer for 30 minutes or until the liquid is absorbed.

moroccan rice ▬

Serves 4

1 tablespoon unsalted
    butter
1 shallot or ½ onion, diced
1 cup rice
¼ cup pine nuts
One 15-ounce can or 2 cups
    chicken broth
½ cup water
1 teaspoon pumpkin pie
    spice
½ teaspoon salt
⅛ teaspoon black pepper
½ cup bacon, cooked and
    chopped
¼ cup raisins

1. In a fry pan over medium heat, melt the butter. Cook the shallot, rice, and pine nuts until the shallot softens.
2. Add the broth, water, pumpkin pie spice, salt, and pepper and bring to a boil. Reduce the heat, cover, and simmer for 30 minutes.
3. When the rice is tender and all the liquid is absorbed, fluff with a fork, fold in the bacon and raisins, and serve.

spanish rice ▬

Serves 4

1 tablespoon olive oil
1 shallot or ½ onion,
    finely diced
½ bell pepper, diced
1 cup rice
1 cup water
One 15-ounce can diced
    tomatoes, undrained
1 teaspoon salt
1 tablespoon chili powder
½ teaspoon garlic powder

1. In a fry pan over medium heat, heat the olive oil. Cook the shallot and bell pepper until tender.
2. Add the remaining ingredients and bring to a boil. Reduce the heat, cover, and simmer for 30 minutes or until the liquid is absorbed.

stocked paella ▬

Serves 6 to 8

½ pound bulk breakfast sausage

2 tablespoons white wine vinegar

6 drops Tabasco or hot sauce

½ pound boneless, skinless chicken, cubed

½ bell pepper, chopped

2 shallots or 1 onion, chopped

1 clove garlic, minced

One 15-ounce can diced tomatoes, undrained

One 10-ounce can mandarin orange segments, undrained

2 tablespoons chili powder

1 teaspoon poultry seasoning

½ teaspoon pumpkin pie spice

½ teaspoon cumin

1 teaspoon salt

1 cup rice

One 15-ounce can or 2 cups chicken broth

½ cup frozen peas, thawed

6 ounces shrimp, thawed, peeled but tails left on, and deveined

1. Preheat the oven to 400°F. Spray a deep-dish pizza pan or 9 by 13-inch baking dish with nonstick spray.

2. Heat a fry pan over medium heat. Brown the sausage, breaking up clumps. Stir in the vinegar and Tabasco. Add the chicken and cook thoroughly. Add the bell pepper, shallots, and garlic and cook until the vegetables soften.

3. In a large mixing bowl, combine the diced tomatoes and mandarin oranges and their juices. Stir in the chili powder, poultry seasoning, pumpkin pie spice, cumin, salt, rice, and broth. Add the sausage and chicken mixture and mix well.

4. Pour into the pizza pan. Bake, uncovered, for 30 minutes.

5. Remove from the oven, stir in the peas, and tuck the shrimp throughout the dish. Place the pan back in the oven and bake for 10 to 15 minutes more, until the rice is tender and the shrimp are pink.

Most of these recipes are made from frozen vegetables, so they are quick and easy.

almond green beans

Serves 4

3 cups frozen cut green beans

1 tablespoon unsalted butter

1 tablespoon olive oil

1 tablespoon lemon juice

1 tablespoon dried minced onion

½ cup sliced or chopped almonds

¼ teaspoon salt

Black pepper

1. Cook the green beans in a saucepan according to the package directions.
2. Drain the beans. Add the remaining ingredients and stir over low heat until combined and warmed through.

cheesy broccoli

Serves 4

2 tablespoons unsalted butter

2 tablespoons flour

½ cup milk

½ teaspoon salt

¼ teaspoon black pepper

3 cups frozen chopped broccoli

½ cup grated Cheddar cheese

1. In a saucepan over medium heat, melt the butter. Whisk in the flour and cook for 1 to 2 minutes, until it bubbles and becomes smooth. Whisk in the milk, salt, and pepper, and cook until thickened.
2. Add the broccoli and cook through.
3. Once cooked, stir in the cheese until melted.

corn casserole

Serves 8

Four 15-ounce cans corn
2 teaspoons sugar
2 teaspoons salt
2 tablespoons unsalted
  butter, melted
3 eggs, beaten
3 green onions, thinly
  sliced
3 cups milk
12 butter crackers, crushed
1 tablespoon herbes de
  Provence

1. Preheat the oven to 350°F. Spray a 9 by 13-inch baking dish with nonstick spray.
2. In a blender, blend 2 cans of the corn with their liquid, the sugar, salt, and butter until smooth. Pour the puree into a mixing bowl.
3. Drain the remaining 2 cans corn. Mix the corn, eggs, green onions, milk, cracker crumbs, and herbes de Provence into the puree. Pour into the baking dish.
4. Bake, uncovered, for 1 hour or until the center sets.

creamy spinach

Serves 4

3 cups frozen spinach
1 tablespoon dried minced
  onion
½ teaspoon garlic powder
Half of an 8-ounce package
  cream cheese, cubed
¼ cup grated Parmesan
  cheese
¼ teaspoon salt
⅛ teaspoon nutmeg

1. Cook the spinach in a saucepan according to the package directions. Drain and squeeze out the excess water. Return to the pot.
2. Stir in the remaining ingredients over low heat until combined and warmed through.

easy asian broccoli

Serves 4

3 cups frozen chopped broccoli
2 tablespoons Dijon mustard
2 tablespoons soy sauce
¼ cup sliced or chopped almonds, toasted

1. Cook the broccoli in a saucepan according to the package directions. Drain off the excess water.
2. Mix together the mustard and soy sauce. Add to the broccoli and toss to coat. Sprinkle with the almonds and serve.

feta peas ▬

Serves 4

2 cups frozen peas
¼ cup crumbled feta cheese
1 tablespoon chopped fresh basil
¼ teaspoon salt
⅛ teaspoon black pepper

1. Cook the peas in a saucepan according to the package directions. Drain off the excess water.
2. Stir in the remaining ingredients over low heat until combined and warmed through.

glazed carrots

Serves 4

1 tablespoon unsalted
    butter
4 cups carrots, cut into
    1-inch chunks, or
    1 pound baby carrots
1 cup beef broth
¼ cup maple syrup
¼ teaspoon salt
⅛ teaspoon black pepper
½ cup chopped toasted
    pecans

1. In a fry pan over medium heat, melt the butter. Add the carrots and stir to coat. Add the beef broth, maple syrup, salt, and pepper. Increase the heat to high and bring to a boil. Cover and cook for 8 to 10 minutes.
2. Uncover and cook until the liquid reduces to a glaze over the carrots, 15 to 20 minutes. Stir in the pecans and serve immediately.

horseradish peas

Serves 4

2 cups frozen peas
¼ teaspoon salt
1 tablespoon unsalted
    butter
1 teaspoon prepared
    horseradish
½ teaspoon Dijon mustard

1. Cook the peas in a saucepan according to the package directions. Drain off the excess water.
2. Stir in the remaining ingredients over low heat until combined and warmed through.

lemon-butter broccoli

Serves 4

2 tablespoons unsalted butter
¼ cup lemon juice
1 teaspoon grated lemon zest
⅛ teaspoon Tabasco or hot sauce
½ teaspoon salt
3 cups frozen chopped broccoli, thawed

1. In a saucepan over medium heat, melt the butter. Stir in the lemon juice and zest, Tabasco, and salt.
2. Add the broccoli and cook until heated through.

olive green beans

Serves 4

3 cups frozen cut green beans
1 tablespoon olive oil
10 green or Kalamata olives, chopped
1 medium tomato, diced
¼ teaspoon garlic powder
¼ cup pine nuts, toasted

1. Cook the green beans in a saucepan according to the package directions. Drain off the excess water.
2. Stir in the remaining ingredients over low heat until combined and warmed through.

stuffed spicy bell pepper boats

Serves 4 to 8

½ pound bulk breakfast sausage

1½ cups cooked rice

½ cup grated Parmesan cheese

¼ teaspoon Tabasco or hot sauce

½ cup ranch dressing

½ cup chopped black olives

One 15-ounce can corn, drained

4 bell peppers, cut in half lengthwise and seeded

1. Preheat the oven to 375°F.
2. Brown the sausage in a fry pan and drain off the excess grease.
3. In a mixing bowl, mix together the sausage, rice, Parmesan, Tabasco, ranch dressing, olives, and corn. Fill a pepper half with one-eighth of the mixture. Repeat with the remaining peppers and filling. Place in a 9 by 13-inch baking dish.
4. Bake for 30 to 45 minutes, until the peppers begin to brown and pucker.

---

main dish or side?

Although we say that this dish serves four, that is as an entrée. If using these as a side dish, make with or without the sausage and serve up to eight.

sweet carrot bake

Serves 4

4 cups peeled and chopped carrot

½ cup granulated sugar

2 eggs, beaten

½ teaspoon salt

4 tablespoons (½ stick) unsalted butter, melted

½ cup milk

½ teaspoon vanilla extract

½ cup brown sugar

⅓ cup flour

3 tablespoons unsalted butter, softened

½ cup chopped pecans

1. Preheat the oven to 325°F. Spray an 8-inch square baking dish with nonstick spray.

2. Place the carrots in a large saucepan and cover with cold water. Bring to a boil, reduce the heat, and simmer for 20 minutes. Drain the carrots and put in the baking dish.

3. In a mixing bowl, beat together the granulated sugar, eggs, salt, melted butter, milk, and vanilla extract until smooth. Pour over the carrots.

4. Mix together the brown sugar and flour. Cut in the softened butter with a fork or pastry cutter until the mixture is coarse. Stir in the pecans and sprinkle on top.

5. Bake for 30 minutes or until the topping is lightly brown.

sweet carrots

I love carrots! To make this recipe for eight, I double it and bake it in a 9 by 13-inch baking dish for 45 minutes or until the topping is lightly brown.
This dish is so sweet and yummy, it is almost a dessert, but the carrots make it a healthy option. (This is also delicious made with sweet potatoes instead of carrots.)

tomatoes provençal

Serves 4

4 medium tomatoes
¾ cup plain bread crumbs
2 green onions, minced
¼ cup minced fresh basil
2 teaspoons herbes de
    Provence
2 cloves garlic, minced
1 teaspoon salt
¼ teaspoon black pepper
½ cup grated Parmesan
    cheese
2 tablespoons olive oil

1. Preheat the oven to 400°F. Spray a 9 by 13-inch baking dish with nonstick spray.

2. Remove the stem ends from the tomatoes. Cut the tomatoes in half crosswise. Gently remove the interior with a spoon. Place the tomatoes in the baking dish.

3. Mix together the bread crumbs, green onions, basil, herbes de Provence, garlic, salt, pepper, and Parmesan. Sprinkle the mixture over the top of each tomato half. Drizzle the olive oil over the top of the tomatoes.

4. Bake for 20 minutes or until lightly browned on top.

desserts

These bar cookies are a great alternative to your standard cookies and so decadent you can eat them with a fork.

chocolate chip–almond bars

Makes 24

4 eggs
2 cups sugar
⅛ teaspoon salt
2 cups flour
8 ounces (2 sticks) unsalted butter, melted
2 teaspoons almond extract
½ cup sliced or chopped almonds
One 12-ounce bag chocolate chips (2 cups)

1. Preheat the oven to 325°F. Spray a 9 by 13-inch baking dish with nonstick spray.
2. In a mixing bowl, beat together the eggs, sugar, and salt with an electric hand mixer until the eggs turn much lighter yellow, about 2 minutes.
3. Alternate adding the flour and butter to the egg mixture and mix until combined. Add the almond extract and beat until smooth. Fold in the almonds and chocolate chips.
4. Pour into the baking dish. Bake for 35 to 40 minutes, until very light golden.
5. Cool completely in the pan before cutting into squares.

applesauce

To cut down on the fat and calories in these bar cookies, try substituting ½ cup applesauce for one of the sticks of butter. You can generally use applesauce as a substitute for half of the oil or butter in baked dessert recipes to cut fat and calories without sacrificing a moist and delicious result.

chocolate peppermint bars

Makes 24

4 eggs

2 cups sugar

⅛ teaspoon salt

2 cups flour

⅔ cup cocoa powder

8 ounces (2 sticks) unsalted butter, melted

2 teaspoons peppermint extract

One 12-ounce package white chocolate chips (2 cups)

1. Preheat the oven to 325°F. Spray a 9 by 13-inch baking dish with nonstick spray.

2. In a mixing bowl, beat together the eggs, sugar, and salt with an electric hand mixer until the eggs turn much lighter yellow, about 2 minutes.

3. In a separate bowl, mix together the flour and cocoa powder. Alternate adding the flour-cocoa mixture and butter to the egg mixture and mix until combined. Add the peppermint extract and beat until smooth. Fold in the chocolate chips.

4. Pour into the baking dish. Bake for 35 to 40 minutes, until the center is set when tapped.

5. Cool completely in the pan before cutting into squares.

white chocolate–pecan bars

Makes 24

4 eggs

2 cups sugar

⅛ teaspoon salt

2 cups flour

8 ounces (2 sticks) unsalted butter, melted

2 teaspoons vanilla extract

1 cup white chocolate chips

½ cup dried cranberries, chopped

½ cup chopped pecans

1. Preheat the oven to 325°F. Spray a 9 by 13-inch baking dish with nonstick spray.

2. In a mixing bowl, beat together the eggs, sugar, and salt with an electric hand mixer until the eggs turn much lighter yellow, about 2 minutes.

3. Alternate adding the flour and butter to the egg mixture and mix until combined. Add the vanilla extract and beat until smooth. Fold in the chocolate chips, cranberries, and pecans.

4. Pour into the baking dish. Bake for 35 to 40 minutes, until very light golden.

5. Cool completely in the pan before cutting into squares.

Your guests will be shocked that these cakes aren't made from scratch. Because they all start with a yellow cake mix, it limits the potential for mistakes, and you always end up with a moist and delicious dessert.

carrot cake

Serves 8

CAKE

1 box yellow cake mix

3 cups grated carrot

1 cup sour cream or plain yogurt

⅓ cup vegetable oil

3 eggs

1 tablespoon pumpkin pie spice

½ cup pineapple chunks, undrained

⅓ cup raisins

⅓ cup finely chopped pecans

CREAM CHEESE FROSTING

One 8-ounce package cream cheese, softened

2 teaspoons vanilla extract

2 cups confectioners' sugar, sifted through a strainer

2 tablespoons milk, plus more if needed

1. Preheat the oven to 350°F. Spray two 9-inch round cake pans with nonstick spray and cut parchment paper into circles to fit into the bottoms.

2. Combine all the cake ingredients in a large mixing bowl and mix on low speed with an electric hand mixer until just moistened. Pour evenly into the prepared pans.

3. Bake for 30 to 35 minutes, until the cake pulls away from the sides of the pan and is set in the middle. Let the cakes cool for 5 to 10 minutes, then remove from the pans and allow to cool completely on a cooling rack.

4. Blend all the frosting ingredients together with an electric hand mixer. (Add a little more milk if needed to get a spreadable consistency.) Frost the top of one layer and then stack the other layer on top. Frost the sides and top with the remaining frosting.

lemon layer cake

Serves 8

1 box yellow cake mix

1 cup sour cream or plain yogurt

⅓ cup vegetable oil

¼ cup water

¼ cup granulated sugar, plus more for garnish

4 eggs

1 tablespoon lemon juice

LEMON GLAZE

1⅓ cups confectioners' sugar

¼ cup lemon juice

2 teaspoons grated lemon zest

1 cup raspberry jam or jelly

Lemon slices, for garnish

1. Preheat the oven to 350°F. Spray two 9-inch round cake pans with nonstick spray.
2. Using an electric hand mixer, blend together the cake mix, sour cream, oil, water, granulated sugar, eggs, and lemon juice. Pour evenly into the prepared pans.
3. Bake for 25 to 30 minutes, until the cake pulls away from the sides of the pan and is set in the middle. Let the cakes cool for 5 to 10 minutes, then remove them from the pans and allow to cool completely on a cooling rack.
4. In the meantime, mix together the lemon glaze ingredients. When the cakes are cool, put one layer on a serving plate, spread with the raspberry jam, and top with the remaining layer.
5. Drizzle the lemon glaze over the top. Garnish with lemon slices dipped in sugar.

---

cupcakes!

We love cupcakes, not only because they are a huge dessert trend, but also because they make cakes more versatile. (You can make one batch, and serve them for multiple events.) To make our carrot or lemon cake into cupcakes, simply spoon cake batter evenly into 24 lined muffin tins. Bake for 20 to 25 minutes, cool, and frost. (Omit the raspberry jam from the Lemon Layer Cake recipe when making cupcakes.)

pineapple upside-down cake

Serves 8

One 15-ounce can
    pineapple slices,
    undrained
½ cup brown sugar
½ cup finely chopped
    pecans
1 box yellow cake mix
3 eggs
8 tablespoons (1 stick)
    unsalted butter, melted
2 tablespoons pureed ginger

1. Preheat the oven to 325°F. Spray an 8-inch square baking dish with nonstick spray.
2. Drain the pineapple, reserving ⅔ cup of the juice in a mixing bowl. Chop the pineapple.
3. Sprinkle the bottom of the baking dish with the brown sugar, pecans, and chopped pineapple.
4. Add the cake mix, eggs, butter, and ginger to the juice in the mixing bowl. Mix using an electric hand mixer. Spread over the toppings.
5. Bake for 55 to 60 minutes, until the cake begins to pull away from the sides of the pan and is set in the middle.
6. Let cool for 5 to 10 minutes and invert onto a serving platter.

When you use a yellow cake or brownie mix as the base, these cheesecakes are a snap. We like to completely cool and chill cheesecake before serving.

key lime cheesecake

Serves 8

1 box yellow cake mix
2 tablespoons vegetable oil
4 eggs
Two 8-ounce packages
    cream cheese, softened
¾ cup sugar
1½ cups milk
½ cup lime juice

1. Preheat the oven to 350°F. Spray a 9-inch springform pan with nonstick spray.
2. Reserve 1 cup of the cake mix. Combine the remaining cake mix with the vegetable oil and 1 egg with an electric hand mixer. Press into the bottom of the springform pan.
3. Beat together the cream cheese and sugar with the hand mixer. Add the remaining 3 eggs and mix well. Add the reserved cake mix, the milk, and the lime juice and beat until smooth.
4. Pour over the crust. Bake for 1 hour and 15 minutes or until the center is set.
5. Cool to room temperature and then chill in the refrigerator for at least 2 hours. Remove the sides of the springform pan and serve.

mocha cheesecake

Serves 8

1 box brownie mix

2 tablespoons vegetable oil

4 eggs

Two 8-ounce packages
  cream cheese, softened

½ cup sugar

1½ cups milk

1 cup chocolate chips,
  melted

¼ cup brewed strong
  coffee

1. Preheat the oven to 350°F. Spray a 9-inch springform pan with nonstick spray.

2. Reserve 1 cup of the brownie mix. Combine the remaining brownie mix with the vegetable oil and 1 egg with an electric hand mixer. Press into the bottom of the springform pan.

3. Beat together the cream cheese and sugar with the hand mixer. Add the remaining 3 eggs and mix well. Add the reserved brownie mix, the milk, chocolate chips, and coffee and beat until smooth.

4. Pour over the crust. Bake for 1 hour and 15 minutes or until the center is set.

5. Cool to room temperature and then chill in the refrigerator for at least 2 hours. Remove the sides of the springform pan and serve.

---

dessert sauces

Make these cheesecakes even more decadent by topping them with one of our ice cream sundae sauces. Try:

Traditional Cheesecake with Caramel Sauce (page 261)

Mocha Cheesecake with Peanut Butter Sauce (page 262)

Key Lime Cheesecake with Balsamic Raspberry Sauce (page 260)

traditional cheesecake ▬

Serves 8

1 box yellow cake mix
2 tablespoons vegetable oil
4 eggs
Two 8-ounce packages
    cream cheese, softened
½ cup sugar
1½ cups milk
3 tablespoons lemon juice
1 tablespoon vanilla
    extract

1. Preheat the oven to 350°F. Spray a 9-inch springform pan with nonstick spray.

2. Reserve 1 cup of the cake mix. Combine the remaining cake mix with the vegetable oil and 1 egg with an electric hand mixer. Press into the bottom of the springform pan.

3. Beat together the cream cheese and sugar with the hand mixer. Add the remaining 3 eggs and mix well. Add the reserved cake mix, the milk, lemon juice, and vanilla extract and beat until smooth.

4. Pour over the crust. Bake for 1 hour and 15 minutes or until the center is set.

5. Cool to room temperature and then chill in the refrigerator for at least 2 hours. Remove the sides of the springform pan and serve.

Yep! It gets its own section! Enjoy!

chocolate mousse

Serves 4

1¼ cups heavy cream, chilled

¼ teaspoon almond extract or cinnamon

½ cup white or semisweet chocolate chips

1. Place a mixing bowl in the freezer.
2. Heat ¼ cup of the cream in a saucepan over medium heat. As the edges begin to bubble, remove from the heat and stir in the almond extract. Add the chocolate chips and whisk until melted and thoroughly combined.
3. Using an electric hand mixer, beat the remaining cream in the chilled mixing bowl until soft peaks form. Lightly fold the chocolate into the whipped cream, one-quarter at a time, until the chocolate is mixed in.
4. Spoon into individual cups or keep the mousse in the mixing bowl. Chill for at least 1 hour. Serve in individual bowls or glasses.

chocolate truffles

Makes 12

One 12-ounce package chocolate chips (2 cups)

¾ cup heavy cream

2 tablespoons unsalted butter

1 tablespoon brewed coffee

¼ cup cocoa powder, confectioners' sugar, and/or chili powder, for garnish

1. Place the chocolate chips in a mixing bowl. Heat the cream, butter, and coffee in a saucepan just until the mixture starts to boil. Pour the cream mixture over the chocolate chips. Mix until smooth.
2. Chill in the refrigerator for 2½ to 3 hours.
3. With a teaspoon, scoop the mixture out of the bowl. Roll into a ball with your hands. (This gets messy. Do not overwork the chocolate or it will melt in your hands.)
4. Roll the ball around lightly in the cocoa powder, confectioners' sugar, and/or chili powder. Repeat to make 12 balls. Keep chilled. Store in an airtight container.

chocolate ganache

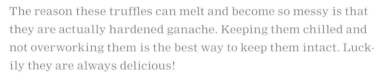

The reason these truffles can melt and become so messy is that they are actually hardened ganache. Keeping them chilled and not overworking them is the best way to keep them intact. Luckily they are always delicious!

Ganache can be an excellent recipe to keep in your back pocket for dipping strawberries or frosting a cake. Simply follow the directions above, but instead of chilling the mixture, use it to dip strawberries or drizzle over cakes while still warm. *Yum yum yum!*

hot cocoa

Serves 2 to 4

3 to 3½ cups milk
¼ cup cocoa powder
¼ cup sugar
½ cup heavy cream
   (optional)
Whipped Cream (page 274),
   for serving (optional)

1. Heat 3 cups milk in a saucepan to the desired temperature.
2. Mix together the cocoa powder and sugar. Add ½ cup milk or cream to create a paste.
3. Remove the saucepan from the heat and mix the cocoa paste into the warm milk until completely dissolved.
4. Try this topped with Whipped Cream.

hot cocoa bar

For winter parties, we love to set up a hot cocoa bar. We pour hot cocoa into a carafe or thermos and lay out yummy toppings around it in small bowls.

These have included candy canes, marshmallows, whipped cream, liqueurs, sprinkles, or whatever we may have. It is fun, delicious, and an unexpected treat.

A childhood favorite worthy of an adult soirée! Make the cookies slightly smaller to yield more sandwiches. These cookies are so good they can even be served without the filling.

brownie cookie sandwich ▬

Makes 12

COOKIES
1 box brownie mix
1 egg
2 tablespoons water
½ cup vegetable oil

BUTTERCREAM
8 tablespoons (1 stick)
    unsalted butter, softened
½ teaspoon vanilla extract
2 cups confectioners' sugar,
    sifted through a strainer
1 tablespoon milk, plus
    more if needed

1. Preheat the oven to 375°F. Cover two jelly roll pans with parchment paper.

2. Mix the cookie ingredients until moistened. Drop the batter by tablespoonfuls onto jelly roll pans 3 inches apart. Repeat until all the dough is used.

3. Bake for 7 to 8 minutes, until the center is set.

4. Cool for 1 minute on the pan. Place on a cooling rack to cool completely.

5. Meanwhile, beat the buttercream ingredients well with an electric hand mixer. Add a little more milk if needed to get a spreadable consistency.

6. To make the sandwiches, scoop out 1 to 2 tablespoons of buttercream and sandwich between two cookies. Store in an airtight container in the refrigerator.

pb&j ice cream sandwich

Makes 12

8 ounces (2 sticks) unsalted butter

1 cup peanut butter

1 cup brown sugar

1 cup granulated sugar

2 eggs

1 teaspoon vanilla extract

2 teaspoons baking soda

½ teaspoon salt

2 cups flour

1 cup dried cranberries or chocolate chips

¾ cup to 1½ cups vanilla ice cream, softened

Chopped pecans and chocolate chips, for garnish

1. Preheat the oven to 350°F. Cover two jelly roll pans with parchment paper.

2. In a mixing bowl, cream together the butter, peanut butter, and sugars with an electric hand mixer. Mix in the eggs and vanilla extract.

3. In a separate bowl, combine the baking soda, salt, and flour. Add the peanut butter mixture and blend together with the hand mixer. Fold in the cranberries. Drop rounded tablespoons of cookie dough onto the jelly roll pan 2 inches apart. Repeat until all the dough is used.

4. Bake for 10 to 12 minutes, until the center is set.

5. Cool the cookies completely on a cooling rack.

6. To make the sandwiches, scoop out 1 to 2 tablespoons of vanilla ice cream and sandwich between two cookies. Roll the sides in chopped pecans and chocolate chips. Serve immediately or wrap the sandwiches individually in aluminum foil and store in the freezer.

sugar cookie sandwich

Makes 18

8 ounces (2 sticks) unsalted butter

1 cup granulated sugar, plus more for sprinkling

1 cup milk plus 1 tablespoon lemon juice (allow to sit for 5 minutes)

2 eggs

½ teaspoon vanilla extract

2 teaspoons baking powder

1 teaspoon baking soda

1 teaspoon salt

3½ cups flour

½ teaspoon cinnamon

CHOCOLATE BUTTERCREAM

8 tablespoons (1 stick) unsalted butter

½ teaspoon vanilla extract

¼ cup cocoa powder

2 cups confectioners' sugar, sifted through a strainer

2 tablespoons milk, plus more if needed

1. Preheat the oven to 350°F. Cover two jelly roll pans with parchment paper.

2. In a mixing bowl, cream together the butter and granulated sugar with an electric hand mixer. Mix in the milk, eggs, and vanilla extract.

3. In a separate bowl, combine the baking powder, baking soda, salt, flour, and cinnamon. Add the butter and sugar mixture and blend together with the hand mixer. Drop 1 to 2 tablespoons of cookie dough onto the jelly roll pan 2 inches apart. Repeat until all the dough is used.

4. Bake for 10 to 12 minutes, until the center is set.

5. Sprinkle with granulated sugar after removing from the oven. Cool the cookies completely on a cooling rack.

6. Meanwhile, beat the chocolate buttercream ingredients well with an electric hand mixer. Add a little more milk if needed to get a spreadable consistency.

7. To make the sandwiches, scoop out 2 tablespoons of chocolate buttercream and sandwich between two cookies. Store in an airtight container in the refrigerator.

These bars are tangy, light, and perfect for summer, although we enjoy them all year-round. Make sure they are cool before sprinkling with confectioners' sugar; otherwise, the sugar will melt into the bars.

lemon bars

Makes 24

5 eggs

1 box yellow cake mix

⅓ cup (5 tablespoons plus 1 teaspoon) unsalted butter, melted

¾ cup lemon juice

1½ cups confectioners' sugar, plus 2 tablespoons for topping

½ teaspoon vanilla extract

2 teaspoons grated lemon zest

1. Preheat the oven to 350°F. Spray a 9 by 13-inch baking dish with nonstick spray.

2. Lightly beat 1 egg. Mix together the cake mix, butter, and egg until crumbly. Press into the bottom of the baking dish. Bake for 20 minutes.

3. Remove from the oven and turn down the temperature to 300°F.

4. Mix together the lemon juice, 1½ cups confectioners' sugar, the vanilla extract, the remaining 4 eggs, and lemon zest. Pour over the partially baked crust. Bake for 30 minutes.

5. Remove from the oven and let cool completely in the pan.

6. Using a strainer, sprinkle 2 tablespoons confectioners' sugar over the cooled bars. Cut into squares and serve.

margarita bars

Makes 24

5 eggs

1 box yellow cake mix

⅓ cup (5 tablespoons plus 1 teaspoon) unsalted butter, melted

¾ cup lime juice

1 cup well-drained mandarin orange segments, chopped

1 cup confectioners' sugar, plus 2 tablespoons for topping

1 teaspoon salt

1. Preheat the oven to 350°F. Spray a 9 by 13-inch baking dish with nonstick spray.

2. Lightly beat 1 egg. Mix together the cake mix, butter, and egg until crumbly. Press into the bottom of the baking dish. Bake for 20 minutes.

3. Remove from the oven and turn down the temperature to 300°F.

4. Mix together the lime juice, orange segments, 1 cup confectioners' sugar, and the remaining 4 eggs. Pour over the partially baked crust. Bake for 30 minutes.

5. Remove from the oven and let cool completely in the pan.

6. Using a strainer, sprinkle 2 tablespoons confectioners' sugar and the salt over the cooled bars. Cut into squares and serve.

raspberry-almond bars

Makes 24

5 eggs

1 box yellow cake mix

⅓ cup (5 tablespoons plus 1 teaspoon) unsalted butter, melted

½ cup raspberry jam or jelly

⅓ cup hot water

1 cup confectioners' sugar, plus 2 tablespoons for topping

½ teaspoon almond extract

1. Preheat the oven to 350°F. Spray a 9 by 13-inch baking dish with nonstick spray.

2. Lightly beat 1 egg. Mix together the cake mix, butter, and egg until crumbly. Press into the bottom of the baking dish. Bake for 20 minutes.

3. Remove from the oven and turn down the temperature to 300°F.

4. Mix together the raspberry jam, water, 1 cup confectioners' sugar, the almond extract, and the remaining 4 eggs. The mixture will be a liquid. Pour over the partially baked crust. Bake for 30 minutes.

5. Remove from the oven and let cool completely in the pan.

6. Using a strainer, sprinkle 2 tablespoons confectioners' sugar over the cooled bars. Cut into squares and serve.

Fruit crisps are traditional comfort food at its best. These one-pan desserts are simple and delicious.

apple crisp

Serves 4

5 cups peeled, cored, and diced apples

1 cup brown sugar

¾ teaspoon pumpkin pie spice

1½ cups finely chopped almonds or pecans

½ cup flour

4 tablespoons (½ stick) unsalted butter, melted

Vanilla ice cream or Whipped Cream (page 274), for serving

1. Preheat the oven to 375°F. Spray an 8-inch square baking dish with nonstick spray.

2. Mix together the apples, ½ cup of the brown sugar, and ½ teaspoon of the pumpkin pie spice. Pour into the baking dish.

3. Mix together the almonds, flour, and butter, and the remaining ½ cup brown sugar and ¼ teaspoon pumpkin pie spice. Sprinkle over the apple mixture. Press down and flatten.

4. Bake for 45 minutes or until bubbly and golden brown. Let cool slightly.

5. Serve with vanilla ice cream or Whipped Cream.

ginger pear crisp

Serves 4

Three 15-ounce cans pears, well drained

1 cup brown sugar

1 tablespoon pureed ginger

½ cup dried cranberries

½ cup finely chopped almonds or pecans

½ cup flour

4 tablespoons (½ stick) unsalted butter, melted

¼ teaspoon pumpkin pie spice

Vanilla ice cream or Whipped Cream (page 274), for serving

1. Preheat the oven to 375°F. Spray an 8-inch square baking dish with nonstick spray.

2. Mix together the pears, ½ cup of the brown sugar, the ginger, and cranberries. Pour into the baking dish.

3. Mix together the almonds, flour, butter, pumpkin pie spice, and the remaining ½ cup brown sugar. Sprinkle over the pear mixture. Press down and flatten.

4. Bake for 30 minutes or until bubbly and golden brown. Let cool slightly.

5. Serve with vanilla ice cream or Whipped Cream.

This section provides an entire arsenal of quick and easy dessert options. Play with different combinations and enjoy!

almond ice cream

Serves 4

2 cups vanilla ice cream, softened
¼ teaspoon almond extract
¼ cup chopped almonds
Green food coloring (optional)

Mix the ice cream, almond extract, and almonds together well. If desired, stir in a few drops of green food coloring. Refreeze if necessary.

softening and refreezing ice cream

We like to soften ice cream by allowing it to sit out on the counter or by microwaving it for 15 seconds at a time. If you soften it to the point where it is pliable but not too soft, you may be able to avoid refreezing. If not, and you need to refreeze, be sure to stir the ice cream regularly to avoid ice crystals.

coffee ice cream ▬

Serves 4

1 cup brewed coffee
2 cups vanilla ice cream,
   softened

1. In a saucepan, bring the coffee to a boil. Boil for 15 minutes to reduce to ¼ cup. Cool.
2. Mix the coffee with the ice cream. Refreeze if necessary.

cookie dough ice cream

Serves 4

2 tablespoons granulated
   sugar
2 tablespoons brown sugar
1 tablespoon unsalted
   butter, softened
½ teaspoon vanilla extract
2 tablespoons flour
¼ cup chocolate chips
2 cups vanilla ice cream,
   softened

Combine the sugars, butter, vanilla extract, flour, and chocolate chips. Stir into the ice cream. Refreeze if necessary.

peanut butter ice cream ▬

Serves 4

¼ cup peanut butter
2 cups vanilla ice cream,
   softened

Melt the peanut butter in a saucepan or microwave. Mix with the ice cream. Refreeze if necessary.

peppermint ice cream

Serves 4

$\frac{1}{8}$ teaspoon peppermint
    extract
2 cups vanilla ice cream,
    softened
Red food coloring (optional)

Mix the peppermint extract and ice cream together well. If desired, stir in a few drops of red food coloring. Refreeze if necessary.

balsamic raspberry sundae

Serves 4

BALSAMIC RASPBERRY
    SAUCE
$\frac{1}{2}$ cup raspberry jam or
    jelly
2 tablespoons balsamic
    vinegar
1 tablespoon sugar
1 tablespoon unsalted
    butter

4 brownies
2 cups vanilla ice cream,
    softened (or desired
    ice cream from above)
$\frac{1}{2}$ cup pine nuts, toasted

1. Combine the sauce ingredients in a saucepan over medium heat. Cook until the mixture has a syrupy consistency.
2. Place the brownies in four bowls. Top each with a scoop of ice cream. Drizzle with sauce and sprinkle with pine nuts.

playing it by ear

We love these sundaes. They are especially great to have available when you aren't sure if guests will be staying for dessert. We make the brownies and sauce ahead of time, and then assemble the sundaes if our guests decide on staying.

caramel brownie sundae

Serves 4

⅔ cup brown sugar

⅔ cup granulated sugar

¼ cup honey

4 tablespoons (½ stick) unsalted butter, softened

1 cup heavy cream

4 brownies

2 cups vanilla ice cream, softened (or desired ice cream from above)

½ cup chopped pecans

1. Combine the sugars and honey in a saucepan over medium heat. Cook until the sugars have melted and the mixture begins to bubble. Remove from the heat and stir in the butter and cream.
2. Place the brownies in four bowls. Top each with a scoop of ice cream. Drizzle with sauce and sprinkle with pecans.

hot fudge brownie sundae

Serves 4

HOT FUDGE SAUCE

1 cup semisweet or white chocolate chips

¾ cup heavy cream

1 teaspoon unsalted butter

1 teaspoon vanilla, peppermint, or almond extract

4 brownies

2 cups vanilla ice cream, softened (or desired ice cream from above)

Peanuts, chopped

1. Place the chocolate chips in a mixing bowl. In a saucepan over medium heat, warm the cream until the edges begin to bubble. Pour immediately over the chocolate chips. Whisk in the butter and extract until smooth.
2. Place the brownies in four bowls. Top each with a scoop of ice cream. Drizzle with sauce and sprinkle with peanuts.

peanut butter brownie sundae

Serves 4

PEANUT BUTTER SAUCE
4 tablespoons (½ stick)
    unsalted butter
1 cup brown sugar
¼ cup milk
½ cup peanut butter
½ teaspoon vanilla extract

4 brownies
2 cups vanilla ice cream,
    softened (or desired ice
    cream from above)
Chocolate chips, chopped

1. Combine the sauce ingredients in a saucepan over medium heat. Cook until the mixture has a syrupy consistency.
2. Place the brownies in four bowls. Top each with a scoop of ice cream. Drizzle with the sauce and sprinkle with chocolate chips.

---

ice cream bar

A wonderful birthday party, graduation, or summer celebration treat is an ice cream bar. In addition to making any of our sundae sauces available to your guests, also try:

Chocolate chips
White chocolate chips
Pecans, peanuts, and/or almonds
Pineapple chunks
Mandarin orange segments
Whipped Cream (page 274)

brownie ice cream pie

Serves 6 to 8

1 box brownie mix

HOT FUDGE SAUCE

1 cup semisweet or white chocolate chips

¾ cup heavy cream

1 teaspoon unsalted butter

1 teaspoon vanilla, peppermint, or almond extract

2 cups vanilla ice cream, softened (or desired ice cream from above)

1. Preheat the oven to 350°F. Spray a 9-inch springform pan with nonstick spray.

2. Prepare the brownie mix according to the package directions. Spread over the bottom of the springform pan. Bake for 30 to 35 minutes, until the center is set. Cool completely.

3. To make the sauce, place the chocolate chips in a mixing bowl. In a saucepan over medium heat, warm the cream until the edges begin to bubble. Pour immediately over the chocolate chips. Whisk in the butter and extract until smooth.

4. Spread the ice cream over the top of the cooled brownies. If the ice cream is too soft, cover and place in the freezer until frozen.

5. Remove the sides of the springform pan. Cut the ice cream pie in wedges and serve immediately drizzled with the sauce.

These desserts are all about cozy comfort food and are wonderful endings to a fall or winter meal. Try these puddings topped with vanilla ice cream or Whipped Cream (page 274).

rice pudding

Serves 4 to 6

4 cups milk
1 cup heavy cream
1 cup rice
⅔ cup sugar
¼ teaspoon salt
½ cup white chocolate chips (optional)
¼ cup maple syrup (optional)
¼ cup chopped pecans (optional)

1. Stir together the milk, the cream, rice, sugar, and salt in a saucepan over medium-high heat until the sugar dissolves and the mixture comes to a boil.

2. Reduce the heat to medium-low and simmer until the pudding is thick and the rice is tender, stirring occasionally, about 45 minutes. Serve warm.

3. For added flavor, try adding ½ cup white chocolate chips or ¼ cup maple syrup and ¼ cup chopped pecans while the rice pudding is still warm.

sandwich bread pudding

Serves 8

2 tablespoons unsalted butter, plus more for the pan

10 slices bread, crusts removed

¾ cup (total) raspberry jam or jelly, apricot preserves, or peanut butter

3 cups milk

1 cup heavy cream

3 eggs

2 cups sugar

2 teaspoons vanilla extract

1 cup chopped pecans (optional)

⅓ cup raisins (optional)

½ cup white or semisweet chocolate chips (optional)

1. Preheat the oven to 375°F. Butter an 8-inch square baking dish.

2. Make five sandwiches with the bread and jam and/or peanut butter. Cut each sandwich into four triangles.

3. Stand the triangles in the baking dish with the points sticking up.

4. Whisk together the milk, cream, eggs, sugar, and vanilla extract. Pour over the bread.

5. Sprinkle with optional toppings as desired. Top the bread points with dollops of butter. Let the bread soak for 10 to 15 minutes.

6. Bake for 45 minutes or until the center is set.

7. Serve warm or at room temperature.

---

heavy cream alternative

Although we love having heavy cream on our list, it does spoil fairly quickly. We try to provide an alternative when possible. In the case of these puddings, try using melted vanilla ice cream instead. Just be sure to use only half the sugar. Enjoy!

Puff pastry is a wonderfully versatile ingredient. We love these puff pastry bites as impressive individual bite-size desserts. The Triangle Puffs are wonderful garnishes for ice cream sundaes.

apple pie bites ▬

Makes 24

1 sheet puff pastry, thawed
⅓ cup applesauce
¼ teaspoon cinnamon
3 tablespoons brown sugar
2 tablespoons finely chopped pecans

1. Preheat the oven to 400°F.
2. Roll out the puff pastry on a floured surface to approximately 11 by 14 inches.
3. With a pizza cutter, cut the pastry into 24 pieces (4 rows, 6 columns). Stretch the pastry pieces slightly and lay in the cups of a mini muffin pan.
4. Mix together the remaining ingredients. Fill each cup with about 1 teaspoon of the mixture, being careful not to overfill. Discard any remaining filling.
5. Bake for 12 to 15 minutes, until the corners begin to brown. Serve immediately.

apricot-almond bites

Makes 24

1 sheet puff pastry, thawed
½ cup apricot preserves
½ teaspoon almond extract
24 whole almonds

1. Preheat the oven to 400°F.
2. Roll out the puff pastry on a floured surface to approximately 11 by 14 inches.
3. With a pizza cutter, cut the pastry into 24 pieces (4 rows, 6 columns). Stretch the pastry pieces slightly and lay in the cups of a mini muffin pan.
4. Mix together the apricot preserves and almond extract. Fill each cup with about 1 teaspoon of the mixture, being careful not to overfill. Top cach cup with an almond.
5. Bake for 12 to 15 minutes, until the corners begin to brown. Serve immediately.

pecan pie bites ▰

Makes 24

1 sheet puff pastry, thawed
2 tablespoons unsalted butter, melted
½ cup brown sugar
1 egg, lightly beaten
1 teaspoon vanilla extract
24 pecan halves

1. Preheat the oven to 400°F.
2. Roll out the puff pastry on a floured surface to approximately 11 by 14 inches.
3. With a pizza cutter, cut the pastry into 24 pieces (4 rows, 6 columns). Stretch the pastry pieces slightly and lay in the cups of a mini muffin pan.
4. Mix together the butter, sugar, egg, and vanilla extract. Fill each cup with about 1 teaspoon of the mixture, being careful not to overfill. Top each cup with a pecan half.
5. Bake for 12 to 15 minutes, until the corners begin to brown. Serve immediately.

raspberry cheesecake bites ▬

Makes 24

1 sheet puff pastry,
  thawed
4 ounces cream cheese,
  softened
¼ cup confectioners'
  sugar
¼ cup raspberry jam

1. Preheat the oven to 400°F.
2. Roll out the puff pastry on a floured surface to approximately 11 by 14 inches.
3. With a pizza cutter, cut the pastry into 24 pieces (4 rows, 6 columns). Stretch the pastry pieces slightly and lay in the cups of a mini muffin pan.
4. Mix together the cream cheese, confectioners' sugar, and raspberry jam. Fill each cup with about 1 teaspoon of the mixture, being careful not to overfill.
5. Bake for 12 to 15 minutes, until the corners begin to brown. Serve immediately.

triangle puffs ▬

Makes 12

**1 sheet puff pastry,
thawed**
1 egg
1 tablespoon milk
2 teaspoons cinnamon
⅓ cup sugar

1. Preheat the oven to 350°F. Cover a jelly roll pan with parchment paper.
2. Cut the pastry with a pizza cutter into 12 triangles. Place on the jelly roll pan.
3. Beat the egg lightly and mix in the milk. Brush over the triangles.
4. Mix the cinnamon and sugar and sprinkle over the triangles.
5. Bake for 10 minutes or until golden. Serve immediately or at room temperature. To reduce stress, make these Triangle Puffs the day ahead and store them in an airtight container.

---

easy and elegant

A quick yet elegant dessert is to serve these puff pastry triangles with a scoop of vanilla ice cream in a martini glass, drizzled with one of our sundae sauces.

These cookies are a perfect way to celebrate any holiday or occasion. Grab your kids and your favorite cookie cutter and make some memories.

cutout sugar cookies

Makes 36

SUGAR COOKIE DOUGH

12 tablespoons (1½ sticks) unsalted butter

1 cup sugar

1 egg

2 teaspoons vanilla extract

2¾ cups flour

1 teaspoon baking powder

½ teaspoon salt

Egg wash (1 egg beaten with 1 tablespoon water) (optional)

Sugar sprinkles (optional)

SUGAR COOKIE ICING

2 cups confectioners' sugar

½ teaspoon almond extract

3 tablespoons milk, plus more if needed

Food coloring, as desired

Decorations (optional)

1. To make the sugar cookies, cream together the butter and sugar. Beat in the egg and vanilla extract.

2. In a separate bowl, mix together the flour, baking powder, and salt. Add to the butter mixture and mix until incorporated.

3. Separate the dough into two balls. Wrap each in plastic wrap and then in aluminum foil, and chill for at least 1 hour. (The dough can also be frozen at this point. Wrap in aluminum foil over the plastic wrap.)

4. Preheat the oven to 350°F. Cover a jelly roll pan with parchment paper.

5. On a floured surface, roll out the dough until it is an even ¼ inch thick. Cut out with cookie cutters and place on the jelly roll pan. Keep rolling and cutting the dough until it is all used.

6. To save time, roll the dough into 1-inch balls, place on the pan, and press gently down to flatten a bit.

7. If you will be frosting the cookies, bake for 8 to 10 minutes, until they are slightly golden.

8. To save time, brush cookies with the egg wash and sprinkle with sugar sprinkles. Bake for 8 to 10 minutes until light golden brown.
9. Cool completely on a rack.
10. To make the icing, sift the confectioners' sugar into a bowl. Add the almond extract and milk. Mix together well. Add more milk, 1 teaspoon at a time, until the icing is a drizzling consistency.
11. Stir in a few drops of food coloring, if desired.
12. Frost the cooled cookies. Decorate, if desired. Allow to dry. Store in an airtight container and either refrigerate or freeze.

make ahead

You can make this recipe ahead of time at several stages in the process. Freeze the dough, unfrosted cookies, or frosted cookies. Thaw at room temperature and proceed with the recipe—or eat! This is a wonderful way to be prepared ahead of time for your celebration.

These tarts share our shortbread crust and a lot of flavor. Both are served chilled and make an impressive presentation.

mandarin orange cream tart

Serves 8

SHORTBREAD CRUST

8 tablespoons (1 stick) unsalted butter, softened

½ cup confectioners' sugar

1 cup flour

⅛ teaspoon salt

12 ounces white chocolate chips, melted

¼ cup heavy cream

One 8-ounce package cream cheese, softened

¼ cup apricot preserves

2 tablespoons water

One 10-ounce can mandarin orange segments, well drained

1. Preheat the oven to 350°F.

2. Beat together the butter and sugar with an electric hand mixer. Gradually mix in the flour and salt until the mixture is made up of small crumbles. Press the mixture onto the bottom and up the sides of a 9-inch pie plate. Prick the crust all over with a fork. Bake for 15 to 20 minutes, until golden brown. Cool completely.

3. Beat together the melted chocolate chips and the cream. Add the cream cheese and continue to mix. Spread over the crust.

4. In a saucepan, heat the apricot preserves and water and stir until smooth. Mix in the mandarin oranges and heat through. Pour over the filling.

5. Chill the tart for at least 1 hour before serving.

peanut butter tart

Serves 8

SHORTBREAD CRUST

8 tablespoons (1 stick) unsalted butter, softened

½ cup confectioners' sugar

1 cup flour

⅛ teaspoon salt

¾ cup peanut butter

One 8-ounce package cream cheese, softened

½ cup confectioners' sugar

2 cups vanilla ice cream, softened

Hot Fudge Sauce (page 261), for serving (optional)

1. Preheat the oven to 350°F.

2. To make the shortbread crust, beat together the butter and sugar with an electric hand mixer. Gradually mix in the flour and salt until the mixture is made up of small crumbles. Press the mixture onto the bottom and up the sides of a 9-inch pie plate. Prick the crust all over with a fork. Bake for 15 to 20 minutes, until golden brown. Cool completely.

3. Mix the peanut butter, cream cheese, sugar, and ice cream together and spread over the crust. Chill until firm.

4. Try serving topped with Hot Fudge sauce.

You'll never go back to store-bought whipped cream again. A great way to use up your heavy cream, and a delicious treat on ice cream, cheesecakes, tarts, and hot cocoa.

whipped cream

Serves 4 to 6

1 cup heavy cream
2 tablespoons sugar
1 teaspoon vanilla
   extract

1. Chill a mixing bowl in the freezer for about 10 minutes.
2. With an electric hand mixer, beat the cream until soft peaks form.
3. Lightly fold in the sugar and vanilla extract until incorporated. Chill before serving.

breakfast or brunch

Biscotti, in Italian, is used as a general word for "cookies." They are usually twice-baked and served with a cup of coffee or tea.

anise and pine nut biscotti ▬

Makes 24

1 box yellow cake mix
¾ cup flour
8 tablespoons (1 stick) unsalted butter, melted and cooled
2 teaspoons vanilla extract
2 eggs
2 tablespoons aniseed or fennel seed, crushed
¼ cup pine nuts

1. Preheat the oven to 350°F. Position a rack in the center of the oven. Place parchment paper over a jelly roll pan.
2. Combine all the ingredients in a large mixing bowl. Mix with an electric hand mixer on low speed until well blended, 2 to 3 minutes, scraping down the sides of the bowl. (The mixture will be very thick.)
3. Transfer the dough to the jelly roll pan. With your hands, form two rectangles, each approximately 14 by 3 by ¾ inches. Leave 3 to 4 inches between the rectangles.
4. Bake for 30 to 35 minutes, until firm to the touch. Remove from the oven (leave the oven on) and cool on the pan for 10 minutes.
5. Cutting on the pan, use a sharp knife to slice each rectangle into ¾-inch-thick slices on the diagonal. Turn the slices on their flat sides and return to the oven.
6. Bake for 10 minutes more. Remove from the oven and let cool completely on the pan.

chocolate-cranberry biscotti

Makes 24

1 box yellow cake mix
¼ cup flour
8 tablespoons (1 stick) unsalted butter, melted and cooled
2 teaspoons vanilla extract
2 eggs
½ cup cocoa powder
⅓ cup white chocolate chips
⅓ cup dried cranberries

1. Preheat the oven to 350°F. Position a rack in the center of the oven. Place parchment paper over a jelly roll pan.

2. In a large mixing bowl, mix together the cake mix, flour, butter, vanilla extract, eggs, and cocoa powder with an electric hand mixer on low speed until well blended, 2 to 3 minutes, scraping down the sides of the bowl. Fold in the chocolate chips and cranberries. (The mixture will be very thick.)

3. Transfer the dough to the jelly roll pan. With your hands, form two rectangles, each approximately 14 by 3 by ¾ inches. Leave 3 to 4 inches between the rectangles.

4. Bake for 30 to 35 minutes, until firm to the touch. Remove from the oven (leave the oven on) and cool on the pan for 10 minutes.

5. Cutting on the pan, use a sharp knife to slice each rectangle into ¾-inch-thick slices on the diagonal. Turn the slices on their flat sides and return to the oven.

6. Bake for 10 minutes more. Remove from the oven and let cool completely on the pan.

ginger-pecan biscotti ▬

Makes 24

1 box yellow cake mix
¾ cup flour
8 tablespoons (1 stick)
   unsalted butter,
   melted and cooled
2 teaspoons vanilla
   extract
2 eggs
2 tablespoons pureed ginger
⅓ cup chopped pecans

1. Preheat the oven to 350°F. Position a rack in the center of the oven. Place parchment paper over a jelly roll pan.

2. In a large mixing bowl, mix together the cake mix, flour, butter, vanilla extract, eggs, and ginger with an electric hand mixer on low speed until well blended, 2 to 3 minutes, scraping down the sides of the bowl. Fold in the pecans. (The mixture will be very thick.)

3. Transfer the dough to the jelly roll pan. With your hands, form two rectangles, each approximately 14 by 3 by ¾ inches. Leave 3 to 4 inches between the rectangles.

4. Bake for 30 to 35 minutes, until firm to the touch. Remove from the oven (leave the oven on) and cool on the pan for 10 minutes.

5. Cutting on the pan, use a sharp knife to slice each rectangle into ¾-inch-thick slices on the diagonal. Turn the slices on their flat sides and return to the oven.

6. Bake for 10 minutes more. Remove from the oven and let cool completely on the pan.

coffee talk

Biscotti are easy to make and a great treat to have on hand. They store well in a plastic container for those impromptu coffee dates. Freezing is a great option to keep them fresher longer. Take out only what you need. Set out at room temperature an hour or so before serving.

These breakfast potatoes add a lot of flavor and a decidedly
"diner" feel to any breakfast. Great for dinnertime "breakfasts."

hash browns

Serves 4

3 cups peeled and grated
   potatoes (russet, Yukon
   Gold, or sweet)
1 teaspoon salt
¼ teaspoon black pepper
3 tablespoons vegetable oil
2 tablespoons unsalted
   butter

1. Put the potatoes into a mixing bowl. Mix with the salt and pepper.

2. Heat half of the oil and butter in a large fry pan. Spread the potatoes over the bottom of the pan. Press flat with the back of a spatula. Cook for about 10 minutes over medium-low heat without disturbing, until the bottom is golden brown.

3. Cut into quarters and flip in sections, adding the remaining butter and oil as you go.

4. Cook the second side until golden brown on the bottom, about 10 minutes. Serve immediately.

home fries

Serves 4

2 tablespoons vegetable oil

2 tablespoons unsalted butter

¼ cup diced shallot or onion

¼ bell pepper, diced

3 cups peeled and cubed (½-inch cubes) potatoes (russet, Yukon Gold, or sweet), parboiled

1 teaspoon salt

¼ teaspoon black pepper

Tabasco or hot sauce

1. Heat the oil and butter in a fry pan over medium heat until the butter is melted.

2. Add the shallot and bell pepper and cook for 8 to 10 minutes, until softened.

3. Add the potatoes and cook, covered, for 8 to 10 minutes, until the potatoes are crisp and brown.

4. Season with salt and pepper, add Tabasco to taste, and serve.

---

parboiling potatoes

This is an extra step, but it allows your potatoes to be tender without scorching the outside or having them take forever to cook through.

Cover the potatoes with water in a stockpot. Bring to a boil, reduce the heat to low, and cook for 10 minutes. Drain and rinse with cold water to cool the potatoes for handling.

potato pancakes

Serves 4

3 cups peeled and grated
  potatoes (russet,
  Yukon Gold, or sweet)

¼ cup grated shallot or
  onion

2 eggs, lightly beaten

3 tablespoons flour

2 teaspoons salt

¼ teaspoon black pepper

2 tablespoons vegetable oil

Applesauce, for serving
  (optional)

Sour cream, for serving
  (optional)

1. Drain the excess liquid from the potatoes and put them in
   a mixing bowl.

2. Add the shallot to the potatoes. Stir in the eggs, flour,
   salt, and pepper.

3. Heat the oil in a fry pan. With ½-cup measuring cup,
   pour the potato mixture into the hot oil.

4. Fry over medium heat, 3 to 4 minutes per side, until
   golden brown, then drain on paper towels.

5. Serve with applesauce or sour cream, if desired.

This yummy cinnamon loaf is perfect for a holiday morning, or when you have out-of-town guests.

cinnamon roll loaf ▬

Serves 4 to 6

1 pound frozen bread dough
¾ cup granulated sugar
1 tablespoon cinnamon
8 tablespoons (1 stick) unsalted butter, melted

CREAM CHEESE ICING
¼ cup cream cheese
¼ cup confectioners' sugar
About 2 tablespoons milk

1. In a greased loaf pan, set the bread dough, covered, overnight to thaw and rise.
2. When ready to bake, preheat the oven to 350°F.
3. Mix together the sugar and cinnamon in a mixing bowl. Cut the bread dough into 1-inch cubes with kitchen scissors. Roll the cubes in the cinnamon-sugar.
4. Place half the dough cubes back in the loaf pan. Drizzle with half the butter. Top with the remaining dough cubes. Pour the rest of the butter over the top. Sprinkle any remaining cinnamon-sugar over the top.
5. Bake for 40 to 45 minutes, until golden brown.
6. Let sit for 5 minutes. Invert onto a serving platter. Turn right side up again.
7. To make the icing, beat together the cream cheese and sugar. Add milk to create a glaze consistency. Spread over the top of the loaf while the bread is still warm.
8. Let cool slightly before slicing. Or serve warm and pull apart.

Choose from raspberry, apricot, or chocolate variations. Crazy good!

cream cheese coffee cake ▬

Serves 8

2⅓ cups flour, plus more for the pan

1 cup sugar

12 tablespoons (1½ sticks) unsalted butter

½ teaspoon baking powder

½ teaspoon baking soda

¼ teaspoon salt

¾ cup sour cream or plain yogurt

1 teaspoon almond extract

2 eggs

One 8-ounce package cream cheese, softened

½ cup raspberry jam or jelly, apricot preserves, or chocolate chips

½ cup sliced almonds

1. Preheat the oven to 350°F. Grease and flour the bottom of a 9-inch springform pan.

2. In a large mixing bowl, combine the flour and ¾ cup of the sugar and mix well. With a fork or pizza cutter, cut in the butter until the mixture is coarse crumbs. Remove and reserve 1 cup.

3. To the remaining crumb mixture, add the baking powder, baking soda, salt, sour cream, almond extract, and 1 egg. Mix until just blended. Press the mixture onto the bottom of the pan and up the sides.

4. In a small bowl, combine the cream cheese, the remaining ¼ cup sugar, and the remaining egg. Blend well. Pour into the crust-lined pan. Carefully spoon the jam or chocolate chips evenly over the cream cheese mixture. Sprinkle the reserved crumb mixture and the almonds over the top.

5. Bake for 1 hour and 10 minutes or until the filling is set and the top is golden brown.

6. Let cool for 15 minutes in the pan.

7. Remove the sides of the pan and serve.

---

easy-spread jam

If you are having any difficulty spreading the jelly, jam, or preserves on top of the coffee cake, try microwaving it for just a few seconds. This will make it much easier to spread!

These egg dishes cover just about any flavor combination you are looking for. The strata and bakes provide a make-ahead option, and the omelettes are just delicious.

black bean strata

Serves 4

1 cup salsa

1 cup drained and rinsed black beans

10 flour tortillas (8-inch or fajita size), cut into 1-inch strips

1 cup grated Cheddar cheese

1 cup sour cream or plain yogurt

1 cup milk

½ teaspoon salt

4 eggs, beaten

¼ cup thinly sliced green onion

1. Spray an 8-inch square baking dish with nonstick spray.
2. Combine the salsa and beans in a mixing bowl.
3. Place one-third of the tortilla strips in the prepared dish. Top with one-third of the cheese and about half of the salsa mixture. Repeat with half of the remaining tortilla strips, half of the remaining cheese, and the remaining salsa mixture. Top with the remaining tortilla strips.
4. Whisk together the sour cream, milk, salt, and eggs until well blended. Stir in the green onion. Pour over the tortilla strips. Sprinkle with the remaining cheese. Cover and chill for 8 hours or overnight.
5. Preheat the oven to 350°F. Remove the dish from the refrigerator. Let sit at room temperature for 10 minutes.
6. Cover with aluminum foil and bake for 20 minutes. Uncover and bake for an additional 15 minutes or until lightly browned.

breakfast burritos

Serves 4

6 eggs

¼ teaspoon salt

½ cup salsa, plus more for serving

8 ounces bulk breakfast sausage, cooked and crumbled

1 cup shredded Cheddar cheese

4 flour tortillas (8-inch or fajita size), or 8 slices bread, toasted

Sour cream, for serving

1. In a bowl, beat the eggs with the salt. Coat a fry pan with nonstick spray. Over medium heat, begin to scramble the eggs. Before they are completely cooked, add the salsa, sausage, and cheese. Heat all the ingredients thoroughly.

2. If using tortillas, warm them in the microwave between two paper towels. This should take only 15 to 30 seconds on high.

3. Place one-quarter of the filling on each tortilla and wrap up like a burrito, or make four sandwiches with toast. Serve with extra salsa and sour cream.

scrambled egg tip

No need to add anything to your eggs—like milk or water—to make them delicious. What you do need for fluffy scrambled eggs is air. Whisk the eggs for a couple of minutes, allowing them to get frothy. As you cook them, make sure that you let the eggs sit for just a minute to start to set before you begin to push them with a spatula or flat wooden spoon toward the middle. This gives you fluffy and slightly larger curds.

crab and cream cheese omelette

Serves 1

3 eggs
¼ teaspoon salt
Black pepper
1 teaspoon olive oil
¼ cup chopped imitation
  crabmeat or drained
  canned lump crabmeat
2 tablespoons cream cheese,
  cubed
¼ teaspoon dill weed

1. Whisk the eggs in a mixing bowl, getting plenty of air into them so they become fluffy. Once the eggs have become frothy, mix in the salt and pepper to taste.

2. Heat the olive oil in a nonstick fry pan over medium heat. Pour in the eggs. The bottom layer of the omelette will start to cook and solidify. Pull back the edges slightly toward the center of the pan, and tip the pan to allow more of the liquid to run to the edge and begin to cook. Repeat all the way around the edge until the base layer of the omelette is cooked and firm.

3. Sprinkle in the remaining ingredients.

4. Reduce the heat, fold over the omelette, and cover the fry pan to allow the center to cook for 2 to 3 minutes more. Slide onto a plate and serve.

eggs benedict ▬

Serves 4

4 slices bread, cut into circles and toasted

4 slices ham, cut into circles

POACHED EGGS

4 eggs

4 cups water

1 teaspoon lemon juice

½ teaspoon salt

HOLLANDAISE SAUCE

2 egg yolks

1 tablespoon lemon juice

¼ teaspoon salt

4 tablespoon (½ stick) unsalted butter

1. Place the toast circles on dinner plates. Top the toast with the ham slices.

2. To make the poached eggs, crack the eggs into individual small bowls. Bring the water to a boil and reduce immediately to a simmer. Stir in the lemon juice and salt. Gently pour each egg into the simmering water. Cover and cook for 3 minutes. Remove the eggs from the water and place the eggs on top of the ham.

3. While the eggs are cooking, make the hollandaise sauce: Place the egg yolks, lemon juice, and salt in a blender or food processor. Blend at top speed for 2 minutes. In the meantime, melt the butter in a saucepan over medium heat until foaming. With the blender or food processor running, pour the hot butter in a thin stream into the egg yolk mixture. By the time two-thirds of the butter is in the blender, the sauce should be thick.

4. Drizzle over the poached eggs and serve.

ham and cheese bake

Serves 4

5 eggs

¾ cup milk

1 tablespoon yellow
    mustard

½ teaspoon salt

¼ teaspoon black pepper,
    or to taste

4 slices bread, cut into
    cubes

1 cup diced ham

¾ cup grated Cheddar
    cheese

1. Spray an 8-inch square baking dish with nonstick spray.

2. In a mixing bowl, whisk together the eggs, milk,
   mustard, salt, and pepper.

3. Spread the bread cubes on the bottom of the baking dish.
   Top with the ham and cheese. Pour the eggs over the top.
   Cover and refrigerate overnight.

4. Preheat the oven to 350°F.

5. Bake for about 50 minutes, until the center is puffed and
   set.

make more!

These bake recipes are so easy and
delicious, they are perfect for large
groups. To serve eight, double the recipe and place in a 9 by 13-inch baking
dish. Bake for approximately 1 hour.

sausage and bell pepper bake ▬

Serves 4

5 eggs

¾ cup milk

1 tablespoon yellow mustard

½ teaspoon salt

¼ teaspoon black pepper, or to taste

4 slices bread, cut into cubes

8 ounces bulk breakfast sausage, cooked and crumbled

¼ cup diced bell pepper

¼ cup diced shallot or onion

¾ cup grated Cheddar cheese

1. Spray an 8-inch square baking dish with nonstick spray.
2. In a mixing bowl, whisk together the eggs, milk, mustard, salt, and black pepper.
3. Spread the bread cubes on the bottom of the baking dish. Top with the sausage, bell pepper, shallot, and cheese. Pour the eggs over the top. Cover and refrigerate overnight.
4. Preheat the oven to 350°F.
5. Bake for about 50 minutes, until the center is puffed and set.

spinach and red pepper bake

Serves 4

5 eggs

¾ cup milk

1 tablespoon yellow
mustard

½ teaspoon salt

¼ teaspoon black pepper,
or to taste

4 slices bread, cut into
cubes

1 cup spinach, thawed and
squeezed dry

2 roasted red peppers,
drained and diced

¾ cup grated Cheddar
cheese

1. Spray an 8-inch square baking dish with nonstick spray.

2. In a mixing bowl, whisk together the eggs, milk,
mustard, salt, and black pepper.

3. Spread the bread cubes on the bottom of the baking
dish. Top with the spinach, roasted red peppers, and
cheese. Pour the eggs over the top. Cover and refrigerate
overnight.

4. Preheat the oven to 350°F.

5. Bake for about 50 minutes, until the center is puffed and
set.

double it!

These bake recipes are so easy and delicious, they are perfect for large groups.
To serve eight, double the recipe and
place in a 9 by 13-inch baking dish.
Bake for approximately 1 hour.

tomato-basil egg white omelette

Serves 1

4 egg whites
¼ teaspoon salt
Black pepper
1 teaspoon olive oil
½ medium tomato, thinly
   sliced
1 tablespoon finely chopped
   fresh basil
2 tablespoons grated
   Parmesan cheese or
   crumbled feta

1. Whisk the egg whites in a mixing bowl, getting plenty of air into them so they become fluffy. Once the egg whites have become frothy, mix in the salt and pepper to taste.

2. Heat the olive oil in a nonstick fry pan over medium heat. Pour in the egg whites. The bottom layer of the omelette will start to cook and solidify. Pull back the edges slightly toward the center of the pan, and tip the pan to allow more of the liquid to run to the edge and begin to cook. Repeat all the way around the edge until the base layer of the omelette is cooked and firm.

3. Lay the tomato slices on one half of the omelette. Sprinkle on the remaining ingredients.

4. Reduce the heat, fold over the omelette, and cover the fry pan to allow the center to cook for 2 to 3 minutes more. Slide onto a plate and serve.

western omelette

Serves 1

3 eggs
¼ teaspoon salt
Black pepper
1 teaspoon olive oil
¼ cup diced ham
2 tablespoons diced bell
    pepper
2 tablespoons diced shallot
    or onion
¼ cup shredded Cheddar
    cheese

1. Whisk the eggs in a mixing bowl, getting plenty of air into them so they become fluffy. Once the eggs have become frothy, mix in the salt and black pepper to taste.
2. Heat the olive oil in a nonstick fry pan over medium heat. Pour in the eggs. The bottom layer of the omelette will start to cook and solidify. Pull back the edges slightly toward the center of the pan, and tip the pan to allow more of the liquid to run to the edge and begin to cook. Repeat all the way around the edge until the base layer of the omelette is cooked and firm.
3. Sprinkle on the remaining ingredients.
4. Reduce the heat, fold over the omelette, and cover the fry pan to allow the center to cook for 2 to 3 minutes more. Slide onto a plate and serve.

These casseroles are a simple and delicious make-ahead breakfast with a bread pudding consistency. The recipes serve four. To serve eight, double the recipe, use a 9 by 13-inch baking dish, and bake for 1 hour and 10 minutes or until the center is set.

apricot-stuffed french toast bake

Serves 4

4 ounces cream cheese, softened

2 tablespoons sour cream or plain yogurt

½ cup apricot preserves

9 slices bread, crusts removed

3 eggs

6 tablespoons sugar

1½ cups milk

1 teaspoon vanilla extract

1 teaspoon cinnamon

Maple syrup, for serving

1. Spray an 8-inch square baking dish with nonstick spray.
2. Beat together the cream cheese and sour cream until well combined.
3. Spread about 2 teaspoons of preserves on one side of 3 slices of bread. Spread one-third of the cream cheese mixture over the preserves. Lay the bread, coated side down, in the baking dish. (Cut 1 slice of bread in half to fit it in the baking dish.) Continue until all the bread and fillings have been used up, making three bread layers.
4. In a mixing bowl, whisk together the eggs, ¼ cup of the sugar, the milk, and vanilla extract. Pour evenly over the bread. Mix the remaining 2 tablespoons sugar with the cinnamon and sprinkle over the top. Cover and refrigerate overnight or for at least 2 hours.
5. Preheat the oven to 350°F.
6. Bake for 1 hour. Let sit for 10 minutes and serve with maple syrup.

cinnamon french toast bake

Serves 4

4 tablespoons (½ stick)
   unsalted butter,
   melted
2 teaspoons cinnamon
½ cup brown sugar
9 slices bread, crusts
   removed
3 eggs
4 tablespoons granulated
   sugar
1½ cups milk
1 teaspoon vanilla extract
Maple syrup, for serving

1. Spray an 8-inch square baking dish with nonstick spray.
2. Mix together the butter, 1 teaspoon of the cinnamon, and the brown sugar. Sprinkle one-third of the butter mixture over the bottom of the baking dish. Lay 3 slices of bread on top of the butter. (Cut 1 slice of bread in half to fit it in the baking dish.) Continue until all the bread and butter have been used up, making three bread layers.
3. In a mixing bowl, whisk together the eggs, 2 tablespoons of the granulated sugar, the milk, and vanilla extract. Pour evenly over the bread. Mix the remaining 2 tablespoons granulated sugar with the remaining 1 teaspoon cinnamon, and sprinkle over the top. Cover and refrigerate overnight or for at least 2 hours.
4. Preheat the oven to 350°F.
5. Bake for 1 hour. Let sit for 10 minutes and serve with maple syrup.

raspberry french toast bake ▬

Serves 4

½ cup white chocolate chips
½ cup finely chopped pecans
¼ cup raspberry jam or jelly
9 slices bread, crusts removed
3 eggs
4 tablespoons sugar
1½ cups milk
1 teaspoon vanilla extract
1 teaspoon cinnamon
Maple syrup, for serving

1. Spray an 8-inch square baking dish with nonstick spray.
2. Sprinkle one-third each of the chocolate chips and pecans over the bottom of the pan. Spread about 1 teaspoon of jam on one side of each of 3 slices of bread. Lay the bread, jam side down, in the baking dish. (Cut 1 slice of bread in half to fit it in the baking dish.) Continue until all the chocolate, nuts, jam, and bread have been used up, making three bread layers.
3. In a mixing bowl, whisk together the eggs, 2 tablespoons of the sugar, the milk, and vanilla extract. Pour evenly over the bread. Mix the remaining 2 tablespoons sugar with the cinnamon and sprinkle over the top. Cover and refrigerate overnight or for at least 2 hours.
4. Preheat the oven to 350°F.
5. Bake for 1 hour. Let sit for 10 minutes and serve with maple syrup.

Take your favorite pancake mix up a few notches with these delicious and creative additions! We prefer to buy mixes that are not "complete," because "complete" mixes, which require you to add only water, limit your options. If you do use a "complete" mix, make the batter according to the package directions.

apple-cinnamon pancakes

Serves 4

1½ cups pancake mix
¾ cup milk
1 tablespoon vegetable oil
1 egg
½ teaspoon cinnamon
1 apple, peeled, cored, and thinly sliced
Maple syrup, for serving

1. Mix together all the ingredients except the syrup until just combined. Some lumps are acceptable.
2. Heat a fry pan over medium heat. Spray with nonstick spray.
3. Pour ¼ cup pancake batter onto the pan as many times as the size of the pan allows. When bubbles form on the top of the entire pancake, flip and cook for 1 to 2 minutes more.
4. Serve warm with maple syrup.

warm maple syrup

We like to serve warm maple syrup with loaded pancakes. It is a simple step with a decadent result. Simply warm over low heat in a saucepan or in the microwave in a microwave-safe bowl for 30 seconds at a time until warmed through.

pigs-in-a-blanket pancakes

Serves 4

1½ cups pancake mix
¾ cup milk
1 tablespoon vegetable
   oil
1 egg
¼ cup cooked and
   crumbled bulk
   breakfast sausage
   or cooked and finely
   chopped bacon
Maple syrup, for serving

1. Mix together all the ingredients except the syrup until just combined. Some lumps are acceptable.
2. Heat a fry pan over medium heat. Spray with nonstick spray.
3. Pour ¼ cup pancake batter onto the pan as many times as the size of the pan allows. When bubbles form on the top of the entire pancake, flip and cook for 1 to 2 minutes more.
4. Serve warm with maple syrup.

pineapple pancakes

Serves 4

1½ cups pancake mix
¾ cup milk
1 tablespoon vegetable oil
1 egg
¼ cup well-drained and
   finely chopped
   pineapple
Maple syrup, for serving

1. Mix together all the ingredients except the syrup until just combined. Some lumps are acceptable.
2. Heat a fry pan over medium heat. Spray with nonstick spray.
3. Pour ¼ cup pancake batter onto the pan as many times as the size of the pan allows. When bubbles form on the top of the entire pancake, flip and cook for 1 to 2 minutes more.
4. Serve warm with maple syrup.

turtle pancakes

Serves 4

PANCAKES

1½ cups pancake mix

¾ cup milk

1 tablespoon vegetable oil

1 egg

¼ cup chocolate chips

2 tablespoons chopped
   pecans

CARAMEL SAUCE

⅔ cup brown sugar

⅔ cup granulated sugar

¼ cup honey

4 tablespoons (½ stick)
   unsalted butter

1 cup heavy cream

1. Mix together the pancake ingredients until just combined. Some lumps are acceptable.

2. Heat a fry pan over medium heat. Spray with nonstick spray.

3. Pour ¼ cup pancake batter onto the pan as many times as the size of the pan allows. When bubbles form on the top of the entire pancake, flip and cook for 1 to 2 minutes more. Keep warm.

4. To make the caramel sauce, stir together the sugars, honey, and butter in a saucepan over medium heat until the mixture bubbles. Remove from the heat and stir in the cream. Drizzle over the pancakes.

All of these quiches have three crust options. Choose a cracker crust, a puff pastry crust, or crustless.

cracker quiche crust

Makes one 9-inch crust

Approximately 35 butter
  crackers
4 tablespoons (½ stick)
  unsalted butter, melted

1. Preheat the oven to 350°F.
2. Place the crackers in a resealable storage bag and crush with a rolling pin. You need 1½ cups crumbs. Mix the crumbs and butter. Press firmly onto the bottom and up the sides of a 9-inch pie plate. Bake for 10 minutes.
3. Remove from the oven. Pour in the filling of your choice (see the following pages).
4. Return to the oven. Bake for 45 minutes or until the center has set.

puff pastry quiche crust

Makes 12 (individual quiches)

1 sheet puff pastry,
  thawed

1. Preheat the oven to 400°F.
2. Roll out the puff pastry on a floured surface to approximately 11 by 14 inches. With a pizza cutter, cut the sheet into 12 pieces (3 rows, 4 columns). Stretch the pastry squares slightly and lay into muffin pan cups.
3. Fill the cups with the filling of your choice.
4. Bake for 20 minutes or until the corners begin to brown.

broccoli and cheese quiche

Serves 4 to 6

Cracker Quiche Crust
(page 299) or Puff
Pastry Quiche Crust
(page 299), optional

1 cup frozen chopped
broccoli

1 cup shredded Cheddar
cheese

4 eggs

½ cup milk

½ cup heavy cream, sour
cream, or plain yogurt

2 tablespoons dried
minced onion

½ teaspoon salt

Black pepper

1. For a crustless quiche, preheat the oven to 375°F and spray a 9-inch pie plate with nonstick spray. Otherwise, choose a crust and prepare it.

2. Sprinkle the pie plate or crust(s) with the broccoli and cheese.

3. Whisk together the eggs, milk, cream, onion, salt, and pepper to taste. Pour the egg mixture over the broccoli and cheese.

4. Bake the crustless version for 45 minutes or until the center is set, or bake according to the preferred crust option. Let sit for approximately 5 minutes, then serve.

5. To make a spinach and cheese quiche, substitute 1 cup frozen spinach, thawed, drained, and squeezed dry, for the broccoli. Proceed as above.

---

large brunches

Smaller bite-size quiches are great to serve for large groups. Use any of these quiche recipes with 2 puff pastry sheets cut up to fill 48 mini muffin cups. Use only 1 teaspoon of the quiche filling and bake at 400°F for 12 to 15 minutes.

---

ham and apple quiche

Serves 4 to 6

Cracker Quiche Crust (page 299) or Puff Pastry Crust (page 299), optional

1 cup shredded Cheddar cheese

1 cup diced ham

1 apple, peeled, cored, and grated

½ teaspoon cinnamon

½ cup heavy cream, sour cream, or plain yogurt

½ cup milk

4 eggs

2 tablespoons yellow mustard

⅛ teaspoon garlic powder

½ teaspoon salt

1. For a crustless quiche, preheat the oven to 375°F and spray a 9-inch pie plate with nonstick spray. Otherwise, choose a crust and prepare it.

2. Toss together the cheese, ham, apple, and cinnamon. Pour into the pie plate or crust(s).

3. Whisk together the cream, milk, eggs, mustard, garlic powder, and salt. Pour the egg mixture over the ham mixture.

4. Bake the crustless version for 45 minutes or until the center is set, or bake according to the preferred crust option. Let sit for approximately 5 minutes, then serve.

mushroom–red pepper quiche

Serves 4 to 6

Cracker Quiche Crust (page 299) or Puff Pastry Quiche Crust (page 299), optional

One 4-ounce can sliced or cut mushrooms, drained

1 roasted red pepper, drained and diced

½ cup shredded mozzarella cheese

½ cup crumbled feta cheese

½ cup milk

½ cup heavy cream, sour cream, or plain yogurt

4 eggs

½ teaspoon salt

¼ teaspoon black pepper

1. For a crustless quiche, preheat the oven to 375°F and spray a 9-inch pie plate with nonstick spray. Otherwise, choose a crust and prepare it.

2. Sprinkle the pie plate or crust(s) with the mushrooms, roasted red pepper, and cheeses.

3. Whisk together the milk, cream, eggs, salt, and black pepper. Pour the egg mixture over the filling.

4. Bake the crustless version for 45 minutes or until the center is set, or bake according to the preferred crust option. Let sit for approximately 5 minutes, then serve.

quiche lorraine ▬

Serves 4 to 6

Cracker Quiche Crust
(page 299) or Puff
Pastry Quiche Crust
(page 299), optional

4 slices bacon, cooked
and crumbled (see
Bacon Cooking Tip
on page 52)

½ cup shredded
mozzarella cheese

½ cup grated Parmesan
cheese

4 eggs

½ cup milk

½ cup heavy cream,
sour cream, or
plain yogurt

¼ teaspoon salt

⅛ teaspoon black pepper

⅛ teaspoon nutmeg

1. For a crustless quiche, preheat the oven to 375°F and
   spray a 9-inch pie plate with nonstick spray. Otherwise,
   choose a crust and prepare it.

2. Sprinkle the pie plate or crust(s) with the bacon and
   cheeses.

3. Whisk together the eggs, milk, cream, salt, pepper, and
   nutmeg. Pour the egg mixture over the filling.

4. Bake the crustless version for 45 minutes or until the
   center is set, or bake according to the preferred crust
   option. Let sit for approximately 5 minutes, then serve.

These scones are flaky and delicious. Try them for breakfast, brunch, or anytime.

cheddar-herb scones

Makes 12

1¾ cups flour

4 teaspoons baking powder

1 tablespoon sugar

½ teaspoon salt

5 tablespoons cold unsalted butter, cut into pieces

⅓ cup milk

¼ cup sour cream or plain yogurt

1 teaspoon herbes de Provence

½ cup shredded Cheddar cheese

1. Preheat the oven to 400°F. Cover a jelly roll pan with parchment paper.
2. Sift the flour, baking powder, sugar, and salt together into a mixing bowl. Cut the butter into the mixture, using a pastry cutter or fork, until the mixture is crumbly.
3. Stir in the milk and sour cream just until combined. Fold in the herbes de Provence and cheese.
4. Roll into 2-inch balls and place on the jelly roll pan about 2 inches apart. Flatten lightly.
5. Bake for 10 to 15 minutes, until golden brown.
6. Cool on a rack and store in an airtight container.

chocolate chip scones

Makes 12

1¾ cups flour
4 teaspoons baking
   powder
⅓ cup sugar
⅛ teaspoon salt
5 tablespoons cold
   unsalted butter,
   cut into pieces
⅓ cup milk
¼ cup sour cream or
   plain yogurt
1 teaspoon vanilla extract
½ cup chocolate chips

1. Preheat the oven to 400°F. Cover a jelly roll pan with parchment paper.
2. Sift the flour, baking powder, sugar, and salt together into a mixing bowl. Cut the butter into the mixture, using a pastry cutter or fork, until the mixture is crumbly.
3. Stir in the milk, sour cream, and vanilla extract just until combined. Fold in the chocolate chips.
4. Roll into 2-inch balls and place on the jelly roll pan about 2 inches apart. Flatten lightly.
5. Bake for 10 to 15 minutes, until golden brown.
6. Cool on a rack and store in an airtight container.

cinnamon chip scones ▬

Makes 12

CINNAMON CHIPS
3 tablespoons sugar
1 tablespoon cinnamon
2 teaspoons unsalted
    butter
2 teaspoons honey

1¾ cups flour
4 teaspoons baking powder
⅓ cup sugar
⅛ teaspoon salt
5 tablespoons cold
    unsalted butter,
    cut into pieces
⅓ cup milk
¼ cup sour cream or
    plain yogurt
1 teaspoon vanilla extract

1. To make the cinnamon chips, preheat the oven to 250°F. Cover a jelly roll pan with aluminum foil.
2. In a bowl, combine the sugar, cinnamon, butter, and honey with a fork until crumbly and evenly blended. Spread onto the jelly roll pan. Bake for 30 to 40 minutes, until melted and bubbly. Cool completely on the pan. Break into small pieces.
3. Preheat the oven to 400°F. Cover a jelly roll pan with parchment paper.
4. Sift the flour, baking powder, sugar, and salt together into a mixing bowl. Cut the butter into the mixture, using a pastry cutter or fork, until the mixture is crumbly.
5. Stir in the milk, sour cream, and vanilla extract just until combined. Fold in the cinnamon chips.
6. Roll into 2-inch balls and place on the jelly roll pan about 2 inches apart. Flatten lightly.
7. Bake for 10 to 15 minutes, until golden brown.
8. Cool on a rack and store in an airtight container.

---

save a step

These cinnamon chips are super-good. However, if you don't have time to take that extra step, just add the extra sugar and cinnamon to the scone batter. The scones will still be cinnalicious!

lemon-apricot scones

Makes 12

2¼ cups flour

4 teaspoons baking
   powder

½ cup sugar

⅛ teaspoon salt

6 tablespoons (¾ stick)
   cold unsalted butter,
   cut into pieces

⅓ cup lemon juice

2 teaspoons grated lemon
   zest

¼ cup apricot preserves

½ cup sour cream or plain
   yogurt

1. Preheat the oven to 400°F. Cover a jelly roll pan with parchment paper.
2. Sift the flour, baking powder, sugar, and salt together into a mixing bowl. Cut the butter into the mixture, using a pastry cutter or fork, until the mixture is crumbly.
3. Stir in the lemon juice, lemon zest, apricot preserves, and sour cream just until combined.
4. Roll into 2-inch balls and place on the jelly roll pan about 2 inches apart. Flatten lightly.
5. Bake for 10 to 15 minutes, until golden brown.
6. Cool on a rack and store in an airtight container.

acknowledgments

The Stocked Kitchen would not be possible without the support and help of so many people. We are very thankful for all of you who have believed in this concept and extended, willingly, your time, talent, and love.

special thanks to:

Sue Beecham. We are forever grateful for your photos, kindness, and friendship. You are so very talented and such fun to work with. We will always fondly remember taste-testing cold "photo session" food with you and Jason.
Sue Beecham Photography, LLC
www.suebeechamphoto.com

Andrea Shepherd. Thank you so much for your willingness to help, particularly with recipe testing and product marketing. You are lovely and a joy.

Christi, Dawn, and Karen, our original testers. Thank you so much for your friendship, enthusiasm, and great ideas!

from sarah

To my children, who are the greatest happiness of my life, thank you both for your patience and love. To my parents, Sue and Norb, I am so thankful for all of your love, support, and hard work. This book would not exist without you. Mom and Grandma, thank you for teaching me that love is the most important ingredient in great cooking. To my brother, Pete, thank you for your support, guidance, and love. I am so grateful for you, Andrea, and my new little niece or nephew! To Christi and Megan, who, no matter how much time passes, are always there for me. Thank you for your input and encouragement. To my wonderful in-law family—Larry, Mary, Jack, Cheryl, Lando, and Lukus—for all your love, enthusiasm, and support. And to the love of my life, Larry, you are the best person I have ever known. I am thankful, every day, for you and the life we have created together.

from stacey

I live every day for my children and hope that I might inspire them. Thank you to Andrew and Charlie for teaching me, just as much as I teach you. To my friends and family, especially my parents, in-laws, and sisters, thank you all for your guidance, love, and support as I chase my dream. I could never have accomplished all of this without all of you. To my best friend, Karen, thank you for all your love, encouragement, and honesty. Our friendship is unwavering, and I am grateful for that. To my husband, Craig, thank you for believing in me and inspiring me to be a better person. I am always in awe of your patience and kindness, and I look forward to growing old together. I love you.

Last, to all the mothers before us who invented a better way to do something, you are our inspiration.

the stocked heart

For more information about this not-for-profit organization, go to
www.thestockedheart.org

index

ingredient index

f

Fennel seed, 115, 185, 276

Feta cheese, 56, 77, 85, 95, 106, 108, 140, 154, 174, 175, 182, 193, 230, 302

Flank steak, 45, 71, 88, 90, 91, 92, 93, 94, 95, 96, 97, 98, 99, 100, 101, 127, 128, 129, 140, 141, 142, 143, 144, 146, 147, 149, 150, 164, 179, 180, 181, 182, 183, 184, 185, 186, 187, 188, 189

Flour, 73, 74, 75, 76, 77, 117, 121, 127, 128, 139, 142, 144, 147, 149, 170, 181, 186, 191, 192, 199, 201, 228, 234, 238, 239, 240, 251, 252, 256, 257, 259, 266, 267, 268, 272, 273, 276, 277, 278, 281, 283, 299, 304, 305, 306, 307

Flour tortillas, 85, 86, 148, 168, 169, 188, 191, 198, 199, 202, 206, 209, 213, 284, 285

Food coloring, 258, 260

g

Garlic, 55, 57, 60, 80, 84, 91, 95, 106, 108, 115, 120, 122, 124, 126, 127, 130, 134, 138, 139, 140, 141, 142, 143, 147, 156, 157, 162, 163, 164, 169, 171, 172, 175, 181, 182, 184, 186, 187, 188, 189, 193, 194, 204, 205, 206, 208, 209, 210, 216, 224, 227, 235

Garlic powder, 57, 58, 61, 62, 70, 72, 74, 75, 76, 85, 91, 98, 101, 107, 109, 123, 132, 135, 149, 154, 177, 185, 191, 192, 193, 198, 199, 206, 213, 222, 226, 229, 232, 301

Ginger, 72, 74, 75, 79, 83, 84, 94, 106, 143, 158, 163, 164, 172, 175, 176, 186, 189, 206, 214, 225, 243, 257, 278

Gorgonzola cheese, 59, 71, 90, 96, 99, 100, 154, 166, 180, 190

Great Northern beans, 55, 108, 130, 215, 216

Green beans, 122, 170, 228, 232

Green olives, 64, 67, 73, 76, 85, 89, 154, 184, 193, 232

Green onions, 63, 68, 69, 70, 72, 74, 75, 78, 86, 88, 89, 90, 92, 93, 94, 98, 99, 100, 105, 106, 107, 108, 112, 129, 139, 143, 158, 191, 201, 205, 206, 223, 225, 235, 284

Grill seasoning, 53, 71, 137, 153, 173, 174, 179, 180, 182, 184, 187, 190, 200, 220, 221

Ground beef/turkey/chicken, 70, 122, 123, 138, 145, 146, 149, 154, 191, 192, 193, 194, 195, 196, 197, 198, 199

h

Ham, 77, 86, 91, 92, 93, 96, 97, 99, 100, 112, 121, 130, 148, 154, 167, 215, 222, 287, 288, 292, 301

Heavy cream, 125, 168, 202, 247, 248, 249, 261, 263, 264, 265, 272, 274, 298, 300, 301, 302, 303

Herbes de Provence, 61, 64, 68, 99, 110, 166, 181, 184, 193, 204, 235, 304

Honey, 72, 79, 96, 97, 101, 112, 115, 143, 155, 158, 162, 163, 164, 172, 173, 206, 210, 261, 298, 306

Horseradish, 64, 65, 68, 71, 180, 190, 208, 231

Hot sauce, *see* Tabasco/hot sauce

i

Italian seasoning, 95, 98, 106, 107, 122, 124, 126, 138, 142, 145, 150, 154, 162, 163, 194, 195

k

Kalamata olives, 64, 73, 76, 85, 89, 154, 184, 193, 232

Ketchup, 64, 71, 74, 83, 92, 109, 128, 190, 196, 197, 208, 214

Kidney beans, 100, 108, 122, 123, 126, 146, 213, 214

l

Lemon juice, 55, 62, 64, 68, 78, 85, 89, 91, 93,
  95, 96, 97, 98, 106, 107, 108, 112, 139, 140,
  143, 158, 162, 163, 164, 172, 173, 174, 184, 201,
  204, 207, 208, 210, 225, 228, 232, 242, 246,
  253, 287, 307
Lemons, 162, 232, 242, 253, 307
Lettuce, 63, 70, 71, 72, 88, 89, 90, 91, 92, 93, 94,
  95, 96, 97, 98, 99, 100, 101, 173, 194, 198, 199
Limes or lime juice, 26, 81, 102, 104, 146, 163,
  169, 188, 205, 209, 210, 244, 254

m

Mandarin oranges, 78, 94, 96, 106, 115, 227,
  254, 272
Maple syrup, 71, 190, 214, 231, 264, 293, 294,
  295, 296, 297
Mayonnaise, 61, 62, 66, 68, 69, 76, 91, 93, 94,
  97, 102, 103, 105, 106, 109, 110, 111, 112, 113,
  173, 175, 178, 194, 198, 201, 207, 208
Milk, 69, 91, 93, 97, 102, 103, 105, 117, 118, 121,
  129, 139, 141, 142, 143, 144, 147, 148, 173, 196,
  201, 203, 219, 220, 222, 223, 228, 229, 234,
  241, 243, 244, 245, 246, 249, 250, 252, 262,
  264, 265, 269, 282, 284, 288, 289, 290, 293,
  294, 295, 296, 297, 298, 300, 301, 302, 303,
  304, 305, 306
Mozzarella cheese, 60, 69, 73, 133, 138, 154,
  156, 157, 158, 159, 167, 168, 170, 171, 202, 222,
  302, 303
Mushrooms, 69, 70, 71, 75, 128, 138, 149, 154,
  159, 186, 190, 203, 206, 213, 302
Mustard, *see* Dijon mustard, Yellow
  mustard

n

Nutmeg, 61, 76, 105, 129, 139, 142, 144, 147, 198,
  229, 303

o

Olive oil, 55, 56, 58, 60, 64, 77, 78, 80, 81, 88, 89,
  90, 91, 95, 98, 99, 107, 108, 109, 115, 117, 118,
  120, 124, 125, 128, 134, 135, 140, 144, 145,
  150, 151, 152, 156, 157, 162, 163, 164, 165,
  166, 171, 179, 180, 181, 182, 183, 184, 186, 187,
  200, 212, 215, 216, 220, 221, 226, 228, 232,
  235, 286, 291, 292
Onion, dried minced, *see* Dried minced onion
Onions, 71, 78, 81, 88, 101, 109, 115, 118, 120,
  121, 122, 123, 124, 125, 126, 127, 128, 130,
  138, 140, 142, 145, 149, 154, 155, 157, 166,
  169, 176, 178, 181, 182, 186, 188, 189, 209,
  212, 214, 215, 216, 224, 226, 227, 280, 281,
  289, 292; *see also* Green onion

p

Pancake mix, 207, 296, 297, 298
Parmesan cheese, 56, 60, 69, 88, 89, 91, 98,
  118, 122, 132, 134, 138, 139, 141, 142, 144, 147,
  150, 154, 156, 157, 167, 171, 175, 187, 194, 216,
  222, 229, 233, 291, 303
Pasta, penne, 105, 106, 107, 108, 122, 138, 148,
  149
Pasta, thin, 106, 141, 142, 143, 144, 145, 146,
  147, 150
Peanut butter, 55, 59, 143, 158, 164, 172, 206,
  251, 259, 262, 265, 273
Peanuts, 59, 68, 79, 96, 175, 261, 263
Pears, 99, 101, 166, 257
Peas, 56, 63, 92, 93, 97, 105, 118, 141, 167, 170,
  175, 197, 227, 230, 231

recipe index

the
grocery
list

get more grocery lists

Go to www.thestockedkitchen.com for more information.

The Stocked Kitchen Grocery List

pantry

- ☐ applesauce
- ☐ apricot preserves
- ☐ artichoke hearts, marinated
- ☐ barbecue sauce
- ☐ beans, black (15 oz.)*
- ☐ beans, Great Northern/ cannellini (15 oz.)*
- ☐ beans, kidney (15 oz.)*
- ☐ bread crumbs, plain
- ☐ broth, beef (15 oz.)*
- ☐ broth, chicken (15 oz.)*
- ☐ coffee, regular and decaf
- ☐ corn (15 oz.)
- ☐ honey
- ☐ horseradish, prepared
- ☐ ketchup
- ☐ mandarin orange segments (10 oz.)*
- ☐ maple syrup
- ☐ mayonnaise
- ☐ mushrooms (4 oz.)*
- ☐ mustard, Dijon
- ☐ mustard, yellow
- ☐ olives, black (4 oz.)*
- ☐ olives, green or Kalamata
- ☐ pancake mix (not "complete")
- ☐ peanut butter, creamy
- ☐ pears (15 oz.)*
- ☐ pineapple, slices or chunks (20 oz.)*
- ☐ ranch or buttermilk dressing
- ☐ raspberry jam or jelly
- ☐ relish, sweet or dill
- ☐ Tabasco/hot sauce
- ☐ tomatoes, diced (15 oz.)*
- ☐ tomato paste (6 oz.)*
- ☐ tomato sauce (15 oz.)*
- ☐ vinegar, balsamic
- ☐ vinegar, red wine
- ☐ vinegar, white wine
- ☐ Worcestershire sauce

international

- ☐ egg noodles
- ☐ pasta, penne/rotini/ farfalle
- ☐ pasta, string
- ☐ rice, jasmine or brown
- ☐ roasted red peppers (jar)
- ☐ salsa
- ☐ soy sauce

snacks, crackers, and bread

- ☐ bread loaf, white or wheat
- ☐ butter crackers
- ☐ pita bread
- ☐ tortilla chips

spices

- ☐ aniseed or fennel seed
- ☐ black pepper
- ☐ chili powder
- ☐ cinnamon, ground
- ☐ cumin, ground
- ☐ curry powder
- ☐ dill weed
- ☐ garlic powder
- ☐ grill seasoning
- ☐ herbes de Provence
- ☐ Italian seasoning
- ☐ nutmeg, ground
- ☐ onion, dried minced
- ☐ poultry seasoning
- ☐ pumpkin pie spice
- ☐ red pepper flakes
- ☐ salt, table/sea salt

baking

- ☐ baking powder
- ☐ baking soda
- ☐ brownie mix (8 by 8-inch pan size)*
- ☐ cake mix, yellow
- ☐ chocolate chips, semisweet
- ☐ chocolate chips, white
- ☐ cocoa powder

- ☐ extract, almond
- ☐ extract, peppermint
- ☐ extract, vanilla
- ☐ flour, all-purpose
- ☐ food coloring
- ☐ nonstick spray
- ☐ nuts, almonds
- ☐ nuts, peanuts
- ☐ nuts, pecans
- ☐ oil, extra virgin olive
- ☐ oil, vegetable
- ☐ sugar, confectioners'
- ☐ sugar, granulated
- ☐ sugar, light brown

refrigerated

- ☐ butter, unsalted
- ☐ cheese, blue or Gorgonzola
- ☐ cheese, Cheddar
- ☐ cheese, feta
- ☐ cheese, mozzarella
- ☐ cheese, Parmesan
- ☐ cream cheese
- ☐ cream, heavy
- ☐ eggs (large)
- ☐ milk
- ☐ sour cream or plain yogurt
- ☐ tortillas, flour (8-inch fajita size)

freezer

- ☐ bread dough (loaf or ball)
- ☐ broccoli, chopped
- ☐ green beans, cut
- ☐ peas
- ☐ puff pastry sheets
- ☐ shrimp (raw)
- ☐ spinach (bag), chopped
- ☐ vanilla ice cream

meat, chicken, and seafood

- ☐ bacon
- ☐ bulk (ground) breakfast sausage

- ☐ chicken breast (boneless, skinless)
- ☐ chicken thighs (boneless, skinless)
- ☐ crabmeat, imitation or canned lump
- ☐ flank steak or skirt steak
- ☐ ground beef, turkey, or chicken
- ☐ ham, sliced or whole

produce

- ☐ apples
- ☐ basil, fresh
- ☐ bell pepper, red or green
- ☐ cabbage and carrot mix
- ☐ carrots
- ☐ celery
- ☐ cranberries, dried
- ☐ cucumber, English
- ☐ garlic cloves
- ☐ ginger, minced (tube or jar)
- ☐ green onions
- ☐ lemon juice
- ☐ lemons
- ☐ lettuce, head or mixed greens
- ☐ lime juice
- ☐ pine nuts
- ☐ potatoes, russet, sweet, Yukon Gold
- ☐ raisins
- ☐ shallots or onions
- ☐ tomatoes

other supplies

- ☐ aluminum foil
- ☐ parchment paper
- ☐ plastic wrap
- ☐ skewers, wooden
- ☐ storage bags, resealable gallon
- ☐ toothpicks

The Stocked Kitchen Grocery List

pantry

- [ ] applesauce
- [ ] apricot preserves
- [ ] artichoke hearts, marinated
- [ ] barbecue sauce
- [ ] beans, black (15 oz.)*
- [ ] beans, Great Northern/ cannellini (15 oz.)*
- [ ] beans, kidney (15 oz.)*
- [ ] bread crumbs, plain
- [ ] broth, beef (15 oz.)*
- [ ] broth, chicken (15 oz.)*
- [ ] coffee, regular and decaf
- [ ] corn (15 oz.)
- [ ] honey
- [ ] horseradish, prepared
- [ ] ketchup
- [ ] mandarin orange segments (10 oz.)*
- [ ] maple syrup
- [ ] mayonnaise
- [ ] mushrooms (4 oz.)*
- [ ] mustard, Dijon
- [ ] mustard, yellow
- [ ] olives, black (4 oz.)*
- [ ] olives, green or Kalamata
- [ ] pancake mix (not "complete")
- [ ] peanut butter, creamy
- [ ] pears (15 oz.)*
- [ ] pineapple, slices or chunks (20 oz.)*
- [ ] ranch or buttermilk dressing
- [ ] raspberry jam or jelly
- [ ] relish, sweet or dill
- [ ] Tabasco/hot sauce
- [ ] tomatoes, diced (15 oz.)*
- [ ] tomato paste (6 oz.)*
- [ ] tomato sauce (15 oz.)*
- [ ] vinegar, balsamic
- [ ] vinegar, red wine
- [ ] vinegar, white wine
- [ ] Worcestershire sauce

international

- [ ] egg noodles
- [ ] pasta, penne/rotini/ farfalle
- [ ] pasta, string
- [ ] rice, jasmine or brown
- [ ] roasted red peppers (jar)
- [ ] salsa
- [ ] soy sauce

snacks, crackers, and bread

- [ ] bread loaf, white or wheat
- [ ] butter crackers
- [ ] pita bread
- [ ] tortilla chips

spices

- [ ] aniseed or fennel seed
- [ ] black pepper
- [ ] chili powder
- [ ] cinnamon, ground
- [ ] cumin, ground
- [ ] curry powder
- [ ] dill weed
- [ ] garlic powder
- [ ] grill seasoning
- [ ] herbes de Provence
- [ ] Italian seasoning
- [ ] nutmeg, ground
- [ ] onion, dried minced
- [ ] poultry seasoning
- [ ] pumpkin pie spice
- [ ] red pepper flakes
- [ ] salt, table/sea salt

baking

- [ ] baking powder
- [ ] baking soda
- [ ] brownie mix (8 by 8-inch pan size)*
- [ ] cake mix, yellow
- [ ] chocolate chips, semisweet
- [ ] chocolate chips, white
- [ ] cocoa powder
- [ ] extract, almond
- [ ] extract, peppermint
- [ ] extract, vanilla
- [ ] flour, all-purpose
- [ ] food coloring
- [ ] nonstick spray
- [ ] nuts, almonds
- [ ] nuts, peanuts
- [ ] nuts, pecans
- [ ] oil, extra virgin olive
- [ ] oil, vegetable
- [ ] sugar, confectioners'
- [ ] sugar, granulated
- [ ] sugar, light brown

refrigerated

- [ ] butter, unsalted
- [ ] cheese, blue or Gorgonzola
- [ ] cheese, Cheddar
- [ ] cheese, feta
- [ ] cheese, mozzarella
- [ ] cheese, Parmesan
- [ ] cream cheese
- [ ] cream, heavy
- [ ] eggs (large)
- [ ] milk
- [ ] sour cream or plain yogurt
- [ ] tortillas, flour (8-inch fajita size)

freezer

- [ ] bread dough (loaf or ball)
- [ ] broccoli, chopped
- [ ] green beans, cut
- [ ] peas
- [ ] puff pastry sheets
- [ ] shrimp (raw)
- [ ] spinach (bag), chopped
- [ ] vanilla ice cream

meat, chicken, and seafood

- [ ] bacon
- [ ] bulk (ground) breakfast sausage
- [ ] chicken breast (boneless, skinless)
- [ ] chicken thighs (boneless, skinless)
- [ ] crabmeat, imitation or canned lump
- [ ] flank steak or skirt steak
- [ ] ground beef, turkey, or chicken
- [ ] ham, sliced or whole

produce

- [ ] apples
- [ ] basil, fresh
- [ ] bell pepper, red or green
- [ ] cabbage and carrot mix
- [ ] carrots
- [ ] celery
- [ ] cranberries, dried
- [ ] cucumber, English
- [ ] garlic cloves
- [ ] ginger, minced (tube or jar)
- [ ] green onions
- [ ] lemon juice
- [ ] lemons
- [ ] lettuce, head or mixed greens
- [ ] lime juice
- [ ] pine nuts
- [ ] potatoes, russet, sweet, Yukon Gold
- [ ] raisins
- [ ] shallots or onions
- [ ] tomatoes

other supplies

- [ ] aluminum foil
- [ ] parchment paper
- [ ] plastic wrap
- [ ] skewers, wooden
- [ ] storage bags, resealable gallon
- [ ] toothpicks

The Stocked Kitchen Grocery List

pantry

- [ ] applesauce
- [ ] apricot preserves
- [ ] artichoke hearts, marinated
- [ ] barbecue sauce
- [ ] beans, black (15 oz.)*
- [ ] beans, Great Northern/ cannellini (15 oz.)*
- [ ] beans, kidney (15 oz.)*
- [ ] bread crumbs, plain
- [ ] broth, beef (15 oz.)*
- [ ] broth, chicken (15 oz.)*
- [ ] coffee, regular and decaf
- [ ] corn (15 oz.)
- [ ] honey
- [ ] horseradish, prepared
- [ ] ketchup
- [ ] mandarin orange segments (10 oz.)*
- [ ] maple syrup
- [ ] mayonnaise
- [ ] mushrooms (4 oz.)*
- [ ] mustard, Dijon
- [ ] mustard, yellow
- [ ] olives, black (4 oz.)*
- [ ] olives, green or Kalamata
- [ ] pancake mix (not "complete")
- [ ] peanut butter, creamy
- [ ] pears (15 oz.)*
- [ ] pineapple, slices or chunks (20 oz.)*
- [ ] ranch or buttermilk dressing
- [ ] raspberry jam or jelly
- [ ] relish, sweet or dill
- [ ] Tabasco/hot sauce
- [ ] tomatoes, diced (15 oz.)*
- [ ] tomato paste (6 oz.)*
- [ ] tomato sauce (15 oz.)*
- [ ] vinegar, balsamic
- [ ] vinegar, red wine
- [ ] vinegar, white wine
- [ ] Worcestershire sauce

international

- [ ] egg noodles
- [ ] pasta, penne/rotini/ farfalle
- [ ] pasta, string
- [ ] rice, jasmine or brown
- [ ] roasted red peppers (jar)
- [ ] salsa
- [ ] soy sauce

snacks, crackers, and bread

- [ ] bread loaf, white or wheat
- [ ] butter crackers
- [ ] pita bread
- [ ] tortilla chips

spices

- [ ] aniseed or fennel seed
- [ ] black pepper
- [ ] chili powder
- [ ] cinnamon, ground
- [ ] cumin, ground
- [ ] curry powder
- [ ] dill weed
- [ ] garlic powder
- [ ] grill seasoning
- [ ] herbes de Provence
- [ ] Italian seasoning
- [ ] nutmeg, ground
- [ ] onion, dried minced
- [ ] poultry seasoning
- [ ] pumpkin pie spice
- [ ] red pepper flakes
- [ ] salt, table/sea salt

baking

- [ ] baking powder
- [ ] baking soda
- [ ] brownie mix (8 by 8-inch pan size)*
- [ ] cake mix, yellow
- [ ] chocolate chips, semisweet
- [ ] chocolate chips, white
- [ ] cocoa powder
- [ ] extract, almond
- [ ] extract, peppermint
- [ ] extract, vanilla
- [ ] flour, all-purpose
- [ ] food coloring
- [ ] nonstick spray
- [ ] nuts, almonds
- [ ] nuts, peanuts
- [ ] nuts, pecans
- [ ] oil, extra virgin olive
- [ ] oil, vegetable
- [ ] sugar, confectioners'
- [ ] sugar, granulated
- [ ] sugar, light brown

refrigerated

- [ ] butter, unsalted
- [ ] cheese, blue or Gorgonzola
- [ ] cheese, Cheddar
- [ ] cheese, feta
- [ ] cheese, mozzarella
- [ ] cheese, Parmesan
- [ ] cream cheese
- [ ] cream, heavy
- [ ] eggs (large)
- [ ] milk
- [ ] sour cream or plain yogurt
- [ ] tortillas, flour (8-inch fajita size)

freezer

- [ ] bread dough (loaf or ball)
- [ ] broccoli, chopped
- [ ] green beans, cut
- [ ] peas
- [ ] puff pastry sheets
- [ ] shrimp (raw)
- [ ] spinach (bag), chopped
- [ ] vanilla ice cream

meat, chicken, and seafood

- [ ] bacon
- [ ] bulk (ground) breakfast sausage
- [ ] chicken breast (boneless, skinless)
- [ ] chicken thighs (boneless, skinless)
- [ ] crabmeat, imitation or canned lump
- [ ] flank steak or skirt steak
- [ ] ground beef, turkey, or chicken
- [ ] ham, sliced or whole

produce

- [ ] apples
- [ ] basil, fresh
- [ ] bell pepper, red or green
- [ ] cabbage and carrot mix
- [ ] carrots
- [ ] celery
- [ ] cranberries, dried
- [ ] cucumber, English
- [ ] garlic cloves
- [ ] ginger, minced (tube or jar)
- [ ] green onions
- [ ] lemon juice
- [ ] lemons
- [ ] lettuce, head or mixed greens
- [ ] lime juice
- [ ] pine nuts
- [ ] potatoes, russet, sweet, Yukon Gold
- [ ] raisins
- [ ] shallots or onions
- [ ] tomatoes

other supplies

- [ ] aluminum foil
- [ ] parchment paper
- [ ] plastic wrap
- [ ] skewers, wooden
- [ ] storage bags, resealable gallon
- [ ] toothpicks

The Stocked Kitchen Grocery List

pantry

- [ ] applesauce
- [ ] apricot preserves
- [ ] artichoke hearts, marinated
- [ ] barbecue sauce
- [ ] beans, black (15 oz.)*
- [ ] beans, Great Northern/ cannellini (15 oz.)*
- [ ] beans, kidney (15 oz.)*
- [ ] bread crumbs, plain
- [ ] broth, beef (15 oz.)*
- [ ] broth, chicken (15 oz.)*
- [ ] coffee, regular and decaf
- [ ] corn (15 oz.)
- [ ] honey
- [ ] horseradish, prepared
- [ ] ketchup
- [ ] mandarin orange segments (10 oz.)*
- [ ] maple syrup
- [ ] mayonnaise
- [ ] mushrooms (4 oz.)*
- [ ] mustard, Dijon
- [ ] mustard, yellow
- [ ] olives, black (4 oz.)*
- [ ] olives, green or Kalamata
- [ ] pancake mix (not "complete")
- [ ] peanut butter, creamy
- [ ] pears (15 oz.)*
- [ ] pineapple, slices or chunks (20 oz.)*
- [ ] ranch or buttermilk dressing
- [ ] raspberry jam or jelly
- [ ] relish, sweet or dill
- [ ] Tabasco/hot sauce
- [ ] tomatoes, diced (15 oz.)*
- [ ] tomato paste (6 oz.)*
- [ ] tomato sauce (15 oz.)*
- [ ] vinegar, balsamic
- [ ] vinegar, red wine
- [ ] vinegar, white wine
- [ ] Worcestershire sauce

international

- [ ] egg noodles
- [ ] pasta, penne/rotini/ farfalle
- [ ] pasta, string
- [ ] rice, jasmine or brown
- [ ] roasted red peppers (jar)
- [ ] salsa
- [ ] soy sauce

snacks, crackers, and bread

- [ ] bread loaf, white or wheat
- [ ] butter crackers
- [ ] pita bread
- [ ] tortilla chips

spices

- [ ] aniseed or fennel seed
- [ ] black pepper
- [ ] chili powder
- [ ] cinnamon, ground
- [ ] cumin, ground
- [ ] curry powder
- [ ] dill weed
- [ ] garlic powder
- [ ] grill seasoning
- [ ] herbes de Provence
- [ ] Italian seasoning
- [ ] nutmeg, ground
- [ ] onion, dried minced
- [ ] poultry seasoning
- [ ] pumpkin pie spice
- [ ] red pepper flakes
- [ ] salt, table/sea salt

baking

- [ ] baking powder
- [ ] baking soda
- [ ] brownie mix (8 by 8-inch pan size)*
- [ ] cake mix, yellow
- [ ] chocolate chips, semisweet
- [ ] chocolate chips, white
- [ ] cocoa powder
- [ ] extract, almond
- [ ] extract, peppermint
- [ ] extract, vanilla
- [ ] flour, all-purpose
- [ ] food coloring
- [ ] nonstick spray
- [ ] nuts, almonds
- [ ] nuts, peanuts
- [ ] nuts, pecans
- [ ] oil, extra virgin olive
- [ ] oil, vegetable
- [ ] sugar, confectioners'
- [ ] sugar, granulated
- [ ] sugar, light brown

refrigerated

- [ ] butter, unsalted
- [ ] cheese, blue or Gorgonzola
- [ ] cheese, Cheddar
- [ ] cheese, feta
- [ ] cheese, mozzarella
- [ ] cheese, Parmesan
- [ ] cream cheese
- [ ] cream, heavy
- [ ] eggs (large)
- [ ] milk
- [ ] sour cream or plain yogurt
- [ ] tortillas, flour (8-inch fajita size)

freezer

- [ ] bread dough (loaf or ball)
- [ ] broccoli, chopped
- [ ] green beans, cut
- [ ] peas
- [ ] puff pastry sheets
- [ ] shrimp (raw)
- [ ] spinach (bag), chopped
- [ ] vanilla ice cream

meat, chicken, and seafood

- [ ] bacon
- [ ] bulk (ground) breakfast sausage
- [ ] chicken breast (boneless, skinless)
- [ ] chicken thighs (boneless, skinless)
- [ ] crabmeat, imitation or canned lump
- [ ] flank steak or skirt steak
- [ ] ground beef, turkey, or chicken
- [ ] ham, sliced or whole

produce

- [ ] apples
- [ ] basil, fresh
- [ ] bell pepper, red or green
- [ ] cabbage and carrot mix
- [ ] carrots
- [ ] celery
- [ ] cranberries, dried
- [ ] cucumber, English
- [ ] garlic cloves
- [ ] ginger, minced (tube or jar)
- [ ] green onions
- [ ] lemon juice
- [ ] lemons
- [ ] lettuce, head or mixed greens
- [ ] lime juice
- [ ] pine nuts
- [ ] potatoes, russet, sweet, Yukon Gold
- [ ] raisins
- [ ] shallots or onions
- [ ] tomatoes

other supplies

- [ ] aluminum foil
- [ ] parchment paper
- [ ] plastic wrap
- [ ] skewers, wooden
- [ ] storage bags, resealable gallon
- [ ] toothpicks

The Stocked Kitchen Grocery List

pantry

- ☐ applesauce
- ☐ apricot preserves
- ☐ artichoke hearts, marinated
- ☐ barbecue sauce
- ☐ beans, black (15 oz.)*
- ☐ beans, Great Northern/ cannellini (15 oz.)*
- ☐ beans, kidney (15 oz.)*
- ☐ bread crumbs, plain
- ☐ broth, beef (15 oz.)*
- ☐ broth, chicken (15 oz.)*
- ☐ coffee, regular and decaf
- ☐ corn (15 oz.)
- ☐ honey
- ☐ horseradish, prepared
- ☐ ketchup
- ☐ mandarin orange segments (10 oz.)*
- ☐ maple syrup
- ☐ mayonnaise
- ☐ mushrooms (4 oz.)*
- ☐ mustard, Dijon
- ☐ mustard, yellow
- ☐ olives, black (4 oz.)*
- ☐ olives, green or Kalamata
- ☐ pancake mix (not "complete")
- ☐ peanut butter, creamy
- ☐ pears (15 oz.)*
- ☐ pineapple, slices or chunks (20 oz.)*
- ☐ ranch or buttermilk dressing
- ☐ raspberry jam or jelly
- ☐ relish, sweet or dill
- ☐ Tabasco/hot sauce
- ☐ tomatoes, diced (15 oz.)*
- ☐ tomato paste (6 oz.)*
- ☐ tomato sauce (15 oz.)*
- ☐ vinegar, balsamic
- ☐ vinegar, red wine
- ☐ vinegar, white wine
- ☐ Worcestershire sauce

international

- ☐ egg noodles
- ☐ pasta, penne/rotini/ farfalle
- ☐ pasta, string
- ☐ rice, jasmine or brown
- ☐ roasted red peppers (jar)
- ☐ salsa
- ☐ soy sauce

snacks, crackers, and bread

- ☐ bread loaf, white or wheat
- ☐ butter crackers
- ☐ pita bread
- ☐ tortilla chips

spices

- ☐ aniseed or fennel seed
- ☐ black pepper
- ☐ chili powder
- ☐ cinnamon, ground
- ☐ cumin, ground
- ☐ curry powder
- ☐ dill weed
- ☐ garlic powder
- ☐ grill seasoning
- ☐ herbes de Provence
- ☐ Italian seasoning
- ☐ nutmeg, ground
- ☐ onion, dried minced
- ☐ poultry seasoning
- ☐ pumpkin pie spice
- ☐ red pepper flakes
- ☐ salt, table/sea salt

baking

- ☐ baking powder
- ☐ baking soda
- ☐ brownie mix (8 by 8-inch pan size)*
- ☐ cake mix, yellow
- ☐ chocolate chips, semisweet
- ☐ chocolate chips, white
- ☐ cocoa powder
- ☐ extract, almond
- ☐ extract, peppermint
- ☐ extract, vanilla
- ☐ flour, all-purpose
- ☐ food coloring
- ☐ nonstick spray
- ☐ nuts, almonds
- ☐ nuts, peanuts
- ☐ nuts, pecans
- ☐ oil, extra virgin olive
- ☐ oil, vegetable
- ☐ sugar, confectioners'
- ☐ sugar, granulated
- ☐ sugar, light brown

refrigerated

- ☐ butter, unsalted
- ☐ cheese, blue or Gorgonzola
- ☐ cheese, Cheddar
- ☐ cheese, feta
- ☐ cheese, mozzarella
- ☐ cheese, Parmesan
- ☐ cream cheese
- ☐ cream, heavy
- ☐ eggs (large)
- ☐ milk
- ☐ sour cream or plain yogurt
- ☐ tortillas, flour (8-inch fajita size)

freezer

- ☐ bread dough (loaf or ball)
- ☐ broccoli, chopped
- ☐ green beans, cut
- ☐ peas
- ☐ puff pastry sheets
- ☐ shrimp (raw)
- ☐ spinach (bag), chopped
- ☐ vanilla ice cream

meat, chicken, and seafood

- ☐ bacon
- ☐ bulk (ground) breakfast sausage
- ☐ chicken breast (boneless, skinless)
- ☐ chicken thighs (boneless, skinless)
- ☐ crabmeat, imitation or canned lump
- ☐ flank steak or skirt steak
- ☐ ground beef, turkey, or chicken
- ☐ ham, sliced or whole

produce

- ☐ apples
- ☐ basil, fresh
- ☐ bell pepper, red or green
- ☐ cabbage and carrot mix
- ☐ carrots
- ☐ celery
- ☐ cranberries, dried
- ☐ cucumber, English
- ☐ garlic cloves
- ☐ ginger, minced (tube or jar)
- ☐ green onions
- ☐ lemon juice
- ☐ lemons
- ☐ lettuce, head or mixed greens
- ☐ lime juice
- ☐ pine nuts
- ☐ potatoes, russet, sweet, Yukon Gold
- ☐ raisins
- ☐ shallots or onions
- ☐ tomatoes

other supplies

- ☐ aluminum foil
- ☐ parchment paper
- ☐ plastic wrap
- ☐ skewers, wooden
- ☐ storage bags, resealable gallon
- ☐ toothpicks

The Stocked Kitchen Grocery List

pantry

- ☐ applesauce
- ☐ apricot preserves
- ☐ artichoke hearts, marinated
- ☐ barbecue sauce
- ☐ beans, black (15 oz.)*
- ☐ beans, Great Northern/ cannellini (15 oz.)*
- ☐ beans, kidney (15 oz.)*
- ☐ bread crumbs, plain
- ☐ broth, beef (15 oz.)*
- ☐ broth, chicken (15 oz.)*
- ☐ coffee, regular and decaf
- ☐ corn (15 oz.)
- ☐ honey
- ☐ horseradish, prepared
- ☐ ketchup
- ☐ mandarin orange segments (10 oz.)*
- ☐ maple syrup
- ☐ mayonnaise
- ☐ mushrooms (4 oz.)*
- ☐ mustard, Dijon
- ☐ mustard, yellow
- ☐ olives, black (4 oz.)*
- ☐ olives, green or Kalamata
- ☐ pancake mix (not "complete")
- ☐ peanut butter, creamy
- ☐ pears (15 oz.)*
- ☐ pineapple, slices or chunks (20 oz.)*
- ☐ ranch or buttermilk dressing
- ☐ raspberry jam or jelly
- ☐ relish, sweet or dill
- ☐ Tabasco/hot sauce
- ☐ tomatoes, diced (15 oz.)*
- ☐ tomato paste (6 oz.)*
- ☐ tomato sauce (15 oz.)*
- ☐ vinegar, balsamic
- ☐ vinegar, red wine
- ☐ vinegar, white wine
- ☐ Worcestershire sauce

international

- ☐ egg noodles
- ☐ pasta, penne/rotini/ farfalle
- ☐ pasta, string
- ☐ rice, jasmine or brown
- ☐ roasted red peppers (jar)
- ☐ salsa
- ☐ soy sauce

snacks, crackers, and bread

- ☐ bread loaf, white or wheat
- ☐ butter crackers
- ☐ pita bread
- ☐ tortilla chips

spices

- ☐ aniseed or fennel seed
- ☐ black pepper
- ☐ chili powder
- ☐ cinnamon, ground
- ☐ cumin, ground
- ☐ curry powder
- ☐ dill weed
- ☐ garlic powder
- ☐ grill seasoning
- ☐ herbes de Provence
- ☐ Italian seasoning
- ☐ nutmeg, ground
- ☐ onion, dried minced
- ☐ poultry seasoning
- ☐ pumpkin pie spice
- ☐ red pepper flakes
- ☐ salt, table/sea salt

baking

- ☐ baking powder
- ☐ baking soda
- ☐ brownie mix (8 by 8-inch pan size)*
- ☐ cake mix, yellow
- ☐ chocolate chips, semisweet
- ☐ chocolate chips, white
- ☐ cocoa powder

- ☐ extract, almond
- ☐ extract, peppermint
- ☐ extract, vanilla
- ☐ flour, all-purpose
- ☐ food coloring
- ☐ nonstick spray
- ☐ nuts, almonds
- ☐ nuts, peanuts
- ☐ nuts, pecans
- ☐ oil, extra virgin olive
- ☐ oil, vegetable
- ☐ sugar, confectioners'
- ☐ sugar, granulated
- ☐ sugar, light brown

refrigerated

- ☐ butter, unsalted
- ☐ cheese, blue or Gorgonzola
- ☐ cheese, Cheddar
- ☐ cheese, feta
- ☐ cheese, mozzarella
- ☐ cheese, Parmesan
- ☐ cream cheese
- ☐ cream, heavy
- ☐ eggs (large)
- ☐ milk
- ☐ sour cream or plain yogurt
- ☐ tortillas, flour (8-inch fajita size)

freezer

- ☐ bread dough (loaf or ball)
- ☐ broccoli, chopped
- ☐ green beans, cut
- ☐ peas
- ☐ puff pastry sheets
- ☐ shrimp (raw)
- ☐ spinach (bag), chopped
- ☐ vanilla ice cream

meat, chicken, and seafood

- ☐ bacon
- ☐ bulk (ground) breakfast sausage

- ☐ chicken breast (boneless, skinless)
- ☐ chicken thighs (boneless, skinless)
- ☐ crabmeat, imitation or canned lump
- ☐ flank steak or skirt steak
- ☐ ground beef, turkey, or chicken
- ☐ ham, sliced or whole

produce

- ☐ apples
- ☐ basil, fresh
- ☐ bell pepper, red or green
- ☐ cabbage and carrot mix
- ☐ carrots
- ☐ celery
- ☐ cranberries, dried
- ☐ cucumber, English
- ☐ garlic cloves
- ☐ ginger, minced (tube or jar)
- ☐ green onions
- ☐ lemon juice
- ☐ lemons
- ☐ lettuce, head or mixed greens
- ☐ lime juice
- ☐ pine nuts
- ☐ potatoes, russet, sweet, Yukon Gold
- ☐ raisins
- ☐ shallots or onions
- ☐ tomatoes

other supplies

- ☐ aluminum foil
- ☐ parchment paper
- ☐ plastic wrap
- ☐ skewers, wooden
- ☐ storage bags, resealable gallon
- ☐ toothpicks

The Stocked Kitchen Grocery List

pantry

- [ ] applesauce
- [ ] apricot preserves
- [ ] artichoke hearts, marinated
- [ ] barbecue sauce
- [ ] beans, black (15 oz.)*
- [ ] beans, Great Northern/ cannellini (15 oz.)*
- [ ] beans, kidney (15 oz.)*
- [ ] bread crumbs, plain
- [ ] broth, beef (15 oz.)*
- [ ] broth, chicken (15 oz.)*
- [ ] coffee, regular and decaf
- [ ] corn (15 oz.)
- [ ] honey
- [ ] horseradish, prepared
- [ ] ketchup
- [ ] mandarin orange segments (10 oz.)*
- [ ] maple syrup
- [ ] mayonnaise
- [ ] mushrooms (4 oz.)*
- [ ] mustard, Dijon
- [ ] mustard, yellow
- [ ] olives, black (4 oz.)*
- [ ] olives, green or Kalamata
- [ ] pancake mix (not "complete")
- [ ] peanut butter, creamy
- [ ] pears (15 oz.)*
- [ ] pineapple, slices or chunks (20 oz.)*
- [ ] ranch or buttermilk dressing
- [ ] raspberry jam or jelly
- [ ] relish, sweet or dill
- [ ] Tabasco/hot sauce
- [ ] tomatoes, diced (15 oz.)*
- [ ] tomato paste (6 oz.)*
- [ ] tomato sauce (15 oz.)*
- [ ] vinegar, balsamic
- [ ] vinegar, red wine
- [ ] vinegar, white wine
- [ ] Worcestershire sauce

international

- [ ] egg noodles
- [ ] pasta, penne/rotini/ farfalle
- [ ] pasta, string
- [ ] rice, jasmine or brown
- [ ] roasted red peppers (jar)
- [ ] salsa
- [ ] soy sauce

snacks, crackers, and bread

- [ ] bread loaf, white or wheat
- [ ] butter crackers
- [ ] pita bread
- [ ] tortilla chips

spices

- [ ] aniseed or fennel seed
- [ ] black pepper
- [ ] chili powder
- [ ] cinnamon, ground
- [ ] cumin, ground
- [ ] curry powder
- [ ] dill weed
- [ ] garlic powder
- [ ] grill seasoning
- [ ] herbes de Provence
- [ ] Italian seasoning
- [ ] nutmeg, ground
- [ ] onion, dried minced
- [ ] poultry seasoning
- [ ] pumpkin pie spice
- [ ] red pepper flakes
- [ ] salt, table/sea salt

baking

- [ ] baking powder
- [ ] baking soda
- [ ] brownie mix (8 by 8-inch pan size)*
- [ ] cake mix, yellow
- [ ] chocolate chips, semisweet
- [ ] chocolate chips, white
- [ ] cocoa powder
- [ ] extract, almond
- [ ] extract, peppermint
- [ ] extract, vanilla
- [ ] flour, all-purpose
- [ ] food coloring
- [ ] nonstick spray
- [ ] nuts, almonds
- [ ] nuts, peanuts
- [ ] nuts, pecans
- [ ] oil, extra virgin olive
- [ ] oil, vegetable
- [ ] sugar, confectioners'
- [ ] sugar, granulated
- [ ] sugar, light brown

refrigerated

- [ ] butter, unsalted
- [ ] cheese, blue or Gorgonzola
- [ ] cheese, Cheddar
- [ ] cheese, feta
- [ ] cheese, mozzarella
- [ ] cheese, Parmesan
- [ ] cream cheese
- [ ] cream, heavy
- [ ] eggs (large)
- [ ] milk
- [ ] sour cream or plain yogurt
- [ ] tortillas, flour (8-inch fajita size)

freezer

- [ ] bread dough (loaf or ball)
- [ ] broccoli, chopped
- [ ] green beans, cut
- [ ] peas
- [ ] puff pastry sheets
- [ ] shrimp (raw)
- [ ] spinach (bag), chopped
- [ ] vanilla ice cream

meat, chicken, and seafood

- [ ] bacon
- [ ] bulk (ground) breakfast sausage
- [ ] chicken breast (boneless, skinless)
- [ ] chicken thighs (boneless, skinless)
- [ ] crabmeat, imitation or canned lump
- [ ] flank steak or skirt steak
- [ ] ground beef, turkey, or chicken
- [ ] ham, sliced or whole

produce

- [ ] apples
- [ ] basil, fresh
- [ ] bell pepper, red or green
- [ ] cabbage and carrot mix
- [ ] carrots
- [ ] celery
- [ ] cranberries, dried
- [ ] cucumber, English
- [ ] garlic cloves
- [ ] ginger, minced (tube or jar)
- [ ] green onions
- [ ] lemon juice
- [ ] lemons
- [ ] lettuce, head or mixed greens
- [ ] lime juice
- [ ] pine nuts
- [ ] potatoes, russet, sweet, Yukon Gold
- [ ] raisins
- [ ] shallots or onions
- [ ] tomatoes

other supplies

- [ ] aluminum foil
- [ ] parchment paper
- [ ] plastic wrap
- [ ] skewers, wooden
- [ ] storage bags, resealable gallon
- [ ] toothpicks

The Stocked Kitchen Grocery List

pantry

- [ ] applesauce
- [ ] apricot preserves
- [ ] artichoke hearts, marinated
- [ ] barbecue sauce
- [ ] beans, black (15 oz.)*
- [ ] beans, Great Northern/ cannellini (15 oz.)*
- [ ] beans, kidney (15 oz.)*
- [ ] bread crumbs, plain
- [ ] broth, beef (15 oz.)*
- [ ] broth, chicken (15 oz.)*
- [ ] coffee, regular and decaf
- [ ] corn (15 oz.)
- [ ] honey
- [ ] horseradish, prepared
- [ ] ketchup
- [ ] mandarin orange segments (10 oz.)*
- [ ] maple syrup
- [ ] mayonnaise
- [ ] mushrooms (4 oz.)*
- [ ] mustard, Dijon
- [ ] mustard, yellow
- [ ] olives, black (4 oz.)*
- [ ] olives, green or Kalamata
- [ ] pancake mix (not "complete")
- [ ] peanut butter, creamy
- [ ] pears (15 oz.)*
- [ ] pineapple, slices or chunks (20 oz.)*
- [ ] ranch or buttermilk dressing
- [ ] raspberry jam or jelly
- [ ] relish, sweet or dill
- [ ] Tabasco/hot sauce
- [ ] tomatoes, diced (15 oz.)*
- [ ] tomato paste (6 oz.)*
- [ ] tomato sauce (15 oz.)*
- [ ] vinegar, balsamic
- [ ] vinegar, red wine
- [ ] vinegar, white wine
- [ ] Worcestershire sauce

international

- [ ] egg noodles
- [ ] pasta, penne/rotini/ farfalle
- [ ] pasta, string
- [ ] rice, jasmine or brown
- [ ] roasted red peppers (jar)
- [ ] salsa
- [ ] soy sauce

snacks, crackers, and bread

- [ ] bread loaf, white or wheat
- [ ] butter crackers
- [ ] pita bread
- [ ] tortilla chips

spices

- [ ] aniseed or fennel seed
- [ ] black pepper
- [ ] chili powder
- [ ] cinnamon, ground
- [ ] cumin, ground
- [ ] curry powder
- [ ] dill weed
- [ ] garlic powder
- [ ] grill seasoning
- [ ] herbes de Provence
- [ ] Italian seasoning
- [ ] nutmeg, ground
- [ ] onion, dried minced
- [ ] poultry seasoning
- [ ] pumpkin pie spice
- [ ] red pepper flakes
- [ ] salt, table/sea salt

baking

- [ ] baking powder
- [ ] baking soda
- [ ] brownie mix (8 by 8-inch pan size)*
- [ ] cake mix, yellow
- [ ] chocolate chips, semisweet
- [ ] chocolate chips, white
- [ ] cocoa powder
- [ ] extract, almond
- [ ] extract, peppermint
- [ ] extract, vanilla
- [ ] flour, all-purpose
- [ ] food coloring
- [ ] nonstick spray
- [ ] nuts, almonds
- [ ] nuts, peanuts
- [ ] nuts, pecans
- [ ] oil, extra virgin olive
- [ ] oil, vegetable
- [ ] sugar, confectioners'
- [ ] sugar, granulated
- [ ] sugar, light brown

refrigerated

- [ ] butter, unsalted
- [ ] cheese, blue or Gorgonzola
- [ ] cheese, Cheddar
- [ ] cheese, feta
- [ ] cheese, mozzarella
- [ ] cheese, Parmesan
- [ ] cream cheese
- [ ] cream, heavy
- [ ] eggs (large)
- [ ] milk
- [ ] sour cream or plain yogurt
- [ ] tortillas, flour (8-inch fajita size)

freezer

- [ ] bread dough (loaf or ball)
- [ ] broccoli, chopped
- [ ] green beans, cut
- [ ] peas
- [ ] puff pastry sheets
- [ ] shrimp (raw)
- [ ] spinach (bag), chopped
- [ ] vanilla ice cream

meat, chicken, and seafood

- [ ] bacon
- [ ] bulk (ground) breakfast sausage
- [ ] chicken breast (boneless, skinless)
- [ ] chicken thighs (boneless, skinless)
- [ ] crabmeat, imitation or canned lump
- [ ] flank steak or skirt steak
- [ ] ground beef, turkey, or chicken
- [ ] ham, sliced or whole

produce

- [ ] apples
- [ ] basil, fresh
- [ ] bell pepper, red or green
- [ ] cabbage and carrot mix
- [ ] carrots
- [ ] celery
- [ ] cranberries, dried
- [ ] cucumber, English
- [ ] garlic cloves
- [ ] ginger, minced (tube or jar)
- [ ] green onions
- [ ] lemon juice
- [ ] lemons
- [ ] lettuce, head or mixed greens
- [ ] lime juice
- [ ] pine nuts
- [ ] potatoes, russet, sweet, Yukon Gold
- [ ] raisins
- [ ] shallots or onions
- [ ] tomatoes

other supplies

- [ ] aluminum foil
- [ ] parchment paper
- [ ] plastic wrap
- [ ] skewers, wooden
- [ ] storage bags, resealable gallon
- [ ] toothpicks

* approximate sizes

www.thestockedkitchen.com

The Stocked Kitchen Grocery List

pantry

- [ ] applesauce
- [ ] apricot preserves
- [ ] artichoke hearts, marinated
- [ ] barbecue sauce
- [ ] beans, black (15 oz.)*
- [ ] beans, Great Northern/ cannellini (15 oz.)*
- [ ] beans, kidney (15 oz.)*
- [ ] bread crumbs, plain
- [ ] broth, beef (15 oz.)*
- [ ] broth, chicken (15 oz.)*
- [ ] coffee, regular and decaf
- [ ] corn (15 oz.)
- [ ] honey
- [ ] horseradish, prepared
- [ ] ketchup
- [ ] mandarin orange segments (10 oz.)*
- [ ] maple syrup
- [ ] mayonnaise
- [ ] mushrooms (4 oz.)*
- [ ] mustard, Dijon
- [ ] mustard, yellow
- [ ] olives, black (4 oz.)*
- [ ] olives, green or Kalamata
- [ ] pancake mix (not "complete")
- [ ] peanut butter, creamy
- [ ] pears (15 oz.)*
- [ ] pineapple, slices or chunks (20 oz.)*
- [ ] ranch or buttermilk dressing
- [ ] raspberry jam or jelly
- [ ] relish, sweet or dill
- [ ] Tabasco/hot sauce
- [ ] tomatoes, diced (15 oz.)*
- [ ] tomato paste (6 oz.)*
- [ ] tomato sauce (15 oz.)*
- [ ] vinegar, balsamic
- [ ] vinegar, red wine
- [ ] vinegar, white wine
- [ ] Worcestershire sauce

international

- [ ] egg noodles
- [ ] pasta, penne/rotini/ farfalle
- [ ] pasta, string
- [ ] rice, jasmine or brown
- [ ] roasted red peppers (jar)
- [ ] salsa
- [ ] soy sauce

snacks, crackers, and bread

- [ ] bread loaf, white or wheat
- [ ] butter crackers
- [ ] pita bread
- [ ] tortilla chips

spices

- [ ] aniseed or fennel seed
- [ ] black pepper
- [ ] chili powder
- [ ] cinnamon, ground
- [ ] cumin, ground
- [ ] curry powder
- [ ] dill weed
- [ ] garlic powder
- [ ] grill seasoning
- [ ] herbes de Provence
- [ ] Italian seasoning
- [ ] nutmeg, ground
- [ ] onion, dried minced
- [ ] poultry seasoning
- [ ] pumpkin pie spice
- [ ] red pepper flakes
- [ ] salt, table/sea salt

baking

- [ ] baking powder
- [ ] baking soda
- [ ] brownie mix (8 by 8-inch pan size)*
- [ ] cake mix, yellow
- [ ] chocolate chips, semisweet
- [ ] chocolate chips, white
- [ ] cocoa powder
- [ ] extract, almond
- [ ] extract, peppermint
- [ ] extract, vanilla
- [ ] flour, all-purpose
- [ ] food coloring
- [ ] nonstick spray
- [ ] nuts, almonds
- [ ] nuts, peanuts
- [ ] nuts, pecans
- [ ] oil, extra virgin olive
- [ ] oil, vegetable
- [ ] sugar, confectioners'
- [ ] sugar, granulated
- [ ] sugar, light brown

refrigerated

- [ ] butter, unsalted
- [ ] cheese, blue or Gorgonzola
- [ ] cheese, Cheddar
- [ ] cheese, feta
- [ ] cheese, mozzarella
- [ ] cheese, Parmesan
- [ ] cream cheese
- [ ] cream, heavy
- [ ] eggs (large)
- [ ] milk
- [ ] sour cream or plain yogurt
- [ ] tortillas, flour (8-inch fajita size)

freezer

- [ ] bread dough (loaf or ball)
- [ ] broccoli, chopped
- [ ] green beans, cut
- [ ] peas
- [ ] puff pastry sheets
- [ ] shrimp (raw)
- [ ] spinach (bag), chopped
- [ ] vanilla ice cream

meat, chicken, and seafood

- [ ] bacon
- [ ] bulk (ground) breakfast sausage
- [ ] chicken breast (boneless, skinless)
- [ ] chicken thighs (boneless, skinless)
- [ ] crabmeat, imitation or canned lump
- [ ] flank steak or skirt steak
- [ ] ground beef, turkey, or chicken
- [ ] ham, sliced or whole

produce

- [ ] apples
- [ ] basil, fresh
- [ ] bell pepper, red or green
- [ ] cabbage and carrot mix
- [ ] carrots
- [ ] celery
- [ ] cranberries, dried
- [ ] cucumber, English
- [ ] garlic cloves
- [ ] ginger, minced (tube or jar)
- [ ] green onions
- [ ] lemon juice
- [ ] lemons
- [ ] lettuce, head or mixed greens
- [ ] lime juice
- [ ] pine nuts
- [ ] potatoes, russet, sweet, Yukon Gold
- [ ] raisins
- [ ] shallots or onions
- [ ] tomatoes

other supplies

- [ ] aluminum foil
- [ ] parchment paper
- [ ] plastic wrap
- [ ] skewers, wooden
- [ ] storage bags, resealable gallon
- [ ] toothpicks

The Stocked Kitchen Grocery List

pantry

- [ ] applesauce
- [ ] apricot preserves
- [ ] artichoke hearts, marinated
- [ ] barbecue sauce
- [ ] beans, black (15 oz.)*
- [ ] beans, Great Northern/ cannellini (15 oz.)*
- [ ] beans, kidney (15 oz.)*
- [ ] bread crumbs, plain
- [ ] broth, beef (15 oz.)*
- [ ] broth, chicken (15 oz.)*
- [ ] coffee, regular and decaf
- [ ] corn (15 oz.)
- [ ] honey
- [ ] horseradish, prepared
- [ ] ketchup
- [ ] mandarin orange segments (10 oz.)*
- [ ] maple syrup
- [ ] mayonnaise
- [ ] mushrooms (4 oz.)*
- [ ] mustard, Dijon
- [ ] mustard, yellow
- [ ] olives, black (4 oz.)*
- [ ] olives, green or Kalamata
- [ ] pancake mix (not "complete")
- [ ] peanut butter, creamy
- [ ] pears (15 oz.)*
- [ ] pineapple, slices or chunks (20 oz.)*
- [ ] ranch or buttermilk dressing
- [ ] raspberry jam or jelly
- [ ] relish, sweet or dill
- [ ] Tabasco/hot sauce
- [ ] tomatoes, diced (15 oz.)*
- [ ] tomato paste (6 oz.)*
- [ ] tomato sauce (15 oz.)*
- [ ] vinegar, balsamic
- [ ] vinegar, red wine
- [ ] vinegar, white wine
- [ ] Worcestershire sauce

international

- [ ] egg noodles
- [ ] pasta, penne/rotini/ farfalle
- [ ] pasta, string
- [ ] rice, jasmine or brown
- [ ] roasted red peppers (jar)
- [ ] salsa
- [ ] soy sauce

snacks, crackers, and bread

- [ ] bread loaf, white or wheat
- [ ] butter crackers
- [ ] pita bread
- [ ] tortilla chips

spices

- [ ] aniseed or fennel seed
- [ ] black pepper
- [ ] chili powder
- [ ] cinnamon, ground
- [ ] cumin, ground
- [ ] curry powder
- [ ] dill weed
- [ ] garlic powder
- [ ] grill seasoning
- [ ] herbes de Provence
- [ ] Italian seasoning
- [ ] nutmeg, ground
- [ ] onion, dried minced
- [ ] poultry seasoning
- [ ] pumpkin pie spice
- [ ] red pepper flakes
- [ ] salt, table/sea salt

baking

- [ ] baking powder
- [ ] baking soda
- [ ] brownie mix (8 by 8-inch pan size)*
- [ ] cake mix, yellow
- [ ] chocolate chips, semisweet
- [ ] chocolate chips, white
- [ ] cocoa powder
- [ ] extract, almond
- [ ] extract, peppermint
- [ ] extract, vanilla
- [ ] flour, all-purpose
- [ ] food coloring
- [ ] nonstick spray
- [ ] nuts, almonds
- [ ] nuts, peanuts
- [ ] nuts, pecans
- [ ] oil, extra virgin olive
- [ ] oil, vegetable
- [ ] sugar, confectioners'
- [ ] sugar, granulated
- [ ] sugar, light brown

refrigerated

- [ ] butter, unsalted
- [ ] cheese, blue or Gorgonzola
- [ ] cheese, Cheddar
- [ ] cheese, feta
- [ ] cheese, mozzarella
- [ ] cheese, Parmesan
- [ ] cream cheese
- [ ] cream, heavy
- [ ] eggs (large)
- [ ] milk
- [ ] sour cream or plain yogurt
- [ ] tortillas, flour (8-inch fajita size)

freezer

- [ ] bread dough (loaf or ball)
- [ ] broccoli, chopped
- [ ] green beans, cut
- [ ] peas
- [ ] puff pastry sheets
- [ ] shrimp (raw)
- [ ] spinach (bag), chopped
- [ ] vanilla ice cream

meat, chicken, and seafood

- [ ] bacon
- [ ] bulk (ground) breakfast sausage
- [ ] chicken breast (boneless, skinless)
- [ ] chicken thighs (boneless, skinless)
- [ ] crabmeat, imitation or canned lump
- [ ] flank steak or skirt steak
- [ ] ground beef, turkey, or chicken
- [ ] ham, sliced or whole

produce

- [ ] apples
- [ ] basil, fresh
- [ ] bell pepper, red or green
- [ ] cabbage and carrot mix
- [ ] carrots
- [ ] celery
- [ ] cranberries, dried
- [ ] cucumber, English
- [ ] garlic cloves
- [ ] ginger, minced (tube or jar)
- [ ] green onions
- [ ] lemon juice
- [ ] lemons
- [ ] lettuce, head or mixed greens
- [ ] lime juice
- [ ] pine nuts
- [ ] potatoes, russet, sweet, Yukon Gold
- [ ] raisins
- [ ] shallots or onions
- [ ] tomatoes

other supplies

- [ ] aluminum foil
- [ ] parchment paper
- [ ] plastic wrap
- [ ] skewers, wooden
- [ ] storage bags, resealable gallon
- [ ] toothpicks

* approximate sizes

The Stocked Kitchen Grocery List

pantry

- applesauce
- apricot preserves
- artichoke hearts, marinated
- barbecue sauce
- beans, black (15 oz.)*
- beans, Great Northern/ cannellini (15 oz.)*
- beans, kidney (15 oz.)*
- bread crumbs, plain
- broth, beef (15 oz.)*
- broth, chicken (15 oz.)*
- coffee, regular and decaf
- corn (15 oz.)
- honey
- horseradish, prepared
- ketchup
- mandarin orange segments (10 oz.)*
- maple syrup
- mayonnaise
- mushrooms (4 oz.)*
- mustard, Dijon
- mustard, yellow
- olives, black (4 oz.)*
- olives, green or Kalamata
- pancake mix (not "complete")
- peanut butter, creamy
- pears (15 oz.)*
- pineapple, slices or chunks (20 oz.)*
- ranch or buttermilk dressing
- raspberry jam or jelly
- relish, sweet or dill
- Tabasco/hot sauce
- tomatoes, diced (15 oz.)*
- tomato paste (6 oz.)*
- tomato sauce (15 oz.)*
- vinegar, balsamic
- vinegar, red wine
- vinegar, white wine
- Worcestershire sauce

international

- egg noodles
- pasta, penne/rotini/ farfalle
- pasta, string
- rice, jasmine or brown
- roasted red peppers (jar)
- salsa
- soy sauce

snacks, crackers, and bread

- bread loaf, white or wheat
- butter crackers
- pita bread
- tortilla chips

spices

- aniseed or fennel seed
- black pepper
- chili powder
- cinnamon, ground
- cumin, ground
- curry powder
- dill weed
- garlic powder
- grill seasoning
- herbes de Provence
- Italian seasoning
- nutmeg, ground
- onion, dried minced
- poultry seasoning
- pumpkin pie spice
- red pepper flakes
- salt, table/sea salt

baking

- baking powder
- baking soda
- brownie mix (8 by 8-inch pan size)*
- cake mix, yellow
- chocolate chips, semisweet
- chocolate chips, white
- cocoa powder

- extract, almond
- extract, peppermint
- extract, vanilla
- flour, all-purpose
- food coloring
- nonstick spray
- nuts, almonds
- nuts, peanuts
- nuts, pecans
- oil, extra virgin olive
- oil, vegetable
- sugar, confectioners'
- sugar, granulated
- sugar, light brown

refrigerated

- butter, unsalted
- cheese, blue or Gorgonzola
- cheese, Cheddar
- cheese, feta
- cheese, mozzarella
- cheese, Parmesan
- cream cheese
- cream, heavy
- eggs (large)
- milk
- sour cream or plain yogurt
- tortillas, flour (8-inch fajita size)

freezer

- bread dough (loaf or ball)
- broccoli, chopped
- green beans, cut
- peas
- puff pastry sheets
- shrimp (raw)
- spinach (bag), chopped
- vanilla ice cream

meat, chicken, and seafood

- bacon
- bulk (ground) breakfast sausage

- chicken breast (boneless, skinless)
- chicken thighs (boneless, skinless)
- crabmeat, imitation or canned lump
- flank steak or skirt steak
- ground beef, turkey, or chicken
- ham, sliced or whole

produce

- apples
- basil, fresh
- bell pepper, red or green
- cabbage and carrot mix
- carrots
- celery
- cranberries, dried
- cucumber, English
- garlic cloves
- ginger, minced (tube or jar)
- green onions
- lemon juice
- lemons
- lettuce, head or mixed greens
- lime juice
- pine nuts
- potatoes, russet, sweet, Yukon Gold
- raisins
- shallots or onions
- tomatoes

other supplies

- aluminum foil
- parchment paper
- plastic wrap
- skewers, wooden
- storage bags, resealable gallon
- toothpicks

* approximate sizes

www.thestockedkitchen.com

The Stocked Kitchen Grocery List

pantry

- [ ] applesauce
- [ ] apricot preserves
- [ ] artichoke hearts, marinated
- [ ] barbecue sauce
- [ ] beans, black (15 oz.)*
- [ ] beans, Great Northern/ cannellini (15 oz.)*
- [ ] beans, kidney (15 oz.)*
- [ ] bread crumbs, plain
- [ ] broth, beef (15 oz.)*
- [ ] broth, chicken (15 oz.)*
- [ ] coffee, regular and decaf
- [ ] corn (15 oz.)
- [ ] honey
- [ ] horseradish, prepared
- [ ] ketchup
- [ ] mandarin orange segments (10 oz.)*
- [ ] maple syrup
- [ ] mayonnaise
- [ ] mushrooms (4 oz.)*
- [ ] mustard, Dijon
- [ ] mustard, yellow
- [ ] olives, black (4 oz.)*
- [ ] olives, green or Kalamata
- [ ] pancake mix (not "complete")
- [ ] peanut butter, creamy
- [ ] pears (15 oz.)*
- [ ] pineapple, slices or chunks (20 oz.)*
- [ ] ranch or buttermilk dressing
- [ ] raspberry jam or jelly
- [ ] relish, sweet or dill
- [ ] Tabasco/hot sauce
- [ ] tomatoes, diced (15 oz.)*
- [ ] tomato paste (6 oz.)*
- [ ] tomato sauce (15 oz.)*
- [ ] vinegar, balsamic
- [ ] vinegar, red wine
- [ ] vinegar, white wine
- [ ] Worcestershire sauce

international

- [ ] egg noodles
- [ ] pasta, penne/rotini/ farfalle
- [ ] pasta, string
- [ ] rice, jasmine or brown
- [ ] roasted red peppers (jar)
- [ ] salsa
- [ ] soy sauce

snacks, crackers, and bread

- [ ] bread loaf, white or wheat
- [ ] butter crackers
- [ ] pita bread
- [ ] tortilla chips

spices

- [ ] aniseed or fennel seed
- [ ] black pepper
- [ ] chili powder
- [ ] cinnamon, ground
- [ ] cumin, ground
- [ ] curry powder
- [ ] dill weed
- [ ] garlic powder
- [ ] grill seasoning
- [ ] herbes de Provence
- [ ] Italian seasoning
- [ ] nutmeg, ground
- [ ] onion, dried minced
- [ ] poultry seasoning
- [ ] pumpkin pie spice
- [ ] red pepper flakes
- [ ] salt, table/sea salt

baking

- [ ] baking powder
- [ ] baking soda
- [ ] brownie mix (8 by 8-inch pan size)*
- [ ] cake mix, yellow
- [ ] chocolate chips, semisweet
- [ ] chocolate chips, white
- [ ] cocoa powder
- [ ] extract, almond
- [ ] extract, peppermint
- [ ] extract, vanilla
- [ ] flour, all-purpose
- [ ] food coloring
- [ ] nonstick spray
- [ ] nuts, almonds
- [ ] nuts, peanuts
- [ ] nuts, pecans
- [ ] oil, extra virgin olive
- [ ] oil, vegetable
- [ ] sugar, confectioners'
- [ ] sugar, granulated
- [ ] sugar, light brown

refrigerated

- [ ] butter, unsalted
- [ ] cheese, blue or Gorgonzola
- [ ] cheese, Cheddar
- [ ] cheese, feta
- [ ] cheese, mozzarella
- [ ] cheese, Parmesan
- [ ] cream cheese
- [ ] cream, heavy
- [ ] eggs (large)
- [ ] milk
- [ ] sour cream or plain yogurt
- [ ] tortillas, flour (8-inch fajita size)

freezer

- [ ] bread dough (loaf or ball)
- [ ] broccoli, chopped
- [ ] green beans, cut
- [ ] peas
- [ ] puff pastry sheets
- [ ] shrimp (raw)
- [ ] spinach (bag), chopped
- [ ] vanilla ice cream

meat, chicken, and seafood

- [ ] bacon
- [ ] bulk (ground) breakfast sausage
- [ ] chicken breast (boneless, skinless)
- [ ] chicken thighs (boneless, skinless)
- [ ] crabmeat, imitation or canned lump
- [ ] flank steak or skirt steak
- [ ] ground beef, turkey, or chicken
- [ ] ham, sliced or whole

produce

- [ ] apples
- [ ] basil, fresh
- [ ] bell pepper, red or green
- [ ] cabbage and carrot mix
- [ ] carrots
- [ ] celery
- [ ] cranberries, dried
- [ ] cucumber, English
- [ ] garlic cloves
- [ ] ginger, minced (tube or jar)
- [ ] green onions
- [ ] lemon juice
- [ ] lemons
- [ ] lettuce, head or mixed greens
- [ ] lime juice
- [ ] pine nuts
- [ ] potatoes, russet, sweet, Yukon Gold
- [ ] raisins
- [ ] shallots or onions
- [ ] tomatoes

other supplies

- [ ] aluminum foil
- [ ] parchment paper
- [ ] plastic wrap
- [ ] skewers, wooden
- [ ] storage bags, resealable gallon
- [ ] toothpicks

The Stocked Kitchen Grocery List

pantry

- [ ] applesauce
- [ ] apricot preserves
- [ ] artichoke hearts, marinated
- [ ] barbecue sauce
- [ ] beans, black (15 oz.)*
- [ ] beans, Great Northern/ cannellini (15 oz.)*
- [ ] beans, kidney (15 oz.)*
- [ ] bread crumbs, plain
- [ ] broth, beef (15 oz.)*
- [ ] broth, chicken (15 oz.)*
- [ ] coffee, regular and decaf
- [ ] corn (15 oz.)
- [ ] honey
- [ ] horseradish, prepared
- [ ] ketchup
- [ ] mandarin orange segments (10 oz.)*
- [ ] maple syrup
- [ ] mayonnaise
- [ ] mushrooms (4 oz.)*
- [ ] mustard, Dijon
- [ ] mustard, yellow
- [ ] olives, black (4 oz.)*
- [ ] olives, green or Kalamata
- [ ] pancake mix (not "complete")
- [ ] peanut butter, creamy
- [ ] pears (15 oz.)*
- [ ] pineapple, slices or chunks (20 oz.)*
- [ ] ranch or buttermilk dressing
- [ ] raspberry jam or jelly
- [ ] relish, sweet or dill
- [ ] Tabasco/hot sauce
- [ ] tomatoes, diced (15 oz.)*
- [ ] tomato paste (6 oz.)*
- [ ] tomato sauce (15 oz.)*
- [ ] vinegar, balsamic
- [ ] vinegar, red wine
- [ ] vinegar, white wine
- [ ] Worcestershire sauce

international

- [ ] egg noodles
- [ ] pasta, penne/rotini/ farfalle
- [ ] pasta, string
- [ ] rice, jasmine or brown
- [ ] roasted red peppers (jar)
- [ ] salsa
- [ ] soy sauce

snacks, crackers, and bread

- [ ] bread loaf, white or wheat
- [ ] butter crackers
- [ ] pita bread
- [ ] tortilla chips

spices

- [ ] aniseed or fennel seed
- [ ] black pepper
- [ ] chili powder
- [ ] cinnamon, ground
- [ ] cumin, ground
- [ ] curry powder
- [ ] dill weed
- [ ] garlic powder
- [ ] grill seasoning
- [ ] herbes de Provence
- [ ] Italian seasoning
- [ ] nutmeg, ground
- [ ] onion, dried minced
- [ ] poultry seasoning
- [ ] pumpkin pie spice
- [ ] red pepper flakes
- [ ] salt, table/sea salt

baking

- [ ] baking powder
- [ ] baking soda
- [ ] brownie mix (8 by 8-inch pan size)*
- [ ] cake mix, yellow
- [ ] chocolate chips, semisweet
- [ ] chocolate chips, white
- [ ] cocoa powder
- [ ] extract, almond
- [ ] extract, peppermint
- [ ] extract, vanilla
- [ ] flour, all-purpose
- [ ] food coloring
- [ ] nonstick spray
- [ ] nuts, almonds
- [ ] nuts, peanuts
- [ ] nuts, pecans
- [ ] oil, extra virgin olive
- [ ] oil, vegetable
- [ ] sugar, confectioners'
- [ ] sugar, granulated
- [ ] sugar, light brown

refrigerated

- [ ] butter, unsalted
- [ ] cheese, blue or Gorgonzola
- [ ] cheese, Cheddar
- [ ] cheese, feta
- [ ] cheese, mozzarella
- [ ] cheese, Parmesan
- [ ] cream cheese
- [ ] cream, heavy
- [ ] eggs (large)
- [ ] milk
- [ ] sour cream or plain yogurt
- [ ] tortillas, flour (8-inch fajita size)

freezer

- [ ] bread dough (loaf or ball)
- [ ] broccoli, chopped
- [ ] green beans, cut
- [ ] peas
- [ ] puff pastry sheets
- [ ] shrimp (raw)
- [ ] spinach (bag), chopped
- [ ] vanilla ice cream

meat, chicken, and seafood

- [ ] bacon
- [ ] bulk (ground) breakfast sausage
- [ ] chicken breast (boneless, skinless)
- [ ] chicken thighs (boneless, skinless)
- [ ] crabmeat, imitation or canned lump
- [ ] flank steak or skirt steak
- [ ] ground beef, turkey, or chicken
- [ ] ham, sliced or whole

produce

- [ ] apples
- [ ] basil, fresh
- [ ] bell pepper, red or green
- [ ] cabbage and carrot mix
- [ ] carrots
- [ ] celery
- [ ] cranberries, dried
- [ ] cucumber, English
- [ ] garlic cloves
- [ ] ginger, minced (tube or jar)
- [ ] green onions
- [ ] lemon juice
- [ ] lemons
- [ ] lettuce, head or mixed greens
- [ ] lime juice
- [ ] pine nuts
- [ ] potatoes, russet, sweet, Yukon Gold
- [ ] raisins
- [ ] shallots or onions
- [ ] tomatoes

other supplies

- [ ] aluminum foil
- [ ] parchment paper
- [ ] plastic wrap
- [ ] skewers, wooden
- [ ] storage bags, resealable gallon
- [ ] toothpicks

The Stocked Kitchen Grocery List

pantry

- [ ] applesauce
- [ ] apricot preserves
- [ ] artichoke hearts, marinated
- [ ] barbecue sauce
- [ ] beans, black (15 oz.)*
- [ ] beans, Great Northern/ cannellini (15 oz.)*
- [ ] beans, kidney (15 oz.)*
- [ ] bread crumbs, plain
- [ ] broth, beef (15 oz.)*
- [ ] broth, chicken (15 oz.)*
- [ ] coffee, regular and decaf
- [ ] corn (15 oz.)
- [ ] honey
- [ ] horseradish, prepared
- [ ] ketchup
- [ ] mandarin orange segments (10 oz.)*
- [ ] maple syrup
- [ ] mayonnaise
- [ ] mushrooms (4 oz.)*
- [ ] mustard, Dijon
- [ ] mustard, yellow
- [ ] olives, black (4 oz.)*
- [ ] olives, green or Kalamata
- [ ] pancake mix (not "complete")
- [ ] peanut butter, creamy
- [ ] pears (15 oz.)*
- [ ] pineapple, slices or chunks (20 oz.)*
- [ ] ranch or buttermilk dressing
- [ ] raspberry jam or jelly
- [ ] relish, sweet or dill
- [ ] Tabasco/hot sauce
- [ ] tomatoes, diced (15 oz.)*
- [ ] tomato paste (6 oz.)*
- [ ] tomato sauce (15 oz.)*
- [ ] vinegar, balsamic
- [ ] vinegar, red wine
- [ ] vinegar, white wine
- [ ] Worcestershire sauce

international

- [ ] egg noodles
- [ ] pasta, penne/rotini/ farfalle
- [ ] pasta, string
- [ ] rice, jasmine or brown
- [ ] roasted red peppers (jar)
- [ ] salsa
- [ ] soy sauce

snacks, crackers, and bread

- [ ] bread loaf, white or wheat
- [ ] butter crackers
- [ ] pita bread
- [ ] tortilla chips

spices

- [ ] aniseed or fennel seed
- [ ] black pepper
- [ ] chili powder
- [ ] cinnamon, ground
- [ ] cumin, ground
- [ ] curry powder
- [ ] dill weed
- [ ] garlic powder
- [ ] grill seasoning
- [ ] herbes de Provence
- [ ] Italian seasoning
- [ ] nutmeg, ground
- [ ] onion, dried minced
- [ ] poultry seasoning
- [ ] pumpkin pie spice
- [ ] red pepper flakes
- [ ] salt, table/sea salt

baking

- [ ] baking powder
- [ ] baking soda
- [ ] brownie mix (8 by 8-inch pan size)*
- [ ] cake mix, yellow
- [ ] chocolate chips, semisweet
- [ ] chocolate chips, white
- [ ] cocoa powder
- [ ] extract, almond
- [ ] extract, peppermint
- [ ] extract, vanilla
- [ ] flour, all-purpose
- [ ] food coloring
- [ ] nonstick spray
- [ ] nuts, almonds
- [ ] nuts, peanuts
- [ ] nuts, pecans
- [ ] oil, extra virgin olive
- [ ] oil, vegetable
- [ ] sugar, confectioners'
- [ ] sugar, granulated
- [ ] sugar, light brown

refrigerated

- [ ] butter, unsalted
- [ ] cheese, blue or Gorgonzola
- [ ] cheese, Cheddar
- [ ] cheese, feta
- [ ] cheese, mozzarella
- [ ] cheese, Parmesan
- [ ] cream cheese
- [ ] cream, heavy
- [ ] eggs (large)
- [ ] milk
- [ ] sour cream or plain yogurt
- [ ] tortillas, flour (8-inch fajita size)

freezer

- [ ] bread dough (loaf or ball)
- [ ] broccoli, chopped
- [ ] green beans, cut
- [ ] peas
- [ ] puff pastry sheets
- [ ] shrimp (raw)
- [ ] spinach (bag), chopped
- [ ] vanilla ice cream

meat, chicken, and seafood

- [ ] bacon
- [ ] bulk (ground) breakfast sausage
- [ ] chicken breast (boneless, skinless)
- [ ] chicken thighs (boneless, skinless)
- [ ] crabmeat, imitation or canned lump
- [ ] flank steak or skirt steak
- [ ] ground beef, turkey, or chicken
- [ ] ham, sliced or whole

produce

- [ ] apples
- [ ] basil, fresh
- [ ] bell pepper, red or green
- [ ] cabbage and carrot mix
- [ ] carrots
- [ ] celery
- [ ] cranberries, dried
- [ ] cucumber, English
- [ ] garlic cloves
- [ ] ginger, minced (tube or jar)
- [ ] green onions
- [ ] lemon juice
- [ ] lemons
- [ ] lettuce, head or mixed greens
- [ ] lime juice
- [ ] pine nuts
- [ ] potatoes, russet, sweet, Yukon Gold
- [ ] raisins
- [ ] shallots or onions
- [ ] tomatoes

other supplies

- [ ] aluminum foil
- [ ] parchment paper
- [ ] plastic wrap
- [ ] skewers, wooden
- [ ] storage bags, resealable gallon
- [ ] toothpicks

The Stocked Kitchen Grocery List

pantry

- [ ] applesauce
- [ ] apricot preserves
- [ ] artichoke hearts, marinated
- [ ] barbecue sauce
- [ ] beans, black (15 oz.)*
- [ ] beans, Great Northern/ cannellini (15 oz.)*
- [ ] beans, kidney (15 oz.)*
- [ ] bread crumbs, plain
- [ ] broth, beef (15 oz.)*
- [ ] broth, chicken (15 oz.)*
- [ ] coffee, regular and decaf
- [ ] corn (15 oz.)
- [ ] honey
- [ ] horseradish, prepared
- [ ] ketchup
- [ ] mandarin orange segments (10 oz.)*
- [ ] maple syrup
- [ ] mayonnaise
- [ ] mushrooms (4 oz.)*
- [ ] mustard, Dijon
- [ ] mustard, yellow
- [ ] olives, black (4 oz.)*
- [ ] olives, green or Kalamata
- [ ] pancake mix (not "complete")
- [ ] peanut butter, creamy
- [ ] pears (15 oz.)*
- [ ] pineapple, slices or chunks (20 oz.)*
- [ ] ranch or buttermilk dressing
- [ ] raspberry jam or jelly
- [ ] relish, sweet or dill
- [ ] Tabasco/hot sauce
- [ ] tomatoes, diced (15 oz.)*
- [ ] tomato paste (6 oz.)*
- [ ] tomato sauce (15 oz.)*
- [ ] vinegar, balsamic
- [ ] vinegar, red wine
- [ ] vinegar, white wine
- [ ] Worcestershire sauce

international

- [ ] egg noodles
- [ ] pasta, penne/rotini/ farfalle
- [ ] pasta, string
- [ ] rice, jasmine or brown
- [ ] roasted red peppers (jar)
- [ ] salsa
- [ ] soy sauce

snacks, crackers, and bread

- [ ] bread loaf, white or wheat
- [ ] butter crackers
- [ ] pita bread
- [ ] tortilla chips

spices

- [ ] aniseed or fennel seed
- [ ] black pepper
- [ ] chili powder
- [ ] cinnamon, ground
- [ ] cumin, ground
- [ ] curry powder
- [ ] dill weed
- [ ] garlic powder
- [ ] grill seasoning
- [ ] herbes de Provence
- [ ] Italian seasoning
- [ ] nutmeg, ground
- [ ] onion, dried minced
- [ ] poultry seasoning
- [ ] pumpkin pie spice
- [ ] red pepper flakes
- [ ] salt, table/sea salt

baking

- [ ] baking powder
- [ ] baking soda
- [ ] brownie mix (8 by 8-inch pan size)*
- [ ] cake mix, yellow
- [ ] chocolate chips, semisweet
- [ ] chocolate chips, white
- [ ] cocoa powder
- [ ] extract, almond
- [ ] extract, peppermint
- [ ] extract, vanilla
- [ ] flour, all-purpose
- [ ] food coloring
- [ ] nonstick spray
- [ ] nuts, almonds
- [ ] nuts, peanuts
- [ ] nuts, pecans
- [ ] oil, extra virgin olive
- [ ] oil, vegetable
- [ ] sugar, confectioners'
- [ ] sugar, granulated
- [ ] sugar, light brown

refrigerated

- [ ] butter, unsalted
- [ ] cheese, blue or Gorgonzola
- [ ] cheese, Cheddar
- [ ] cheese, feta
- [ ] cheese, mozzarella
- [ ] cheese, Parmesan
- [ ] cream cheese
- [ ] cream, heavy
- [ ] eggs (large)
- [ ] milk
- [ ] sour cream or plain yogurt
- [ ] tortillas, flour (8-inch fajita size)

freezer

- [ ] bread dough (loaf or ball)
- [ ] broccoli, chopped
- [ ] green beans, cut
- [ ] peas
- [ ] puff pastry sheets
- [ ] shrimp (raw)
- [ ] spinach (bag), chopped
- [ ] vanilla ice cream

meat, chicken, and seafood

- [ ] bacon
- [ ] bulk (ground) breakfast sausage
- [ ] chicken breast (boneless, skinless)
- [ ] chicken thighs (boneless, skinless)
- [ ] crabmeat, imitation or canned lump
- [ ] flank steak or skirt steak
- [ ] ground beef, turkey, or chicken
- [ ] ham, sliced or whole

produce

- [ ] apples
- [ ] basil, fresh
- [ ] bell pepper, red or green
- [ ] cabbage and carrot mix
- [ ] carrots
- [ ] celery
- [ ] cranberries, dried
- [ ] cucumber, English
- [ ] garlic cloves
- [ ] ginger, minced (tube or jar)
- [ ] green onions
- [ ] lemon juice
- [ ] lemons
- [ ] lettuce, head or mixed greens
- [ ] lime juice
- [ ] pine nuts
- [ ] potatoes, russet, sweet, Yukon Gold
- [ ] raisins
- [ ] shallots or onions
- [ ] tomatoes

other supplies

- [ ] aluminum foil
- [ ] parchment paper
- [ ] plastic wrap
- [ ] skewers, wooden
- [ ] storage bags, resealable gallon
- [ ] toothpicks

* approximate sizes

The Stocked Kitchen Grocery List

pantry

- [ ] applesauce
- [ ] apricot preserves
- [ ] artichoke hearts, marinated
- [ ] barbecue sauce
- [ ] beans, black (15 oz.)*
- [ ] beans, Great Northern/ cannellini (15 oz.)*
- [ ] beans, kidney (15 oz.)*
- [ ] bread crumbs, plain
- [ ] broth, beef (15 oz.)*
- [ ] broth, chicken (15 oz.)*
- [ ] coffee, regular and decaf
- [ ] corn (15 oz.)
- [ ] honey
- [ ] horseradish, prepared
- [ ] ketchup
- [ ] mandarin orange segments (10 oz.)*
- [ ] maple syrup
- [ ] mayonnaise
- [ ] mushrooms (4 oz.)*
- [ ] mustard, Dijon
- [ ] mustard, yellow
- [ ] olives, black (4 oz.)*
- [ ] olives, green or Kalamata
- [ ] pancake mix (not "complete")
- [ ] peanut butter, creamy
- [ ] pears (15 oz.)*
- [ ] pineapple, slices or chunks (20 oz.)*
- [ ] ranch or buttermilk dressing
- [ ] raspberry jam or jelly
- [ ] relish, sweet or dill
- [ ] Tabasco/hot sauce
- [ ] tomatoes, diced (15 oz.)*
- [ ] tomato paste (6 oz.)*
- [ ] tomato sauce (15 oz.)*
- [ ] vinegar, balsamic
- [ ] vinegar, red wine
- [ ] vinegar, white wine
- [ ] Worcestershire sauce

international

- [ ] egg noodles
- [ ] pasta, penne/rotini/ farfalle
- [ ] pasta, string
- [ ] rice, jasmine or brown
- [ ] roasted red peppers (jar)
- [ ] salsa
- [ ] soy sauce

snacks, crackers, and bread

- [ ] bread loaf, white or wheat
- [ ] butter crackers
- [ ] pita bread
- [ ] tortilla chips

spices

- [ ] aniseed or fennel seed
- [ ] black pepper
- [ ] chili powder
- [ ] cinnamon, ground
- [ ] cumin, ground
- [ ] curry powder
- [ ] dill weed
- [ ] garlic powder
- [ ] grill seasoning
- [ ] herbes de Provence
- [ ] Italian seasoning
- [ ] nutmeg, ground
- [ ] onion, dried minced
- [ ] poultry seasoning
- [ ] pumpkin pie spice
- [ ] red pepper flakes
- [ ] salt, table/sea salt

baking

- [ ] baking powder
- [ ] baking soda
- [ ] brownie mix (8 by 8-inch pan size)*
- [ ] cake mix, yellow
- [ ] chocolate chips, semisweet
- [ ] chocolate chips, white
- [ ] cocoa powder

- [ ] extract, almond
- [ ] extract, peppermint
- [ ] extract, vanilla
- [ ] flour, all-purpose
- [ ] food coloring
- [ ] nonstick spray
- [ ] nuts, almonds
- [ ] nuts, peanuts
- [ ] nuts, pecans
- [ ] oil, extra virgin olive
- [ ] oil, vegetable
- [ ] sugar, confectioners'
- [ ] sugar, granulated
- [ ] sugar, light brown

refrigerated

- [ ] butter, unsalted
- [ ] cheese, blue or Gorgonzola
- [ ] cheese, Cheddar
- [ ] cheese, feta
- [ ] cheese, mozzarella
- [ ] cheese, Parmesan
- [ ] cream cheese
- [ ] cream, heavy
- [ ] eggs (large)
- [ ] milk
- [ ] sour cream or plain yogurt
- [ ] tortillas, flour (8-inch fajita size)

freezer

- [ ] bread dough (loaf or ball)
- [ ] broccoli, chopped
- [ ] green beans, cut
- [ ] peas
- [ ] puff pastry sheets
- [ ] shrimp (raw)
- [ ] spinach (bag), chopped
- [ ] vanilla ice cream

meat, chicken, and seafood

- [ ] bacon
- [ ] bulk (ground) breakfast sausage

- [ ] chicken breast (boneless, skinless)
- [ ] chicken thighs (boneless, skinless)
- [ ] crabmeat, imitation or canned lump
- [ ] flank steak or skirt steak
- [ ] ground beef, turkey, or chicken
- [ ] ham, sliced or whole

produce

- [ ] apples
- [ ] basil, fresh
- [ ] bell pepper, red or green
- [ ] cabbage and carrot mix
- [ ] carrots
- [ ] celery
- [ ] cranberries, dried
- [ ] cucumber, English
- [ ] garlic cloves
- [ ] ginger, minced (tube or jar)
- [ ] green onions
- [ ] lemon juice
- [ ] lemons
- [ ] lettuce, head or mixed greens
- [ ] lime juice
- [ ] pine nuts
- [ ] potatoes, russet, sweet, Yukon Gold
- [ ] raisins
- [ ] shallots or onions
- [ ] tomatoes

other supplies

- [ ] aluminum foil
- [ ] parchment paper
- [ ] plastic wrap
- [ ] skewers, wooden
- [ ] storage bags, resealable gallon
- [ ] toothpicks

* approximate sizes